"The *Travelers' Tales* series is altogether remarkable."
—Jan Morris, author of *Journeys*, *Locations*, and *Hong Kong*

"For the thoughtful traveler, these books are an invaluable resource. There's nothing like them on the market."
—Pico Iyer, author of *Video Night in Kathmandu*

"This is the stuff memories can be duplicated from."
—Karen Krebsbach, *Foreign Service Journal*

"I can't think of a better way to get comfortable with a destination than by delving into *Travelers' Tales*...before reading a guidebook, before seeing a travel agent. The series helps visitors refine their interests and readies them to communicate with the peoples they come in contact with...."
—Paul Glassman, Society of American Travel Writers

"...*Travelers' Tales* is a valuable addition to any predeparture reading list."
—Tony Wheeler, publisher, Lonely Planet Publications

"*Travelers' Tales* delivers something most guidebooks only promise: a real sense of what a country is all about...."
—Steve Silk, *Hartford Courant*

"...*Travelers' Tales* is a useful and enlightening addition to the travel bookshelves...providing a real service for those who enjoy reading first-person accounts of a destination before seeing it for themselves."
—Bill Newlin, publisher, Moon Publications

"The *Travelers' Tales* series should become required reading for anyone visiting a foreign country who wants to truly step off the tourist track and experience another culture, another place, firsthand."
—Nancy Paradis, *St. Petersburg Times*

"Like having been there, done it, seen it. If there's one thing traditional guidebooks lack, it's the really juicy travel information, the personal stories about back alleys and brief encounters. The *Travelers' Tales* series fills this gap with an approach that's all anecdotes, no directions."
—Jim Gullo, *Diversion*

OTHER TRAVELERS' TALES BOOKS

Country and Regional Guides
America, Brazil, France, India, Italy, Japan, Mexico, Nepal,
Spain, Thailand; Grand Canyon, Hawai'i, Hong Kong,
Paris, and San Francisco

Women's Travel
A Woman's Passion for Travel, A Woman's World,
Women in the Wild, A Mother's World, Safety and
Security for Women Who Travel, Gutsy Women,
Gutsy Mamas

Body & Soul
The Road Within, Love & Romance, Food, The Fearless
Diner, The Gift of Travel

Special Interest
There's No Toilet Paper on the Road Less Traveled, The
Penny Pincher's Passport to Luxury Travel, A Dog's World

Footsteps
Kite Strings of the Southern Cross, The Sword of Heaven

TESTOSTERONE PLANET

TRUE STORIES FROM A MAN'S WORLD

TRAVELERS' TALES GUIDES

TESTOSTERONE PLANET

TRUE STORIES FROM A MAN'S WORLD

Collected and Edited by

SEAN O'REILLY, LARRY HABEGGER, AND JAMES O'REILLY

TRAVELERS' TALES

SAN FRANCISCO

Testosterone Planet: True Stories from a Man's World
Collected and Edited by Sean O'Reilly, Larry Habegger, and James O'Reilly

Copyright © 1999 Travelers' Tales, Inc. All rights reserved.

Travelers' Tales and *Travelers' Tales Guides* are trademarks of Travelers' Tales, Inc.

Credits and copyright notices for the individual articles in this collection are given starting on page 295.

We have made every effort to trace the ownership of all copyrighted material and to secure permission from copyright holders. In the event of any question arising as to the ownership of any material, we will be pleased to make the necessary correction in future printings. Contact Travelers' Tales, Inc., 330 Townsend Street, Suite 208, San Francisco, California 94107.

Cover design: Judy Anderson
Interior design: Judy Anderson, Kathryn Heflin, and Susan Bailey
Cover photograph: Copyright © 1995 by Greg Epperson
Page Layout by Cynthia Lamb, using the fonts Bembo and Boulevard

Library of Congress Cataloguing-in-Publication Data

Testosterone Planet: true stories from a man's world / collected and edited by
    Sean O'Reilly, Larry Habegger, and James O'Reilly.—
    1st ed.
        p.   cm. — (Travelers' Tales guides)
    ISBN: 1-885211-43-0
    1. Adventure and adventurers Anecdotes. 2. Travel Anecdotes. 3. Travelers
Anecdotes. I. O'Reilly, Sean. II. Habegger, Larry. III. O'Reilly, James. IV. Series.
G525.T39   1999
910.4—dc21   99-35884
                                                                      CIP

First Edition
Printed in the United States
10 9 8 7 6 5 4 3 2 1

This power within us—this portion of our destiny which belongs neither to heredity nor environment—is wiser than our conscious being, wiser than the rational processes of our culture. It drives us by some mysterious impulse into many actions and many changes that well might seem rash, mistaken, foolish and ill-advised. But as time goes on these actions, these changes, will be found strangely justified. They will turn out to have been after all not debouchings from our true path, but bridle-paths rather, by which we attain, where we least looked to find it, the King's High-road of our fate.

—JOHN COWPER POWYS,
The Meaning of Culture

Table of Contents

Part Two
WHEN THEY HEAR A DIFFERENT DRUMMER

Part Three
IN THEIR OWN SHADOW

Part Four
INTO THE LIGHT

Testosterone Planet: An Introduction

Welcome to a man's world.

What does it mean to be a man, driven by that inescapable and sometimes uncontrollable hormone, testosterone?

It means being subjected to and responsible for senseless acts of depredation, hair-raising gallantry, and moments of unexpected tenderness. It means living on the edge and in the soul, following time-honored paths and breaking new ground in an effort to make your mark in the world. A man's world is the world of gamblers and teachers, hunters and pilgrims, lovers and monks, soldiers and explorers, scholars and princes, fathers and sons. It is both dangerous and benign, a world of adventure and misbehavior, codes and beliefs, intense companionship and high hilarity, and above all, a mindset programmed, in the immortal words of Zane Grey, to hunt, roam, and slay.

If you are a woman and wish to understand the mind and soul of your friend, lover, husband, brother, or son, you may find here pieces of the puzzle that has long had you scratching your head. If you are a man you will better understand the testosterone-driven enigma that is yourself.

Travel to India with Tim Ward in "Fire Beneath the Skin," as he explores the meaning of lust in the arms of a beautiful Buddhist scholar. Solo climb a forbidding peak in Alaska with Jon Krakauer as he tries to understand the mystery of another young man's death in the wild. Laugh at Ray Isle—and yourself—as he fights a large flightless bird in "Wild Turkey," and at

Bill Bryson as he tussles with a know-it-all female on the Appalachian Trail. Suffer with Michael Herr in the cauldron of war and madness, and Slavomir Rawicz on the long road from torture and tyranny to freedom. Explore the wide world of male identity, from the man who tattoos his entire body in "The Blue Man" to the guru in Paul William Roberts's "No Like A-feesh?" who may be more than just human. Go with Phil Cousineau to Ankor Wat in "The Longing," as he journeys to Cambodia with his brother in fulfillment of a promise to his dead father, and rediscover what the community of men can mean to you with William Ashton in "A Room of Men."

But whether you try to scuba dive in the world's deepest cave or rescue someone from a plane crash, what you're really looking for is something deeper. You travel for thrills and adventure, but ultimately you're seeking love and respect. Adventure can help get your life moving, but love and respect must be earned. You know deep down that the faint-hearted do not succeed in a man's world, and you also know that the greatest success comes from giving to the world and to others.

So open *Testosterone Planet* and begin your next adventure. Dimensions of wonder, pain, and delight await you.

—Sean O'Reilly, Larry Habegger, and James O'Reilly

PART ONE

THE THINGS THEY DO

The Perfect Punch in the Face

It was a roundhouse for the ages.

I HAVE A FRIEND NAMED ROD. HE'S A MASTER CABINET-maker. You can see his mastery in his self-confidence, and that part of him that is always far away, occupied with lofty things, like his craft. You can see the mojo in him. To be admitted to his workshop, his sanctum sanctorum in Sonoma, California, is like being admitted into a matador's dressing room before the fight. To be able to watch him work is like being given a private concert by James Brown. And he makes huge money, as master cabinetmakers do.

"What do you want for your birthday?" he asked me, thinking he would show largess with an expensive gift. "You want a Rolex?"

"I want a snuffbox made by you," I said. He seemed disappointed. I told him, "You're a master craftsman. It's what you do. It would be a piece of you and your tradition, going back to, what, Jesus when he was a carpenter. If I have something just for me, made by a master, then I'll feel a little like a master, too. I'll feel privileged."

So he made, just for me, the best cherrywood snuffbox the world has ever seen. Just holding it in my hands, I can feel the mastery and feel I'm holding something Jesus could have made when he was a carpenter in Nazareth. Jesus would have made nothing but the best.

So what, you're wondering, has this got to do with a punch in the face? Well, Pinky Gomez and I trained in the same boxing gym in East San Jose, California. Not such a nice neighborhood, but a good venue for fighters. He was pro, I was amateur. He was magic. It was what he did. To watch him train or fight was to watch a master craftsman at work. I knew, if his mojo held, that in him I was watching a champion being born. I was watching the history of the sport I love being made. I wanted some of his mojo. And that was in his fists. Girlfriend was appalled. What can I say?

But there was more in Pinky's fists than mojo. I learned that he had sparred with Sugar Ray Leonard. Had even tagged him a few times. And Leonard had given Pinky a shiner. Now think about this: Leonard had punched Pinky. Before that Tommy Hearns had punched Leonard. The champ before Hearns had punched him; and on and on back in history. On back to Jake LaMotta, through Sugar Ray Robinson. Back, back to Hammerin' Hank, first holder of a Triple Crown, back, back through the Ring Record to the first championship fights under Marquess of Queensberry rules in New York and London, back in the 1890s when John L. Sullivan fought Gentleman Jim Corbett in the first major fight with gloves and three-minute rounds. Back when "the form" had first been established. In Pinky's fists was a physical, living, blood-pumping link with the history of modern boxing.

"I think you're great, Pinky," I told him. "How 'bout layin' one on me? Right in the face." Pinky grinned. He knew what

I meant. Because of our different weight classes, we would never meet in the ring. It was this or nothing.

"You want it with the glove or without?"

"Don't risk your knuckles."

A looping right cross encased in a nine ounce glove slammed into my left cheekbone, just under the eye. Pinky did it just right. Not hard enough to knock me down, but enough to leave a mark. My eye swelled. My head buzzed. And I was one more link in the chain with Pinky and Hammerin' Hank and all the others. It was a perfect punch in the face.

Richard Sterling is a graduate of the University of California, Berkeley, and a veteran of seven years in the U.S. Navy. While serving in Southeast Asia he first indulged his lasting passions for culinary discovery, adventurous travel, and great literature. He is the author of The Fearless Diner, Dining with Headhunters *and* The Eclectic Gourmet Guide to San Francisco. *He's also the editor of* The Adventure of Food: True Stories of Eating Everything, *and* Travelers' Tales Food: A Taste of the Road *which won a Lowell Thomas silver medal for best travel book. He lives in Berkeley, California.*

JON KRAKAUER

* * *

Devils Thumb

In his quest to understand what made a young Chris McCandless
walk off into the Alaskan bush to his death, the author revisits
a climb he made as a young man.

IN THE FINAL POSTCARD HE SENT TO WAYNE WESTERBERG,
McCandless had written, "If this adventure proves fatal and
you don't ever hear from me again, I want you to know you're
a great man. I now walk into the wild." When the adventure
did indeed prove fatal, this melodramatic declaration fueled
considerable speculation that the boy had been bent on suicide from the beginning, that when he walked into the bush,
he had no intention of ever walking out again. I'm not so
sure, however.

My suspicion that McCandless's death was unplanned, that
it was a terrible accident, comes from reading those few documents he left behind and from listening to the men and
women who spent time with him over the final year of his
life. But my sense of Chris McCandless's intentions comes,
too, from a more personal perspective.

As a youth, I am told, I was willful, self-absorbed, intermit-
tently reckless, moody. I disappointed my father in the usual
ways. Like McCandless, figures of male authority aroused in

me a confusing medley of corked fury and hunger to please. If something captured my undisciplined imagination, I pursued it with a zeal bordering on obsession, and from the age of seventeen until my late twenties that something was mountain climbing.

I devoted most of my waking hours to fantasizing about, and then undertaking, ascents of remote mountains in Alaska and Canada—obscure spires, steep and frightening, that nobody in the world beyond a handful of climbing geeks had ever heard of. Some good actually came of this. By fixing my sights on one summit after another, I managed to keep my bearings through some thick postadolescent fog. Climbing *mattered*. The danger bathed the world in a halogen glow that caused everything—the sweep of the rock, the orange and yellow lichens, the texture of the clouds—to stand out in brilliant relief. Life thrummed at a higher pitch. The world was made real.

In 1977, while brooding on a Colorado bar stool, picking unhappily at my existential scabs, I got it into my head to climb a mountain called the Devils Thumb. An intrusion of diorite sculpted by ancient glaciers into a peak of immense and spectacular proportions, the Thumb is especially imposing from the north: its great north wall, which had never been climbed, rises sheer and clean for 6,000 feet from the glacier at its base, twice the height of Yosemite's El Capitan. I would go to Alaska, ski inland from the sea across 30 miles of glacial ice, and ascend this mighty *nordwand*. I decided, moreover, to do it alone.

I was 23, a year younger than Chris McCandless when he walked into the Alaskan bush. My reasoning, if you can call it that, was inflamed by the scattershot passions of youth and a literary diet overly rich in the works of Nietzsche, Kerouac and John Menlove Edwards, the latter a deeply troubled writer and psychiatrist who, before putting an end to his life with a cyanide capsule in 1958, had been one of the preeminent British rock climbers of the day. Edwards regarded climbing as a "psycho-neurotic tendency"; he climbed not for sport but to find refuge from an inner torment that framed his existence.

As I formulated my plan to climb the Thumb, I was dimly aware that I might be getting in over my head. But that only added to the scheme's appeal. That it wouldn't be easy was the whole point.

I owned a book in which there was a photograph of the Devils Thumb, a black-and-white image taken by an eminent glaciologist named Maynard Miller. In Miller's aerial photo, the mountain looked particularly sinister; a huge fin of exfoliated stone, dark and smeared with ice. The picture held an almost pornographic fascination for me. How would it feel, I wondered, to be balanced on that bladelike summit ridge, worrying over the storm clouds building in the distance, hunched against the wind and dunning cold, contemplating the drop on either side? Could a person keep a lid on his terror long enough to reach the top and get back down?

And if I did pull it off...I was afraid to let myself imagine the triumphant aftermath, lest I invite a jinx. But I never had any doubt that climbing the Devils Thumb would transform my life. How could it not?

I was working then as an itinerant carpenter, framing condominiums in Boulder for $3.50 an hour. One afternoon, after nine hours of humping two-by-tens and driving sixteen-penny nails, I told my boss I was quitting: "No, not in a couple of weeks, Steve; right now was more like what I had in mind." It took me a few hours to clear my tools and other belongings out of the crummy job-site trailer where I'd been squatting. And then I climbed into my car and departed for

Alaska. I was surprised, as always, by how easy the act of leaving was, and how good it felt. The world was suddenly rich with possibility.

The Devils Thumb demarcates the Alaska–British Columbia border east of Petersburg, a fishing village accessible only by boat or plane. There was regular jet service to Petersburg, but the sum of my liquid assets amounted to a 1960 Pontiac Star Chief and $200 in cash, not even enough for a one-way airfare. So I drove as far as Gig Harbor, Washington, abandoned the car, and inveigled a ride on a northbound salmon seiner.

The *Ocean Queen* was a stout, no-nonsense workboat built from thick planks of Alaska yellow cedar, rigged for long-lining and purse seining. In exchange for a ride north, I had only to take regular turns at the helm—a four-hour wheel watch every twelve hours—and help tie endless skates of halibut gear. The slow journey up the Inside Passage unfolded in a gauzy reverie of anticipation. I was underway, propelled by an imperative that was beyond my ability to control or comprehend.

Sunlight glinted off the water as we chugged up the Strait of Georgia. Slopes rose precipitously from the water's edge, bearded in a gloom of hemlock and cedar and devil's club. Gulls wheeled overhead. Off Malcolm Island, the boat split a pod of seven orcas. Their dorsal fins, some as tall as a man, cut the glassy surface within spitting distance of the rail.

Our second night out, two hours before dawn, I was steering from the flying bridge when the head of a mule deer materialized in the spotlight's glare. The animal was in the middle of Fitz Hugh Sound, swimming through the cold black water more than a mile from the Canadian shore. Its retinas burned red in the blinding beam; it looked exhausted and crazed with fear. I swung the wheel to starboard, the boat slid past, and the deer bobbed twice in our wake before vanishing into the darkness.

Most of the Inside Passage follows narrow fjordlike channels. As we passed Dundas Island, though, the vista suddenly widened. To the west now was open ocean, the full sweep of the Pacific, and the boat pitched and rolled on a twelve-foot westerly swell. Waves broke over the rail. In the distance off the starboard bow, a jumble of low, craggy peaks appeared, and my pulse quickened at the sight. Those mountains heralded the approach of my desideratum. We had arrived in Alaska.

Five days out of Gig Harbor, the *Ocean Queen* docked in Petersburg to take on fuel and water. I hopped over the gunwale, shouldered my heavy backpack, and walked down the pier in the rain. At a loss for what to do next, I took refuge under the eaves of the town library and sat on my load.

Petersburg is a small town, and prim by Alaska standards. A tall, loose-limbed woman walked by and struck up a conversation. Her name was Kai, she said, Kai Sandburn. She was cheerful, outgoing, easy to talk to. I confessed my climbing plans to her, and to my relief she neither laughed nor acted as though they were particularly strange. "When the weather's clear," she simply offered, "you can see the Thumb from town. It's pretty. It's over there, right across from Frederick Sound." I followed her outstretched arm, which gestured to the east, at a low wall of clouds.

Kai invited me home for dinner. Later I unrolled my sleeping bag on her floor. Long after she fell asleep, I lay awake in the next room, listening to her peaceful exhalations. I had convinced myself for many months that I didn't really mind the absence of intimacy in my life, the lack of real human connection, but the pleasure I'd felt in this woman's company— the ring of her laughter, the innocent touch of a hand on my arm—exposed my self-deceit and left me hollow and aching.

Petersburg lies on an island; the Devils Thumb is on the mainland, rising from a frozen bald known as the Stikine Ice Cap. Vast and labyrinthine, the ice cap rides the spine of the Boundary Ranges like a carapace, from which the long, blue tongues of numerous glaciers inch down toward the sea under the weight of the ages. To reach the foot of the mountain, I had to find a ride across 25 miles of salt water and then ski 30 miles up one of these glaciers, the Baird, a valley of ice that hadn't seen a human footprint, I was fairly certain, in many, many years.

I shared a ride with some tree planters to the head of Thomas Bay, where I was put ashore on a gravel beach. The broad, rubble-strewn terminus of the glacier was visible a mile away. Half an hour later, I scrambled up its frozen snout and began the long plod to the Thumb. The ice was bare of snow and embedded with a coarse, black grit that crunched beneath the steel points of my crampons.

After 3 or 4 miles I came to the snow line and there exchanged crampons for skis. Putting the boards on my feet cut fifteen pounds from the awful load on my back and made the going faster besides. But the snow concealed many of the glacier's crevasses, increasing the danger.

In Seattle, anticipating this hazard, I'd stopped at a hardware store and purchased a pair of stout aluminum curtain rods, each ten feet long. I lashed the rods together to form a cross, then strapped the rig to the hip belt of my backpack so the poles extended horizontally over the snow. Staggering slowly up the glacier beneath my overloaded pack, bearing this ridiculous metal cross, I felt like an odd sort of *penitente*. Were I to break through the veneer of snow over a hidden crevasse, though, the curtain rods would—I hoped mightily—span the slot and keep me from dropping into the frozen depths of the Baird.

For two days I slogged steadily up the valley of ice. The weather was good, the route obvious and without major obstacles. Because I was alone, however, even the mundane seemed charged with meaning. The ice looked colder and more mysterious, the sky a cleaner shade of blue. The unnamed peaks towering over the glacier were bigger and comelier and infinitely more menacing than they would have been were I in the company of another person. And my emotions were similarly amplified: the highs were higher; the periods of despair were deeper and darker. To a self-possessed young man inebriated with the unfolding drama of his own life, all of this held enormous appeal.

Three days after leaving Petersburg, I arrived beneath the Stikine Ice Cap proper, where the long arm of the Baird joins the main body of ice. Here the glacier spills abruptly over the edge of a high plateau, dropping seaward through a gap between two mountains in a phantasmagoria of shattered ice. As I stared at the tumult from a mile away, for the first time since leaving Colorado, I was truly afraid.

The icefall was crisscrossed with crevasses and tottering seracs. From afar it brought to mind a bad train wreck, as if scores of ghostly white boxcars had derailed at the lip of the ice cap and tumbled down the slope willy-nilly. The closer I got, the more unpleasant it looked. My 10-foot curtain rods seemed a poor defense against crevasses that were 40 feet across and hundreds of feet deep. Before I could plot a logical course through the icefall, the wind came up, and snow began to slant hard out of the clouds, stinging my face and reducing visibility to almost nothing.

For the better part of the day, I groped blindly through the labyrinth in the whiteout, retracing my steps from one dead end to another. Time after time I'd think I'd found a way out, only to wind up in a deep-blue cul-de-sac or stranded atop a detached pillar of ice. My efforts were lent a sense of urgency by the noises emanating from beneath my feet. A madrigal of creaks and sharp reports—the sort of protest a large fir limb makes when it's slowly bent to the breaking point—served as a reminder that it is the nature of glaciers to move, the habits of seracs to topple.

I put a foot through a snow bridge spanning a slot so deep I couldn't see the bottom of it. A little later I broke through another bridge to my waist; the poles kept me out of the 100-foot crevasse, but after I extricated myself, I bent double with dry heaves, thinking about what it would be like to be lying in a pile at the bottom of a crevasse, waiting for death to come, with nobody aware of how or where I'd met my end.

Night had nearly fallen by the time I emerged from the top of the serac slope onto the empty, wind-scoured expanse of the high glacial plateau. In shock and chilled to the core, I skied far enough past the icefall to put its rumblings out of earshot, pitched the tent, crawled into my sleeping bag, and shivered myself into a fitful sleep.

I had planned on spending between three weeks and a month on the Stikine Ice Cap. Not relishing the prospect of carrying a four-week load of food, heavy winter camping gear, and climbing hardware all the way up the Baird on my back, I had paid a bush pilot in Petersburg $150—the last of my cash—to have six cardboard cartons of supplies dropped from an airplane when I reached the foot of the Thumb. On his map I'd showed the pilot exactly where I intended to be and told him to give me three days to get there; he promised to fly over and make the drop as soon thereafter as the weather permitted.

On May 6, I set up a base camp on the ice cap just north-east of the Thumb and waited for the airdrop. For the next four days it snowed, nixing any chance for a flight. Too terrified of crevasses to wander far from camp, I spent most of my time recumbant in the tent—the ceiling was too low to allow my sitting upright—fighting a rising chorus of doubts.

As the days passed, I grew increasingly anxious. I had no radio nor any other means of communicating with the outside world. It had been many years since anyone had visited this part of the Stikine Ice Cap, and many more would likely pass before anyone would again. I was nearly out of stove fuel and down to a single chunk of cheese, my last package of Ramen noodles, and half a box of Cocoa Puffs. This, I figured, could sustain me for three or four more days if need be, but then what would I do? It would take only two days to ski back down the Baird to Thomas Bay, but a week or more might easily pass before a fisherman happened by who could give me a lift back to Petersburg (the tree planters with whom I'd ridden over were camped fifteen miles down the impassable headland-studded coast and could be reached only by boat or plane).

When I went to bed on the evening of May 10, it was still snowing and blowing hard. Hours later I heard a faint, momentary whine, scarcely louder than a mosquito. I tore open the tent door. Most of the clouds had lifted, but there was no airplane in sight. The whine returned, more insistently this time. Then I saw it: a tiny red-and-white fleck high in the western sky, droning my way.

A few minutes later the plane passed directly overhead. The pilot, however, was unaccustomed to glacier flying, and he'd badly misjudged the scale of the terrain. Worried about flying too low and getting nailed by unexpected turbulence, he stayed at least a thousand feet above me—believing all the while he was just off the deck—and never saw my tent in the flat evening light. My waving and screaming were to no avail; from his altitude, I was indistinguishable from a pile of rocks.

For the next hour he circled the ice cap, scanning its barren contours without success. But the pilot, to his credit, appreciated the gravity of my predicament and didn't give up. Frantic, I tied my sleeping bag to the end of one of the curtain rods and waved for all I was worth. The plane banked sharply and headed straight at me.

The pilot buzzed my tent three times in quick succession, dropping two boxes on each pass; then the airplane disappeared over a ridge, and I was alone. As silence again settled over the glacier, I felt abandoned, vulnerable, lost. I realized that I was sobbing. Embarrassed, I halted the blubbering by screaming obscenities until I grew hoarse.

I awoke early on May 11 to clear skies and the relatively warm temperature of 20 degrees Fahrenheit. Startled by the good weather, mentally unprepared to commence the actual climb, I hurriedly packed up a rucksack nonetheless and began skiing toward the base of the Thumb. Two previous Alaska expeditions had taught me that I couldn't afford to waste a rare day of perfect weather.

A small hanging glacier extends out from the lip of the ice cap, leading up and across the north face of the Thumb like a catwalk. My plan was to follow this catwalk to a prominent rock prow in the center of the wall and thereby execute an end run around the ugly, avalanche-swept lower half of the face.

The catwalk turned out to be a series of 50-degree ice fields blanketed with knee-deep powder snow and riddled with crevasses. The depth of the snow made the going slow and exhausting; by the time I front-pointed up the overhanging wall of the uppermost bergschrund, some three or four hours after leaving camp, I was thrashed. And I hadn't even gotten to the real climbing yet. That would begin immediately above, where the hanging glacier gives way to vertical rock.

The rock, exhibiting a dearth of holds and coated with six inches of crumbly rime, did not look promising, but just left of the main prow was a shallow corner glazed with frozen meltwater. This ribbon of ice led straight up for 300 feet, and if the ice proved substantial enough to support the picks of my ice axes, the route might be feasible. I shuffled over to the bottom of the corner and gingerly swung one of my tools into the two-inch-thick ice. Solid and plastic, it was thinner than I would have liked but otherwise encouraging.

The climbing was steep and so exposed it made my head spin. Beneath my Vibram soles, the wall fell away for 3,000 feet to the dirty, avalanche-scarred cirque of the Witches Cauldron Glacier. Above, the prow soared with authority toward the summit ridge, a vertical half mile above. Each time I planted one of my ice axes, that distance shrank by another twenty inches.

All that held me to the mountainside, all that held me to the world, were two thin spikes of chrome molybdenum stuck half an inch into a smear of frozen water, yet the higher I climbed, the more comfortable I became. Early on a difficult climb, especially a difficult solo climb, you constantly feel the abyss pulling at your back. To resist takes a tremendous conscious effort; you don't dare let your guard down for an instant. The siren song of the void puts you on edge; it makes your movements tentative, clumsy, herky-jerky. But as the climb goes on, you grow accustomed to the exposure, you get used to rubbing shoulders with doom, you come to believe in the reliability of your hands and feet and head. You learn to trust your self-control.

By and by, your attention becomes so intensely focused that you no longer notice the raw knuckles, the cramping thighs, the strain of maintaining nonstop concentration. A trancelike state settles over your efforts; the climb becomes a clear-eyed dream. Hours slide by like minutes. The accumulated clutter of day-to-day existence—the lapses of conscience, the unpaid bills, the bungled opportunities, the dust under the couch, the inescapable prison of your genes—all of it is temporarily forgotten, crowded from your thoughts by an overpowering clarity of purpose and by the seriousness of the task at hand.

At such moments, something resembling happiness actually stirs in your chest, but it isn't the sort of emotion you want to lean on very hard. In solo climbing the whole enterprise is held together with little more than chutzpah, not the most reliable adhesive. Late in the day on the north face of the Thumb, I felt the glue disintegrate with a swing of an ice ax.

I'd gained nearly 700 feet of altitude since stepping off the hanging glacier, all of it on crampon front points and the picks of my axes. The ribbon of frozen meltwater had ended 300 feet up and was followed by a crumbly armor of frost feathers. Though just barely substantial enough to support body weight, the rime was plastered over the rock to a thickness of 2 or 3 feet, so I kept plugging upward. The wall, however, had been growing imperceptibly steeper, and as it did so, the frost feathers became thinner. I'd fallen into a slow, hypnotic rhythm—swing, swing; kick, kick; swing, swing; kick, kick— when my left ice ax slammed into a slab of diorite a few inches beneath the rime.

I tried left, then right, but kept striking rock. The frost feathers holding me up, it became apparent, were maybe five inches thick and had the structural integrity of stale corn bread. Below was 3,700 feet of air, and I was balanced on a house of cards. The sour taste of panic rose in my throat. My eyesight blurred, I began to hyperventilate, my calves started to shake. I shuffled a few feet farther to the right, hoping to find thicker ice, but managed only to bend an ice ax on the rock.

Awkwardly, stiff with fear, I started working my way back

down. The rime gradually thickened. After descending about 80 feet, I got back on reasonably solid ground. I stopped for a long time to let my nerves settle, then leaned back from my tools and stared up at the face above, searching for a hint of solid ice, for some variation in the underlying rock strata, for anything that would allow passage over the frosted slabs. I looked until my neck ached, but nothing appeared. The climb was over. The only place to go was down.

After coming down from the side of the Devils Thumb, heavy snow and high winds kept me inside the tent for most of the next three days. The hours passed slowly. In the attempt to hurry them along, I chain-smoked for as long as my supply of cigarettes held out, and I read. When I ran out of reading matter, I was reduced to studying the ripstop pattern woven into the tent ceiling. This I did for hours on end, flat on my back, while engaging in a heated self-debate: should I leave for the coast as soon as the weather broke, or should I stay put long enough to make another attempt on the mountain?

In truth, my escapade on the north face had rattled me, and I didn't want to go up on the Thumb again at all. But the thought of returning to Boulder in defeat wasn't very appealing either. I could all too easily picture the smug expressions of condolence I'd receive from those who'd been certain of my failure from the get-go.

By the third afternoon of the storm, I couldn't stand it any longer: the lumps of frozen snow poking me in the back, the clammy nylon walls brushing against my face, the incredible smell drifting up from the depths of my sleeping bag. I pawed through the mess at my feet until I located a small green sack, in which there was a metal film can continuing the makings of what I'd hoped would be a sort of victory cigar. I'd intended to save it for my return from the summit, but what the hey—

it wasn't looking like I'd be visiting the top anytime soon. I poured most of the can's contents onto a leaf of cigarette paper, rolled it into a crooked joint, and promptly smoked it down to the roach.

The marijuana, of course, only made the tent seem even more cramped, more suffocating, more impossible to bear. It also made me terribly hungry. I decided a little oatmeal would put things right. Making it, however, was a long, ridiculously involved process: a potful of snow had to be gathered outside in the tempest, the stove assembled and lit, the oatmeal and sugar located, the remnants of yesterday's dinner scraped from my bowl. I'd gotten the stove going and was melting the snow when I smelled something burning. A thorough check of the stove and its environs revealed nothing. Mystified, I was ready to chalk it up to my chemically enhanced imagination when I heard something crackle at my back.

I spun around in time to see a bag of garbage—into which I'd tossed the match I'd used to light the stove—flare into a small conflagration. Beating on the fire with my hands, I had it out in a few seconds, but not before a large section of the tent's inner wall vaporized before my eyes. The built-in fly escaped the flames, so it was still more or less weatherproof; now, however, it was approximately 30 degrees colder inside.

My left palm began to sting. Examining it, I noticed the pink welt of a burn. What troubled me most, though, was that the tent wasn't even mine: I'd borrowed the expensive shelter from my father. It was new before my trip—the hangtags had still been attached—and had been lent reluctantly. For several minutes I sat dumbstruck, staring at the wreckage of the tent's once-graceful form amid the acrid scent of singed hair and melted nylon. You had to hand it to me, I thought: I had a knack for living up to the old man's worst expectations.

My father was a volatile, extremely complicated person,

possessed of a brash demeanor that masked deep insecurities. If he ever in his entire life admitted to being wrong, I wasn't there to witness it. But it was my father, a weekend mountaineer, who taught me to climb. He bought me my first rope and ice ax when I was eight years old and led me into the Cascade Range to make an assault on the South Sister, a gentle 10,000-foot volcano not far from our Oregon home. It never occurred to him that I would one day try to shape my life around climbing.

A kind and generous man, Lewis Krakauer loved his five children deeply, in the autocratic way of fathers, but his worldview was colored by a relentlessly competitive nature. Life, as he saw it, was a contest. He read and reread the works of Stephen Potter—the English writer who coined the terms *one-upmanship* and *gamesmanship*—not as social satire but as a manual of practical stratagems. He was ambitious in the extreme, and like Walt McCandless, his aspirations extended to his progeny.

Before I'd even enrolled in kindergarten, he began preparing me for a shining career in medicine—or, failing that, law as a poor consolation. For Christmas and birthdays, I received such gifts as a microscope, a chemistry set, and the *Encyclopaedia Britannica*. From elementary school through high school, my siblings and I were hectored to excel in every class, to win medals in science fairs, to be chosen princess of the prom, to win election to student government. Thereby and only thereby, we learned, could we expect to gain admission to the right college, which in turn would get us into Harvard Medical School: life's one sure path to meaningful success and lasting happiness.

My father's faith in this blueprint was unshakable. It was, after all, the path he had followed to prosperity. But I was not a clone of my father. During my teens, as I came to this realization, I veered gradually from the plotted course, and then sharply. My insurrection prompted a great deal of yelling. The windows of our home rattled with the thunder of ultimatums. By the time I left Corvallis, Oregon, to enroll in a distant college where no ivy grew, I was speaking to my father with a clenched jaw or not at all. When I graduated four years later and did not enter Harvard or any other medical school but became a carpenter and climbing bum instead, the unbridgeable gulf between us widened.

I had been granted unusual freedom and responsibility at an early age, for which I should have been grateful in the extreme, but I wasn't. Instead, I felt oppressed by the old man's expectations. It was drilled into me that anything less than winning was failure. In the impressionable way of sons, I did not consider this rhetorically; I took him at his word. And that's why later, when long-held family secrets came to light, when I noticed that this deity who asked only for perfection was himself less than perfect, that he was in fact not a deity at all—well, I wasn't able to shrug it off. I was consumed instead by a blinding rage. The revelation that he was merely human, and frightfully so, was beyond my power to forgive.

Two decades after the fact, I discovered that my rage was gone, and had been for years. It had been supplanted by a rueful sympathy and something not unlike affection. I came to understand that I had baffled and infuriated my father at least as much as he had baffled and infuriated me. I saw that I had been selfish and unbending and a giant pain in the ass. He'd built a bridge of privilege for me, a hand-paved trestle to the good life, and I repaid him by chopping it down and crapping on the wreckage.

But this epiphany occurred only after the intervention of time and misfortune, when my father's self-satisfied existence had begun to crumble beneath him. It began with the betrayal

of his flesh: 30 years after a bout with polio, the symptoms mys-
teriously flared anew. Crippled muscles withered further,
synapses wouldn't fire, wasted legs refused to ambulate. From
medical journals, he deduced that he was suffering from a newly
identified aliment known as postpolio syndrome. Pain, excruciating at times, filled his days like a shrill and constant noise.

In an ill-advised attempt to halt the decline, he started med-
icating himself. He never went anywhere without a faux
leather valise stuffed with dozens of orange plastic pill bottles.
Every hour or two he would fumble through the drug bag,
squinting at the labels, and shake out tablets of Dexedrine and
Prozac and deprenyl. He gulped pills by the fistful, grimacing,
without water. Used syringes and empty ampoules appeared
on the bathroom sink. To a greater and greater degree, his life
revolved around a self-administered pharmacopoeia of steroids,
amphetamines, mood elevators, and painkillers, and the drugs
addled his once-formidable mind.

As his behavior became more and more irrational, more
and more delusional, the last of his friends were driven away.
My long-suffering mother finally had no choice but to move
out. My father crossed the line into madness and then very
nearly succeeded in taking his own life—an act at which he
made sure I was present.

After the suicide attempt, he was placed in a psychiatric
hospital near Portland. When I visited him there, his arms and
legs were strapped to the rails of his bed. He was ranting
incoherently and had soiled himself. His eyes were wild.
Flashing in defiance one moment, in uncomprehending terror
the next, they rolled far back in their sockets, giving a clear
and chilling view into the state of his tortured mind. When
the nurses tried to change his linens, he thrashed against his
restraints and cursed them, cursed me, cursed the fates. That
his foolproof life plan had in the end transported him here, to

this nightmarish station, was an irony that brought me no pleasure and escaped his notice altogether.

There was another irony he failed to appreciate: his struggle to mold me in his image had been successful after all. The old walrus in fact managed to instill in me a great and burning ambition; it had simply found expression in an unintended pursuit. He never understood that the Devils Thumb was the same as medical school, only different.

I suppose it was this inherited, off-kilter ambition that kept me from admitting defeat on the Stikine Ice Cap after my initial attempt to climb the Thumb had failed, even after nearly burning the tent down. Three days after retreating from my first try, I went up on the north face again. This time I climbed only 120 feet above the bergschrund before lack of composure and the arrival of a snow squall forced me to turn around.

Instead of descending to my base camp on the ice cap, though, I decided to spend the night on the steep flank of the mountain, just below my high point. This proved to be a mistake. By late afternoon the squall had metastasized into another major storm. Snow fell from the clouds at the rate of an inch an hour. As I crouched inside my bivouac sack under the lip of the bergschrund, spindrift avalanches hissed down from the wall above and washed over me like surf, slowly burying my ledge.

It took about twenty minutes for the spindrift to inundate my bivvy sack—a thin nylon envelope shaped exactly like a Baggies sandwich bag, only bigger—to the level of the breathing slit. Four times this happened, and four times I dug myself out. After the fifth burial, I'd had enough. I threw all my gear into my pack and made a break for the base camp.

The descent was terrifying. Because of the clouds, the ground blizzard, and the flat, fading light, I couldn't tell slope from sky. I worried, with ample reason, that I might step

blindly off the top of a serac and end up at the bottom of the
Witches Cauldron, a vertical half mile below. When I finally
arrived on the frozen plain of the ice cap, I found that my
tracks had long since drifted over. I didn't have a clue as to
how to locate the tent on the featureless glacial plateau.
Hoping I'd get lucky and stumble across my camp, I skied in
circles for an hour—until I put a foot into a small crevasse and
realized that I was acting like an idiot—that I should hunker
down right where I was and wait out the storm.

I dug a shallow hole, wrapped myself in the bivvy bag, and
sat on my pack in the swirling snow. Drifts piled up around
me. My feet became numb. A damp chill crept down my chest
from the base of my neck, where spindrift had gotten inside
my parka and soaked my shirt. If only I had a cigarette, I
thought, a single cigarette, I could summon the strength of
character to put a good face on this fucked-up situation, on
the whole fucked-up trip. I pulled the bivvy sack tighter
around my shoulders. The wind ripped at my back. Beyond
shame, I cradled my head in my arms and embarked on an
orgy of self-pity.

I knew that people sometimes died climbing mountains.
But at the age of 23, personal mortality—the idea of my own
death—was still largely outside my conceptual grasp. When I
decamped from Boulder for Alaska, my head swimming with
visions of glory and redemption on the Devils Thumb, it
didn't occur to me that I might be bound by the same cause-
and-effect relationships that governed the actions of others.
Because I wanted to climb the mountain so badly, because I
had thought about the Thumb so intensely for so long, it
seemed beyond the realm of possibility that some minor obstacle like the weather or crevasses or rime-covered rock
might ultimately thwart my will.

At sunset the wind died, and the ceiling lifted 150 feet off the glacier, enabling me to locate my base camp. I made it back to the tent intact, but it was no longer possible to ignore the fact that the Thumb had made hash of my plans. I was forced to acknowledge that by volition alone, however powerful, I was not going to get up the north wall. I saw, finally, that nothing was.

There still existed an opportunity for salvaging the expedition, however. A week earlier I'd skied over to the southeast side of the mountain to take a look at the route by which I'd intended to descend the peak after climbing the north wall, a route that Fred Beckey, the legendary alpinist, had followed in 1946 in making the first ascent of the Thumb. During my reconnaissance, I'd noticed an obviously unclimbed line to the left of the Beckey route—a patchy network of ice angling across the southeast face—that struck me as a relatively easy way to achieve the summit. At the time, I'd considered this route unworthy of my attentions. Now, on the rebound from my calamitous entanglement with the *nordwand*, I was prepared to lower my sights.

On the afternoon of May 15, when the blizzard finally abated, I returned to the southeast face and climbed to the top of a slender ridge that abuts the upper peak like a flying buttress on a Gothic cathedral. I decided to spend the night there, on the narrow crest, 1,600 feet below the summit. The evening sky was cold and cloudless. I could see all the way to tidewater and beyond. At dusk I watched, transfixed, as the lights of Petersburg blinked on in the west. The closest thing I'd had to human contact since the airdrop, the distant lights triggered a flood of emotion that caught me off guard. I imagined people watching baseball on television, eating fried chicken in brightly lit kitchens, drinking beer, making love. When I lay down to sleep, I was overcome by a wrenching loneliness. I'd never felt so alone, ever.

That night I had troubled dreams, of a police bust and vampires and a gangland-style execution. I heard someone whisper, "I think he's in there...." I sat bolt upright and opened my eyes. The sun was about to rise. The entire sky was scarlet. It was still clear, but a thin, wispy scum of cirrus had spread across the upper atmosphere, and a dark line of squalls was visible just above the southwestern horizon. I pulled on my boots and hurriedly strapped on my crampons. Five minutes after waking up, I was climbing away from the bivouac.

I carried no rope, no tent or bivouac gear, no hardware save my ice axes. My plan was to go light and fast, to reach the summit and make it back down before the weather turned. Pushing myself, continually out of breath, I scurried up and to the left, across small snowfields linked by ice-choked clefts and short rock steps. The climbing was almost fun—the rock was covered with large incut holds, and the ice, though thin, never got steeper than 70 degrees—but I was anxious about the storm front racing in from the Pacific, darkening the sky.

I didn't have a watch, but in what seemed like a very short time, I was on the distinctive final ice field. By now the entire sky was smeared with clouds. It looked easier to keep angling to the left but quicker to go straight for the top. Anxious about being caught by a storm high on the peak and without shelter, I opted for the direct route. The ice steepened and thinned. I swung my left ice ax and struck rock. I aimed for another spot, and once again it glanced off unyielding diorite with a dull clank. And again, and again. It was a reprise of my first attempt on the north face. Looking between my legs, I stole a glance at the glacier more than 2,000 feet below. My stomach churned.

Forty-five feet above me, the wall eased back onto the sloping summit shoulder. I clung stiffly to my axes, unmoving, racked by terror and indecision. Again I looked down at the long drop to the glacier, then up, then scraped away the patina of ice above my head. I hooked the pick of my left ax on a nickel-thin lip of rock and weighted it. It held. I pulled my right ax from the ice, reached up, twisted the pick into a crooked half-inch fissure until it jammed. Barely breathing now, I moved my feet up, scrabbling my crampon points across the verglas. Reaching as high as I could with my left arm, I swung the ax gently at the shiny, opaque surface, not knowing what I'd hit beneath it. The pick went in with a solid *whunk*! A few minutes later I was standing on a broad ledge. The summit proper, a slender rock fin sprouting a grotesque meringue of atmospheric ice, stood twenty feet directly above.

The insubstantial frost feathers ensured that those last twenty feet remained hard, scary, onerous. But then suddenly there was no place higher to go. I felt my cracked lips stretch into a painful grin. I was on top of the Devils Thumb.

Fittingly, the summit was a surreal, malevolent place, an improbably slender wedge of rock and rime no wider than a file cabinet. It did not encourage loitering. As I straddled the highest point, the south face fell away beneath my right boot for 2,500 feet; beneath my left boot the north face dropped twice that distance. I took some pictures to prove I'd been there and spent a few minutes trying to straighten a bent pick. Then I stood up, carefully turned around, and headed for home.

One week later I was camped in the rain beside the sea, marveling at the sight of moss, willows, mosquitoes. The salt air carried the rich stink of tidal life. By and by, a small skiff motored into Thomas Bay and pulled up on the beach not far from my tent. The man driving the boat introduced himself as Jim Freeman, a timber faller from Petersburg. It was his day off, he said; he'd made the trip to show his family the glacier and to look for bears. He asked me if I'd "been huntin', or what?"

"No," I replied sheepishly. "Actually, I just climbed the Devils Thumb. I've been here over twenty days."

Freeman fiddled with a deck cleat and said nothing. It became obvious that he didn't believe me. Nor did he seem to approve of my snarled, shoulder-length hair or the way I smelled after having gone three weeks without bathing or changing my clothes. When I asked if he could give me a lift back to town, however, he offered a grudging "I don't see why not."

The water was choppy, and the ride across Frederick Sound took two hours. Freeman gradually warmed to me as we talked. He still wasn't convinced I'd climbed the Thumb, but by the time he steered the skiff into Wrangell Narrows, he pretended to be. After docking the boat, he insisted on buying me a cheeseburger. That evening he invited me to spend the night in a junked step van parked in his backyard.

I lay down in the rear of the old truck for a while but couldn't sleep, so I got up and walked to a bar called Kito's Kave. The euphoria, the overwhelming sense of relief, that had initially accompanied my return to Petersburg faded, and an unexpected melancholy took its place. The people I chatted with in Kito's didn't seem to doubt that I'd been to the top of the Thumb; they just didn't much care. As the night wore on, the place emptied except for me and an old, toothless Tlingit man at a back table. I drank alone, putting quarters into the jukebox, playing the same five songs over and over until the barmaid yelled angrily, "Hey! Give it a fucking rest, kid!" I mumbled an apology, headed for the door, and lurched back to Freeman's step van. There, surrounded by the sweet scent of old motor oil, I lay down on the floorboards next to a gutted transmission and passed out.

Less than a month after sitting on the summit of the Thumb,

I was back in Boulder, nailing up siding on the Spruce Street Townhouses, the same condos I'd been framing when I left for Alaska. I got a raise, to $4 an hour, and at the end of the summer moved out of the job-trailer to a cheap studio apartment west of the downtown mall.

It is easy, when you are young, to believe that what you desire is no less than what you deserve, to assume that if you want something badly enough, it is your God-given right to have it. When I decided to go to Alaska that April, like Chris McCandless, I was a raw youth who mistook passion for insight and acted according to an obscure, gap-ridden logic. I thought climbing the Devils Thumb would fix all that was wrong with my life. In the end, of course, it changed almost nothing. But I came to appreciate that mountains make poor receptacles for dreams. And I lived to tell my tale.

As a young man, I was unlike McCandless in many important regards; most notably, I possessed neither his intellect nor his lofty ideals. But I believe we were similarly affected by the skewed relationships we had with our fathers. And I suspect we had a similar intensity, a similar heedlessness, a similar agitation of the soul.

The fact that I survived my Alaskan adventure and McCandless did not survive his was largely a matter of chance; had I not returned from the Stikine Ice Cap in 1977, people would have been quick to say of me—as they now say of him—that I had a death wish. Eighteen years after the event, I now recognize that I suffered from hubris, perhaps, and an appalling innocence, certainly; but I wasn't suicidal.

At that stage of my youth, death remained as abstract a concept as non-Euclidean geometry or marriage. I didn't yet appreciate its terrible finality or the havoc it could wreak on those who'd entrusted the deceased with their hearts. I was stirred by the dark mystery of mortality. I couldn't resist stealing up to the edge of doom and peering over the brink. The hint of what was concealed in those shadows terrified me, but I caught sight of something in the glimpse, some forbidden and elemental riddle that was no less compelling than the sweet, hidden petals of a woman's sex.

In my case—and, I believe in the case of Chris McCandless— that was very different from wanting to die.

Jon Krakauer is the author of Eiger Dreams: Ventures Among Men and Mountains, Into Thin Air: A Personal Account of the Mt. Everest Disaster, *and* Into the Wild, *from which this story was excerpted. A contributing editor to* Outside, *he writes for many national magazines and newspapers. He lives with his wife in Seattle.*

CHRISTOPHER COOK GILMORE

✦

The World's Most Dangerous Girlfriend

It was a case of sin and magic in the Cambodian jungle.

ALL I HAVE LEFT OF THE BEAUTIFUL AND DANGEROUS MISS
Aien Smi is a picture I took of her one night in Phnom Penh
while she was sleeping. I had others—Aien playing soccer in
high school, Aien firing an M–16 at the range, Aien posing
naked in the jungle—but they disappeared at customs. I had a
little silver fish she gave me at Sharkey's the night a cop went
crazy and shot up the place. That vanished, too.

Miss Aien was eighteen, an athlete, the star of the best girls'
soccer team in Cambodia. Her mother was Vietnamese, killed
by the Khmer Rouge when Aien was two. Her father was
Cambodian; he'd been in the army, a general. By the time I
met Aien he was dead, assassinated three years before in
Anlong Veng. Now she was a prostitute.

Miss Aien was young and wild, destitute and desperate, but
I know she loved me. I could see real love in her eyes when
she looked at me. I could hear it in the Buddhist prayers she
said for me when things got scary. If it was my money that

made her love me, so what? What does it matter why a beautiful girl loves you, as long as she does?

I wrote to her a few months after I left Cambodia—tanks were rolling through the streets of Phnom Penh after yet another political meltdown—but I've had no answer. She could be dead, shot starved to death. She could be in a refugee camp in Thailand, or looking for me in Ho Chi Minh City. I just wish she were back in Phnom Penh with a new boyfriend— another American—to take care of her. I wish I had a picture of her with her eyes open.

When I went to Cambodia nearly two years ago, I wasn't looking for a girlfriend. I'd been in Vietnam for months and already had more girlfriends than you could stuff in ten taxis. What I wanted to do in Cambodia was hang out in jungle temples. I'd met a Japanese archaeology student in Nha Trang who'd just come back from Angkor Wat, and she had intrigued me with her weird tales about the ghostly stone temples, some of them in ruins, some overgrown by vegetation, some with triple towers intact and, she'd claimed, "taller than the Pyramids."

My travel agent told me to fly directly to Angkor Wat and stay out of Phnom Penh. Some of his customers had gone to the Cambodian capital and not come back. At a cyber-café in Ho Chi Minh City, I got an E-mail from New York saying he'd read on the Internet that Cambodia's civil war was heating up and that, whatever I did, I should keep clear of Phnom Penh.

A little bell went off somewhere in my head. When all the angels start walking out of the party, it's time for the fools to rush in. I've been rushing in and out of unpredictable Third-World danger zones all my life, and I'm still here. I've always carried with me the necessary ingredients for survival: confidence and ignorance. And incredible luck.

It was hot as hell the morning I left Ho Chi Minh City. I hired a taxi to take me to the Cambodian border, crossed on foot, made a deal with another cab driver, and by late afternoon was cracking an ice-cold Angkor beer in a room on the fourth floor of the Singapore Hotel, Old China Town, Phnom Penh.

I met You, my motorbike boy, early the next morning. He was waiting outside with a plaid scarf tied around his head and a battered 90cc Honda at the ready. He was nineteen, tall, and good-looking, and he laughed hysterically at everything I said. He offered to work for me full-time, take me anywhere I wanted to go, show me anything I wanted to see, for $7 a day.

"Want a girl?" he asked. No, I said, but I wouldn't mind looking at some. "Looking?" he said. "Looking," I said. Screaming with high-pitched laughter, he twisted the throttle and flung us into traffic.

It was early, only 8 p.m., when we entered the Martini Bar and Disco off Mao Tse-tung Boulevard, but the dance floor was already packed with beautiful women. You and I were the only men in the bar, and I was the only paying customer. I had an Angkor and bought You a Coke, causing more gales of laughter.

Every time I'd point out a pretty girl, he'd stand up and shout "You want her?" I'd shake my head, and he'd crack up. Out of curiosity I asked about prices. "Which one?" he demanded. I nodded toward a breathtaking beauty in platform heels and a black satin minidress.

Before I could stop him, You got up, dashed onto the dance floor, grabbed the girl by the hand, and dragged her over. Giggling madly, she said she was $40 for the night. I thanked her and said I would definitely think about it.

Suddenly I felt something warm and soft rub against my calf. Somehow I knew it wasn't a cat. It was a girl who'd sat

down next to me. I turned and looked full into the face of
Miss Aien Smi.

She was only a kid, maybe not as young as some of the girls,
but damn young. Her skin was flawless, and her hair reached
her waist. She wore red satin Chinese pajamas with short
sleeves and little black slippers. She rubbed my leg with hers.
I rubbed back.

"She my friend!" yelled You over the music. "We graduate
high school together! She number-one girl soccer player of
Cambodia!"

She stared at my face. After a long time, she said solemnly
and with great sincerity, "You very handsome man."

"She only $20!" You shouted in my ear.

Miss Aien may not have been the white-hot smoker that
some of the girls were, but she was very beautiful, and I admired her approach. I bought her a Coke—she never touched
alcohol—and we rubbed legs some more. I asked her to dance.

The DJ played Abba while everybody sang along and did
that dance I call Washing the Car. Aien had nice, high breasts
and a cute little bottom she shook in my face every chance
she got. When we stopped dancing, I kissed her. She kissed
me back.

"We go?" she asked.

You dropped us off at the Singapore. When we got to my
room Miss Aien took over. She locked the door, drew the
curtains, turned out the bright lights, turned on a string of
twinkly ones, and got undressed. I felt like her patient. She
took off my clothes. She gave me a back message, then a leg
massage, then a foot massage. When I tried to talk, she
shushed me.

She had no modesty. I gave her a silk scarf I'd bought in
Hue. She knotted it around her head, and that was all she wore
the rest of the night. After we made love, she found a little

Mini-Maglite flashlight I travel with and switched it on. Slowly she ran the beam over her body, then over mine. She was very curious.

Miss Aien liked to roughhouse. She tickled me, poked me, pinched me, pushed me, punched my arms and legs, wrestled me off the bed and onto the floor. At one point I fought back. I pinned her, sat on top of her, and tried to tell her lovingly that what I really wanted from her was love and passion and sweet tenderness, not combat. She laughed in my face and threw me off like a rag doll.

The next day, You took us out of Phnom Penh to the range, where for a few bucks tourists could fire various weapons. Miss Aien said she'd always wanted to shoot an M-16. I bought her a dozen magazines and drank Angkors with You while she blasted away.

"BAZOOKA!" she screamed.

It only got weirder. One day Aien and I were walking down Monivong Boulevard when we heard gunshots. Aien got in front of me, ready to stop bullets. I saw a man drop to the ground in the middle of an intersection. Two cars sped away in opposite directions.

Aien got the story from a noodle lady. A civilian driving a truck had run into a soldier driving a car. A dispute arose. A cop arrived on a motorbike and joined in. Tired of arguing, the soldier pulled out a gun and shot the cop dead.

It was time to get out of Phnom Penh.

We were on a fast boat—about fifteen minutes up the Tonle Sap River from Phnom Penh and headed for Angkor Wat—when we heard automatic-weapon fire. A hundred yards away, a fisherman standing in a wooden boat pointed an AK-47 at the sky and squeezed off another burst. He was asking us to slow down. This happened three more times on the way to the temples. Each time we just went faster.

I chose our room at the Naga Guest House, in Siem Reap, because it had windows on two sides and I thought it would be breezy and cool in the evenings. But the girl at the desk warned us to keep the wooden shutters closed after dark. The room had been grenaded two weeks before. No one had been hurt, but the owner had just replastered, so would we mind?

For five days all we did was eat, drink, and tour the temples, which are sprawling and labyrinthine. We had an excellent guidebook and a new motorbike boy. His name was also You, so we called him You-two. He was $6 a day. He told us to watch out for unexploded bombs and land mines and to hide if we saw any soldiers in the jungle.

What I liked to do was pick a temple, explore it a bit, then find some gloomy chamber where, deep in the ruins, I could sit quietly and think. This was not Miss Aien's idea of what the temples were for. To her they were obstacle courses, training grounds, places for exercise. She ran everywhere, up and down the stone steps, through the courtyards, round and round the narrow corridors. Often I'd be hidden away in my crypt, searching for inspiration, and her plaid skirt would fly by in a blur.

"BAZOOKA!"

After five days of stone temples, we needed a diversion, so we checked out the town of Siem Reap. In the summer of 1997, Pol Pot was arrested and tried in Anlong Veng, which is only about 80 miles from there. At the time Aien and I were touring temples, Anlong Veng and much of the jungle around it was controlled by Khmer Rouge guerrillas.

I smelled trouble. I began to notice bullet holes in some of the buildings, razor wire and armed soldiers by all the banks, and heavy machine guns mounted on the trucks. I started to get the feeling I was pushing my luck.

Apart from that, money was running low and my visa was about to expire. We took the slow boat back to Phnom Penh and, for our last night together, checked in to the Sun Shine Hotel on the Tonle Sap.

The next morning Aien and I walked down by the river to say goodbye. I gave her all the money I could. I wish I'd given her more, everything I had, my flashlight, my radio. I wish I could have stayed on. But I couldn't.

I told her I'd be back. She looked at the river and didn't say anything. I told her I loved her. She laughed and punched me on the arm. Then she spoke. She pointed at her heart and then at me, and she said, "Only one."

Christopher Cook Gilmore writes for Men's Journal.

⋆ ⋆ ⋆

The Lure of Danger

Nothing makes you feel so alive
as the risk of death.

GOING TO A WAR WAS EASY—A LOT EASIER THAN I IMAGINED it would be. It was 1993, and the Balkan conflict had hit a rolling boil. With some big but unformed thoughts about freelancing in Europe, I flew to Prague, spent a week trying to figure out what to do, and then went down to the train station and bought a ticket for the six-hour ride to Zagreb, Croatia. That evening, I was in a country at war.

There were artillery pieces at the Zagreb terminal and soldiers swaggering around with long knives in their belts. Professionally, I had little reason to be there—I had arrived with no contacts and only a vague idea of how to freelance for newspapers—but that wasn't my real reason for going. Truth be told, I was there because people were hammering away at one another from slit trenches an hour outside of town. I wanted to see that. I wanted to be changed.

This belief, that danger and hardship can alter a person—burnish him somehow, make him complete—is an enduring one. Myths, folk tales, rites of passage are all based on it. It's evident in every initiation rite in the world. The Papago Indians of Arizona used to send their young men out on 40-mile runs through the Mojave Desert. Street gangs in Los Angeles bring new members in by kicking them senseless. Special Forces recruits are regularly reduced to tears by the savageness of their training. The thinking behind all this brutality is that survival will earn the person not only the confidence of others but confidence in himself. Going to Bosnia did have that effect on my life, although not so much because it changed me but because it changed how others saw me. After I came back, people took me seriously. They solicited my opinion. They gave me assignments. They wanted to hear my stories. They made me feel, in short, like an adult.

The reason it took me so long to feel that way, I think, is because we Americans live in such a relentlessly safe society. In terms of the basic necessities for survival—food, shelter, clothing—we have, for the greater part, the concerns of children. Which is fine, because there's absolutely nothing redeeming about suffering. But that security comes at a price. Human beings are designed to overcome obstacles. We are designed to outrun, outkill, and outthink anything that threatens our survival. And when we're not being tested—by the weather, by predators, by other tribes—several million years of evolution go unused.

When I was a kid, I broke into a house and caused a number of bad things to happen that I'd rather not go into. The reason I did this wasn't to bring anyone harm—I wasn't angry, just bored—but because I was absolutely aching for a life-and-death sprint through neighbors' backyards with the cops on my heels. I got it, and the fear it inspired in me—along with the raging sense of power I felt from escaping—was an immense rush. I was testing myself, a desire that's natural and genuine and biologically driven.

A war, obviously, is rife with situations that test you. And as much as I hated the war, I found it hard not to envy the soldiers who were fighting it. They had an urgency, a sense of purpose, that few of us experience in such a sweeping way. Politics aside—and the politics were unconscionable—these men thought they were defending their homes against an enemy, and that must have felt deeply, innately right. I've woken up in the middle of the night because I thought I heard someone in the house and crept downstairs—heart pounding, every sense jacked—with that same sense of rightness. *This is what men do*, I would find myself thinking. *Confront things in the dark.*

In Bosnia, there were a lot of guys walking around who seemed to live that sensation. They were younger men, for the most part—ones who hadn't been to battle yet—but the most extreme example I came across was an older Muslim fighter on the outskirts of Sarajevo. I'd gone to the front with two other reporters, and as we sat in a bunker talking to a commander, a shadow filled the doorway: a man dressed in ragged camo, a red bandanna, dark with sweat, tied around his head. It was a dead-hot summer afternoon, and he'd just made his way up a system of trenches and was headed to the front line, about 100 yards away. The line was a gloomy network of bunkers and blown-up houses that led to within speaking distance of Serb troops; in between was a no-man's-land of rubble and splintered trees through which only stray cats could move safely. Puddles of dried blood marked where soldiers had died in people's kitchens. Bullet shells littered what used to be bathroom floors.

He had a machine gun in his hands and the bright eyes of someone in the throes of religious ecstasy—or a high fever. His entire body appeared to vibrate. Wherever a Serb bullet would send him, I figured, he was already there. He was already in the next place. "I'm going up to fight," he told his commander, looking around at us wildly. "I'm going up there to die."

I thought about that guy a lot afterward. It wasn't bravery I'd witnessed so much as an altered state of mind. He was beyond any interest in what the world had to offer him. He was focused on death the way some people focus on sports, on money, or on sex. The killing and dying he would be exposed to on the front line made everything else in his life look like child's play—which it was. If you exchanged his gun for a bouquet of flowers, he could almost have been headed off on a big date, terrified and at the same time knowing there was nothing else he'd rather be doing. But it would be difficult for an evening of romance, no matter how passionate, to offer anything as compelling as what was being tendered just up the hill: you would either be annihilated or cranked out of your mind with relief that you hadn't been. That's why people play Russian roulette, that's why they sky-dive, that's why they kayak Class VI rapids, and play chicken on treacherous mountain roads. There's no heavier rush than the sudden realization that you're still alive, and if you've ever experienced that high, you either never want to feel it again or you creep back to it over and over, furtively, like a man cheating on his wife every Tuesday afternoon.

I spent several weeks in Sarajevo, and they were long and unpleasant ones. We were always hungry, it was infernally hot, and I never got used to the idea of artillery. The sniping I could handle: I knew where the dangerous streets were, and when I came to them I ran like hell. But shelling was different. Mortar rounds can fall anywhere, at any time, and you don't hear them until just before they explode. You could die without ever having known you were in danger, without ever having known you were about to die. You would simply cease to exist. That kind of random threat tended to make me—and

a lot of other people—obsessively self-interested. The smallest
changes in your routine could conceivably put you in the
wrong place at the wrong time, which made every action
glow with a weird kind of importance. One Sarajevan I met
had lost both legs to a mortar because he'd stopped to talk to
someone on his way home from work. That sort of risk-
taking made me queasy, because skill or bravery didn't matter
in the least; it was just one long game of dice.

After a couple of weeks, I joined a handful of journalists
who were on their way to a town called Split, about 100 miles
to the south. A U.N. armored vehicle delivered us to the airport, where we climbed into a C-130 transport plane. An
hour later, we were walking on beautifully cobbled streets,
trying to figure out where to eat lunch.

There are, of course, moral issues that come with being able
to bail out of someone else's nightmare so easily, and I had expected that. What surprised me, though, given what a chick-
enshit I thought I had been about the dangers in Sarajevo, was
how dull life suddenly seemed without them. In Split, we
were able to cross the road without a second thought, to sit at
a café and order a wonderful meal—and suddenly everything
felt drab and dead. Nothing was exciting; nothing was worth
doing. All I wanted was to go back to that strange city where
everything I did seemed big and important and was, poten-
tially, the last act of my life.

This is a horribly indulgent way to think, but more war
correspondents I've talked to have had the same reaction. A
friend of mine once found himself cowering in an obliterated
apartment building during heavy street fighting in West
Beirut. A sniper was raking his hiding place with gunfire, and
my friend just lay there, wired out of his mind. "I was on the
floor, aware of everything," he told me. "I could sense things I
couldn't see. I could hear people breathing 100 feet away. I

was"—he searched for the words—"completely amped." The feeling was like a drug.

In fact, it was a drug. A lot was going on in my friend's brain at that moment, chemically speaking. Fear causes a neurotransmitter called norepinephrine to be released into the locus coeruleus, the section of the brain that governs the senses. Neurotransmitters move nerve impulses across synapses; the more impulses there are, the more active the brain is. When someone is scared, norepinephrine cranks all five senses—sight, hearing, smell, taste, touch—right off the chart. The body is taking in so much information at once that time seems to pass very slowly. In addition, the sympathetic nervous system slams the body into a state of high alert, the heart rate is sped up, and blood is diverted from the skin and organs to the major muscle groups, where it's needed for fighting or running. Finally, intense exertion floods the body with natural opiates, or endorphins, which dull pain and allow you to focus on the crisis at hand. That's what makes fear pleasurable, what keeps people returning to it again and again. Dopamine, the chemical by-product left over in the brain after a terrifying situation, can stimulate the body for hours. (Dopamine, which rouses the pleasure centers of the brain, is produced during a slew of behaviors—foraging, exploring, biting, feeding—that are integral to survival. Attaching a chemical reward to these actions is probably the body's way of making sure they get done. Dopamine is also released during sex.)

There's fairly good evidence that some people need that "amped" feeling more than others do. The brains of high-sensation seekers seem to automatically dampen the level of stimuli they receive, so they need more stimulation to get the same response. This dampening may be the result of lower base levels of norepinephrine or dopamine, both of which are regulated by an enzyme called monoamine oxidase (MAO). People who go out of their way looking for thrills usually have lower-than-average blood levels of MAO; these lower levels have been statistically linked to such high-risk behaviors as crime, gambling, promiscuity, and reckless driving.

In our insulated society, there are precious few situations that can trigger a high-performance response. And so, like good dopamine enthusiasts, we go out and create them—we get in trouble with the law, take drugs, bet the house in a poker game. And those of us who don't want to destroy our personal lives while putting our bodies on the line pursue extreme sports: big-wave surfing, mountain climbing, cave diving. It's interesting to note that people whose jobs are already dangerous usually have no interest in risky activities. At the end of the day, an iron-worker has already been performing an extreme sport for eight hours. He's triggered his norepinephrine response, he's enjoyed the dopamine rush, and now he wants to relax and leave the risk-taking to people who've been trapped behind a desk.

My MAO levels are unknown to me, but the most deeply content I've ever been in my life was when I was working regularly for tree-removal companies in Massachusetts. If a dead tree is in too tight a place to simply be felled, or if it leans over a house, someone has to go up with ropes and a chain saw and take it down in pieces. That person was me. There was no tree I went up that didn't scare me; every day, on every job, part of me suspected that this was going to be it. And some trees seemed truly sinister: huge old ashes and oaks with dark, heavy bark and a brooding silence that felt like doom. I'd get up into their crowns and clip into my rope and wonder at what point—if the trunk experienced a massive failure or if the rope suddenly broke—I would realize I was going to die.

Concentrated action tends to dispel fear, though, and after an hour or so the tree would lose its malevolence, and I'd be moving around it without any hesitation, roping and cutting and dismantling it section by section. Sometimes I'd achieve a state of focus and physical grace that made falling seem not just unlikely but almost impossible. The roughnecks in Texas have a saying about working with the huge oil-drilling pipes: "Tripping pipe isn't a job, it's a sport." I know exactly what they mean, and on some days I'd go them one better: it isn't a sport, it's a religion. And I mean that literally. Occasionally, in virtually every sport, an athlete will perform so far beyond his ability that not only is he untouchable by others, he's simply at a loss to explain what happened. Usually the experience changes him—or at least his athletic career—for the rest of his life. That's the best—the only—definition of religious epiphany I know.

Like most things worth doing, though, risk-taking can be pushed to horrible extremes—which are, in turn, often highly romanticized. Whether it's a soldier who has thrown himself on a hand grenade or an actor who dies, recklessly, in his prime, the public seemingly can't applaud him enough. The most cynical view of this encouragement of self-destruction is that society has always benefited from having a supply of young men willing to jeopardize their lives for honor or good pay. Timber needs to be cut, skyscrapers need to be built, wars need to be fought. What better way to convince people to do these things than to glorify danger and self-sacrifice?

Even among the higher primates, such as baboons, it's the adolescent males—with low social status and, therefore, no access to females—who are often forced to feed on the periphery of the troop, thus becoming a first line of defense. In case of an encounter with marauding lions, this buys the females and the very young enough time to make it into the safety of treetops. If there is an evolutionary origin for so-called "selfless" heroism, it is that less-developed males have to prove themselves before they are granted any respect. There is no easier way to get a man to risk his life than to suggest he'll be admired for it—or to give him an unarguable reason to obey orders.

Captain Patrick Brown, 45, Ladder Company 69, New York City Fire Department: "In Brooklyn, there was a fire on the second floor of a crack house; the third floor was full of regular people. It was crazy, people hanging out of the window. We put an aerial ladder up and into the fire, and they were screaming. I couldn't even see if the ladder was in a window; I just assumed it was. And I was scared shitless, but I kept going up to the fire and I kept burning and I kept coming back. I just kept saying "I can't fucking do this," and then I just ran up through the smoke and heat—thank God it was the window—and I just crashed right through."

If there is a profile of a classic risk-taker, Brown is it. He is the most highly decorated fireman in New York City. Before that, he was stationed in Quang Tri, Vietnam, with the marines for eighteen months. He came back half-cocked—slept in the backyard, drank too much, got into fights. Finally, in an effort to give himself direction, he joined the fire department. It worked: putting his life on the line thrilled him, and saving people—especially kids—made up for things in Vietnam that he couldn't even talk about. In that Brooklyn fire, he ended up saving a mother and two children. Another time, he supervised the rescue of a man from the twelfth floor of a midtown-Manhattan building. Forced to lower a fire-fighter from the roof to grab the man from a window, Brown and two other firemen had no choice but to hold the rope themselves. When the man they were saving leapt into the dangling fireman's arms, they all almost went hurtling over the edge to the pavement below.

It's very hard to tell from Brown's stories whether he's trying to kill himself or trying to save others. If he's trying to save people, it's hard to understand why he is willing to die to do so. There is an element of redemption to the act, to be sure, but that seems to only hint at the full picture. Ultimately, it's difficult to avoid the conclusion that he simply thrives on crisis. He is unnaturally good at it—good at finding it, good at surviving it, good at swallowing it whole.

"I've always reacted well under intense insane circumstances," says Brown. "Keeping calm and doing the right thing, maybe being very violent when the time came; just being able to react. I mean, a lot of people, they sort of get stunned for a second, like a deer in the headlights. I've never had that problem. I just feel like I'm in a zone, you know? The Japanese would say you're empty. You know what I mean? Empty and ready but full of thoughts."

After twenty years in the department, Brown no longer gets that amped feeling with the bad fires; instead, he enters a flat kind of functionality. He walks through blazes level-headed, jaded, and super aware. Perhaps that's the natural result of a lifetime of taking risks—it's as if there is nothing more to see. One of his closest friends was burned to death in an arson fire. Another fell seven stories from a rooftop. A third endured 40 days in a burn unit before finally dying. In a lot of ways, Brown is tired of it all. In a lot of ways, he says, he's 150 years old.

"But what am I going to do?" he asks. "Retire at half-pay and work a 40-hour week to make the other half I'm not getting?" So Brown just keeps going into fires, pulling people out, trying to keep his crew safe. Danger means something different to him now—it's not a celebration of his strength but a necessary evil, an indictment of the world.

You must have to see a lot of horror to get to that point. I suspect that most people who enjoy danger—river rafters, rock climbers, fledgling war correspondents—haven't seen a lot of true horror. I suspect that most of them—I'm including myself in this category—have never been in a situation they couldn't get helicoptered out of by the end of the day. Still, if jumping from an airplane on weekends keeps you from breaking into houses, then do it. But understand that the scariest situations aren't always the most dangerous, and the most dangerous circumstances don't always produce the greatest epiphanies. The worst experience of Brown's life didn't happen on the scene of a fire but in bed one night after he'd seen the body of a good friend who had burned to death. Brown just lay there, shaking with fear that his dead friend would pay him a visit in the dark.

The situation that changed me the most—that really gave me a new way of looking at the world—was far less dangerous than any number of other things I've done (and done thoughtlessly). Two journalist friends and I were on the tortuous, eight-hour drive from Split to Zagreb, along the Croatian coast, when we heard a far-off rumble that could only be artillery. Even at a great distance, it was so inhumanely loud that it was hard not to wonder if something had simply gone wrong with the planet. The Serbs, apparently, were shelling the temporary bridge at Maslenica, having blown up the real one earlier in the war. When we arrived at Maslenica, traffic was backed up in the safety of a road cut, and every few minutes a 155 mm shell would crash into the flinty hillside above the bridge.

It was a beautiful afternoon, with the Adriatic sparkling below us and the white limestone of the coastal range glaring in the midday sun. We put on our flak jackets, bypassed the line of cars, and headed down the hill in our Peugeot (we'd plated the outside of the doors with steel to protect us from shrapnel). Ahead of us was a transport truck and, incredibly, a German car with a windsurfing board strapped to its roof. We crossed the bridge fast, one shell hitting the hill about 100 yards above us, and arrived safely on the other side.

And there it was again: that wild slamming in the chest, that sudden certainty that there was no life I wanted to be living except this very one, right here, right now. It wasn't the degree of risk, which was surprisingly minimal—it was the idea of it. It was the fact that, for a moment, at least, we had no way of knowing what would happen. And when nothing did—when our lives were handed back to us exactly as they had been before, and we were again laughing and talking as we switchbacked along the steep coast—it was as if we'd been introduced into the world all over again. And for a while, we saw the world as it really was: a fascinating, seemingly limitless place, laid wide open for us to explore as fully as possible. That is the reason to take risks, because otherwise, you don't truly understand what you have to lose.

Sebastian Junger is a contributing editor of Men's Journal *and the author of the bestseller* The Perfect Storm.

RAY ISLE

* * *

Wild Turkey

It's always good to know who's boss.

I WAS AN OUTSIDER. AFTER ALL, DIDN'T I HAVE THE REQUISITES?
Check it out. I'd moved to Austin, Texas, a fine place for
would-be outsiders. I'd found an appropriately shitty job,
working as a reservationist on the 800-number for Sheraton
Hotels. And I had the other crucial outsider qualifications:
The Membership in a Bad Band. The Miserable Hole to Live
In. And, crucially, The Substantially More Put-Together
Girlfriend. Patrizia. Student of law. Beautiful, smart, German.
And understanding. So far.

Despite all this, I felt overcome by the squalor and point-
lessness of my life. Sure, I was an outsider. My fellow reserva-
tionists, mostly Air Force wives from Bergstrom Air Force
Base, could vouch for that:

"You're in a band called The Stumps? That's gross."

"Who'd want to listen to a band called The Stumps?"

Well, no one, except maybe Waxface Jeff, our roadie; but
that might have been an act. We were also his biggest customers for the bad pot he sold out of the house we lived in.

I was beginning to catch on. Being an outsider meant being no one. And given that Patrizia was about to graduate from law school and start making $80,000 a year, my no-one-hood boded ill. Our love was about to have oxygen injected into its veins by the assassin of financial incompatibility. Things, it seemed, were about to suck.

So, a Friday afternoon in late July, I am sitting in my sound-baffled nook, inventing for a lawyer from Detroit the sublime glories of the Sheraton Bora Bora.

"The beach? The beach is fucking gorgeous. White sand, acres of it. You climb down these curving wooden stairs from the hotel—which is on this cliff you've got to fucking see to believe. The water? The water is beyond real. The shit's unearthly. Better than Yves Klein's 'Universal Blue.'"

"What?" The guy's a litigator. Fucking he understands; Yves Klein, no.

"Listen, I don't give a shit about this Klein guy. All I know is I need a room. Two weeks, check out the fourteenth. Make it a suite."

Sipping black coffee, staring out darkened windows at the supraluminant natural world, I watch Patrizia cleave rapidly away through azure, expense-account waters. I see clouds like Egyptian cotton pillowcases, sand like silk. And if I lean over slightly, I can even see myself. On the shore. In a little blue uniform. Raking up the monkey shit.

"OK, this is what I want," the litigator says. "I want a mini-bar, I want a king-size bed, I want—"

I disconnect him. Hey, I'm an outsider, aren't I? Clearly it is time to get out.

"Guadalupe Mountains?" Patrizia was puzzled. Whenever she was puzzled, she looked stern. "What are the Guadalupe Mountains? This is Texas. There are no mountains."

I explained. National Park. Just east of El Paso. Guadalupe Mountain itself, highest point in Texas. Arid. Hostile. Rocky. Cactus. Mesquite. Gila monsters. Rattlesnakes. Bobcats.

"I have advanced torts," Patrizia said, sternly.

"Gosh, Zipa, you ought to get something for that."

Patrizia laughed, so lightly that it wasn't entirely clear whether she was laughing at all. What was clear were the white, sharp tips of her perfect teeth. "Funny," she observed, without a trace of amusement. She hated being called Zipa.

She said, "This is one of those male things, isn't it."

"This is not a 'male' thing."

"No, it's a male thing," she added with certainty. "You should go alone."

Well, good. After about five seconds of thinking about it, I realized Patrizia was right. This was a male thing. High time, too! No more of this namby-pamby, camping-trip B.S. Camping trips were for families and tourists. I could already feel myself puffing up with maleness, like one of those colorful Amazon toads. No sir: if you are 22, disaffected, and not in the company of your girlfriend, one thing you do not do is go on a camping trip. What you do is engage the wilderness one on one. You test yourself. You see what you're made of. It's a pre-Jesus activity, a been-to-the-edge-and-survived trip. It's starving yourself in a pit while eating hallucinogenic mushrooms. It's being Richard Harris in that movie *A Man Called Horse,* where Comanches haul you up in the air by means of sticks stuck through your chest muscles, though I really wasn't keen on anything quite that extreme. In any case, you hunt down personal epiphany and wrest it from the bloody jaws of the unthinking wilderness. That's the general gist of the thing.

"You're right," I told Patrizia. "This is something I need to do. Alone."

"Of course I'm right."

"I'll miss making love under the stars, though."

"Making love under stars is itchy. If you come back, we can make love in the bed."

"If I come back? What the hell's that supposed to mean?"

Patrizia shrugged. "You never know."

Five a.m., a sleepy goodbye kiss from Patrizia still on my lips. I am packing the back of my 1977 Ford Fairlane station wagon with the rudiments of survival. Tent, lantern, sleeping bag, pillow, ground sheet, foam liner, another pillow, backpack, flashlight, rope, camp stove, propane canisters, Walkman, 130 cassette tapes in two faux-leather cases, paperback copies of *Moby Dick, Desert Solitaire,* and *Fear and Loathing in Las Vegas*, a quarter ounce of Waxface's best skunkweed, rolling papers, canned tamales, canned chili, canned beef stew, a canned plum pudding complete with hard sauce (my mother had given it to me for Christmas), cigarettes, jar of instant coffee, styrofoam cooler, beer, more beer, a fifth of Famous Grouse blended Scotch whiskey, bottled water, magnesium flares, topographical maps, SPF 55 sunscreen, $120 in traveler's checks, running shoes, hiking boots, moleskin, insect repellent, oranges, a snakebite kit, several aluminum pots, a can opener, two ten-pound dumb-bells, and a guitar.

Presently Patrizia joins me in the driveway, holding a cup of coffee.

"What?"

She shrugs.

"These are all necessities."

"I did not say anything."

"You were doing that saying something without saying anything thing."

She sips her coffee again. "Have fun," she suggests. "If you kill anything, be sure to bring me back its head."

It was in the hundreds as I rambled up the access road to Dog Canyon campground, the Fairlane bottoming out every 50 feet. I'd decided to skip the south end of the park. Enough of this candy-ass forest shit, I wanted aridity, sterility, the rattlesnake slipping through the eye socket of the cow skull, the sun like God's disapproval. Baking salt flats. Million-year drought.

I had my shirt unbuttoned. I was wearing sunglasses, smoking a Camel. The wind was ruthless. It lunged through the open window and ripped the smoke to shreds. Squinting against it, I felt weathered and tough, Clint Eastwood in high-tops and shorts. There was no one around. The hot, desolate, desert wind cracked past empty picnic tables. Even the garbage cans were brutal. I parked and got out.

An hour later, I was sitting on the picnic table of the site I'd selected, reading *Moby Dick* and batting the persistent desert gnats away from my eyes, nose, and ears. Abruptly the silence, the immense silence, my silence, was rent by a rumbling. A wedge of large men wearing leather and denim roared into the campground on Harleys. Jokers, their jackets said. Fort Worth Chapter. Here was I, holding my book, wearing a baseball cap, sunscreen smeared on my nose like Crisco. If I'd had a jacket like theirs it would have read "lightweight" or maybe "panty-boy" and been embroidered by my mother.

I decided to keep reading, to show my nonchalance. The Jokers disappeared to the far end of the campground. About fifteen minutes later one of them sauntered up. He looked like a 30-year-old version of a kid named Randy Ray I'd gone to junior high with. Motorcycle boots, no shirt, jeans stiff with grease, long red hair in a ponytail, pockmarked skin, gray teeth. A stomach you could crack nuts on. Randy Ray had sat down next to me at lunch once and rather out of the blue informed me in his bolted-down rural Texas accent that the "best thing about them souvenir bats they give away at Astros games" was that you could "wrap yourself some bicycle chain around the big end, get some duct tape on there, make yourself a real good nigger-knocker that way." Then he'd whipped out a butterfly knife, removed my sandwich from my hands, whacked off half of it, said, "thanks, dickweed," and walked off.

This adult version of Randy Ray flipped a glassine envelope onto the table next to me. "You want to buy some crank, man? Good shit."

Hey: I was a *Stump*, man. I knew how to be cool.

"Not today. Thanks anyway." I handed the envelope back to him.

He studied me for a moment. Then he palmed the speed and checked out my campsite. Nylon tent, backpack leaning against the car, styrofoam cooler, guitar, dumbbells.

"What are you doing—camping?"

The amused, boot-to-the-head twist he'd given the word "camping" didn't make me optimistic.

"Yes, I am," I said.

He smiled. I recognized that smile: Bruce Lee smiles just the same way in *Enter the Dragon* right as he's crushing some poor fool's trachea with his foot.

Randy Ray said, "Come on over and party with us later, man. If you're up for it. We're gonna get fucked up."

Thirty minutes away on Highway 90, I found the Guadalupe Salt Flats KOA Kampground, where E. L., the manager, was a very sweet old guy. He even reduced my campground fee by five dollars after I explained that, no, I did not need an electrical hookup for my "recreational vehicle."

★

The following morning I drove to the forested end of the park. I was relieved, even as I felt irked with myself for feeling that relief. But here was normality. The gravel road wound through stands of piñon pine and gray oak. Pale clouds scudded through the hot sky. Birds sang. The air smelled rosiny and fresh. Ahead, the brown-painted cinderblocks of a ranger station rose, inviting, a battered drinking fountain by the door. The U.S. flag fluttered overhead.

"Hey, how you doing, buddy?" the ranger called when I went in. He was a little too friendly for my tastes.

I was doing fine, I muttered, and went through the business of registering for a campsite.

"Tell you what, I'll put you over there by the creek," he said. "That's real nice. One thing, you might want to keep an eye out for the turkey." He nodded, checking slowly over the form I'd filled out. "See, there's this flock of wild Mexican turkeys livin' around here, you might want to keep an eye out for the gander. Kinda thinks the campground's his kingdom." He chuckled, evidently amused by the turkey's territorial delusions.

"A turkey," I said.

"That's right."

With the same nonchalance I'd attempted yesterday, I observed, "Well. It can't be any worse than a motorcycle gang."

"Are they up at the canyon again? Goddamn, those guys are worse than fire ants."

Nothing is more irritating to false nonchalance than real nonchalance. Nevertheless, as I was leaving it occurred to me to ask, "So—what are you supposed to do if this turkey decides it's feeling aggressive?"

The ranger laughed uproariously. I was more irritated. We both waited for him to catch his breath. Finally he did.

"Oh, just make a lot of noise. Yell at him. Shoo him off! That old boy'll get scared, he'll figure out what's what."

Noon. I am pounding the stakes of my tent into the hard-packed West Texas dirt. Shirt off, sweating bare-backed in the sun. Testosterone pumping through the every fiber of my body. This is it, maleness, solitude, *cojones grandes*. I feel strong. I feel powerful and real. Then I hear the gobbling.

It occurred to me, briefly, to pay attention to it. But really, who gave a shit if there were a hundred turkeys roosting in this campground? My run-in with the Jokers had left me analytical and cold, and not very willing to back down. I had come out here to go *mano a mano* with the brutal truth of nature, after all, not to spend my time worrying about fat birds so mindless that if you leave them standing outside in the rain they drown.

The gobbling ululated again, causing me to whack my last tent stake into a pretzel shape. "Damn,"

I said. I looked up. At the top of the dusty rise behind my camp, a large turkey had appeared. It was bronze in color, wings tipped in white. It held its ruddy, wattled neck and head high. It looked something like a rotund vulture, but lower to the ground.

I tossed the useless tent stake aside and stood up.

The turkey paused at the crest. In a sort of Napoleonic moment, it took in the camp and saw me. Its head cocked to attention. Then it gave a particularly strident gobble, and trotted down the slope.

My thoughts, roughly, were these: It's a turkey. Give me a fucking break.

I picked up an aluminum pot and my heavy-duty can opener. Make noise? OK. You got it. I was going to scare the bejesus out of this bird.

So as the turkey came down the hill, I went up to meet it, banging on my pot and yelling, "Shoo! Shoo! Hyah!" and that was when I learned my first lesson in Turkey Behavior 101. What I learned is that turkeys don't give a shit when you make noise. Maybe they don't have ears. I still don't know. I do know that as soon as I got near it, banging away and hollering, amused and very pleased with myself, the turkey leaped into the air. It battered me with its wings, and raked at my face with enormous black claws.

"Jesus Christ!" I said, and ran.

As soon as I got about ten feet between us I turned and started banging on the pot again, harder this time. "Hah! Shoo! Get out of here!" I yelled.

This time the turkey tried to tear my face off.

"Jesus Christ!" I yelled, again, and ran.

We went through this three or four times. Then I punched a hole in the bottom of my pot with the heavy end of the can opener. "Uh oh," I said. The turkey quickly launched a brutal counter-assault, buffeting me and gobbling and trying to crawl up my chest. I flung the pot aside and dashed to my car, thinking for some reason as I did, Good Lord, what if I get hepatitis from this thing?

Therapy can sort out why I feel turkeys might be a source of hepatitis. In the meantime, let's hold me suspended in air, as the car door slams shut, and consider some of the facts of this situation: this is late July on the Texas–New Mexico border. Now, the average temperature in late July along the Texas–New Mexico border is something like 98, 99 degrees, Fahrenheit, but this day in particular happens to be about 105. Even the flies have passed out. The car I have just vaulted into is a dark-blue Ford Fairlane station wagon, circa 1979, with dark-blue vinyl seats. It has been sitting in the direct sun, windows sealed, for something like four hours. And I am wearing shorts, and no shirt.

Soon after entering my recreational vehicle, I realized a moment of extreme lucidity. This was followed by pain. I made a horrible noise, something like a shrill gobble, in fact, and then proceeded to levitate, a skill I had not known I possessed until that moment.

Outside, the turkey took up position on top of my picnic table and started eating my Doritos.

At that point I had my epiphany. I had come to the wilderness looking for an epiphany, of course, and though this was not the epiphany I had hoped for, it would have to do. What occurred to me was that even in the direst of circumstances, trapped in a car as hot as a pizza oven, nagged at by the thought that: (a) you have just been outfought and even outstrategized by a bird most people consider holiday dinner and (b) that back in the civilized world your friends are investing in mutual funds, your girlfriend is checking out Mercedes sports coupes, and you are still buying canned tamales for dinner; despite all this, the wonderful thing about nature is that poverty asks no comparisons there. Even that Detroit lawyer, sunning himself on his fucking Sheraton beach in Bora Bora, could have his legs chewed off by a shark if he didn't watch it.

Whereupon a Range Rover drove into the campsite one down from mine. It parked, and a wiry, balding fellow of about 40 got out and stood, hands on hips, observing the site he'd selected. Moments later a much younger, much taller woman with a hell of a lot more hair than he had (all blonde and rumpled up in a gosh-isn't-athletic-sex-wonderful kind of way) poured herself out of the passenger side of that $40,000 vehicle. She flowed up to him, more liquid than mercury, and started nuzzling his ear. The turkey studied the two of them, then me, and in a turkey insight of startling clarity understood that epiphanies were bullshit.

It returned its attention to my Doritos. The bald guy and his girlfriend opened the swing-back of the Rover and vanished inside. Within moments it began to bounce.

Sexual jealousy, I've found, often leads directly to inspiration. Crouched there, sweating, sucking in the superheated air, trying not to come in contact with any surface, I came to a conclusion. The conclusion was simple: this was fucking ridiculous. This was sad, man. This was pitiful. This was citizenship in the country of the wimps. Randy Ray would have laughed in my face, then eaten my canned plum pudding. Hell, Patrizia probably would have, too. Get real, I told myself. You're a human being. A tool-using creature. And that thing out there?

The turkey, serene in its inarguable turkeyness, not hungry for existential justification (or even anything at all, since it had now finished my Doritos), settled down for what looked like an extended roost on my picnic table. Fuck you, I thought. If I'd had a shotgun at that moment, dinner that night would have been extravagant.

I had no gun. But—call it a second epiphany—it did occur to me that I had a brain.

I moved. The turkey cocked its head and gave a low warning gobble, but I was fast, scuttling from the station wagon, apelike and low to the ground, scooping up stones from the dirt. And as the turkey launched itself from table to earth, I hit it in the ass with a rock.

Success! It seemed worried. I hurled another rock, advancing. That's right, bird, know what you're dealing with? Monkey-boy ascendant! Opposable fucking thumbs! I whipped stones at it. It ran. There's one for terraced farming, pal, and one for irrigation. How about another, for Copernicus?

What about the internal combustion engine? The turkey scooted up the hill, gobbling worriedly. I grabbed more stones. I was filled with righteousness. Screw nature, man, give me civilization! Plug in the amps, kick out the jams, let's hear it for calculus and philosophical inquiry, steel-toed workboots and heavy industry, freeze-dried hiking rations and Gore-Tex, distortion and the Fender Stratocaster.

The turkey? Gobbling in outrage, it topped the rise, and vanished.

"You threw rocks at a bird?"

I was on the pay phone behind the ranger station, talking long-distance to Patrizia in Austin. "You don't understand, this thing was huge!"

"You had a fight with a turkey?"

"Patrizia, listen, the thing was nuts! It was like this giant, rabid bird!"

"You were frightened by a turkey, and so you threw rocks at it? This makes you proud?"

"Well, yes and no," I said. "But it was really very big. Huge, Zipa. Prehistoric."

"Good thing you were alone. I might have shrieked and needed protection."

Ah, sarcasm. How I'd missed it. Patrizia would have needed no protection. She would have snapped the turkey's neck, roasted it over an open fire, then fixed us turkey sandwiches.

Dusk hung over us both, and over the 600 miles between us.

On my way back to the camp I nearly ran smack into the blonde girlfriend of the Range Rover pilot as she delicately stepped from the women's porto-can.

"You're the guy just one up from us, aren't you?" she said, in her melted-butter voice.

I admitted this was true. Then I asked her if she was enjoying her camping trip.

"My God, last night we partied with this motorcycle gang, the Jokers? I was freaked out of my wits. But Alan, my boyfriend, he was great with them, they loved him. It was amazing. He's in criminal defense in Dallas. He deals with guys like them all the time."

No, no pride. But even if you can't squeeze pride out of the aged lemon of life, sometimes you can still recover a few small, sour drops of victory:

I am heating my tamales for dinner when out of the dark heart of the night the primordial gobbling rises again. It bubbles up like oil, undaunted and instinctual. And down on the flatlands, the balding guy waves up to me. He's looking a little desperate. His girlfriend is huddled behind their picnic table. He's dodging and feinting as the turkey advances.

He yells, "Excuse me, buddy, but do you know what we're supposed to do about this thing?"

Panty-boy. Lightweight. "Oh sure, just make a lot of noise! It'll get scared and run away."

I figure five minutes. Maybe ten. More than enough. Then, hormones humming like magic, I can head down into that violent darkness and save them.

Ray Isle is a New York writer currently working on a novel, Last Days of the My-T-Fine. *He writes fiction and non-fiction for magazines such as* Terra Nova, Utne Reader, *and* Plowshares. *Even though he has been attacked by not only a wild turkey, but blue jays, a skunk, and several dogs, he still tries to go camping whenever he can.*

FRANK McCOURT

$\star\ ^{\star}\ \star$

A Fine Boyo

A young Irishman learns a lesson in Limerick.

THE BOYS AT THE POST OFFICE TELL ME I'M LUCKY TO GET THE Carmody family telegram, a shilling tip, one of the biggest tips you'll ever get in Limerick. So why am I getting it? I'm the junior boy. They say, Well, sometimes Theresa Carmody answers the door. She has the consumption and they're afraid of catching it from her. She's seventeen, in and out of the sanatorium, and she'll never see eighteen. The boys at the post office say sick people like Theresa know there's little time left and that makes them mad for love and romance and everything. Everything. That's what the consumption does to you, say the boys at the post office.

I cycle through wet November streets thinking of that shilling tip, and as I turn into the Carmody street the bicycle slides out from under me and I skid along the ground scraping my face and tearing open the back of my hand. Theresa Carmody opens the door. She has red hair. She has green eyes like the fields beyond Limerick. Her cheeks are bright pink and her skin is a fierce white. She says, Oh, you're all wet and bleeding.

I skidded on my bike.

Come in and I'll put something on your cuts.

I wonder, Should I go in? I might get the consumption and that will be the end of me. I want to be alive when I'm fifteen, and I want the shilling tip.

Come in. You'll perish standing there.

She puts on the kettle for the tea. Then she dabs iodine on my cuts, and I try to be a man and not whimper. She says, Oh, you're a great bit of a man. Go into the parlor and dry yourself before the fire. Look, why don't you take off your pants and dry them on the screen of the fire?

Ah, no.

Ah, do.

I will.

I drape my pants over the screen. I sit there watching the steam rise, and I watch myself rise, and I worry she might come in and see me in my excitement.

There she is with a plate of bread and jam and two cups of tea. Lord, she says, you might be a scrawny bit of a fellow but that's a fine boyo you have there.

She puts the plate and the cups on a table by the fire, and there they stay. With her thumb and forefinger she takes the tip of my excitement and leads me across the room to a green sofa against the wall and all the time my head is filled with sin and iodine and fear of consumption and the shilling tip and her green eyes and she's on the sofa don't stop or I'll die and she's crying and I'm crying for I don't know what's happening to me if I'm killing myself catching consumption from her mouth I'm riding to heaven I'm falling off a cliff and if this is a sin I don't give a fiddler's fart.

We take our ease on the sofa a while till she says, Don't you have more telegrams to deliver? And when we sit up she gives a little cry, Oh, I'm bleeding.

What's up with you?

I think it's because it's the first time.

I tell her, Wait a minute. I bring the bottle from the kitchen and splash the iodine on her injury. She leaps from the sofa, dances around the parlor like a wild one and runs into the kitchen to douse herself with water. After she dries herself, she says, Lord, you're very innocent. You're not supposed to be pouring iodine on girls like that.

I thought you were cut.

For weeks after that, I deliver the telegram. Sometimes we have the excitement on the sofa, but there are other days she has the cough and you can see the weakness on her. She never tells me she has the weakness. She never tells me she has the consumption. The boys at the post office say I must have been having a great time with the shilling tip and Theresa Carmody. I never tell them I stopped taking the shilling tip. I never tell them about the green sofa and the excitement. I never tell them of the pain that comes when she opens the door and I can see the weakness on her and all I want to do then is make tea for her and sit with my arms around her on the green sofa.

One Saturday I'm told to deliver the telegram to Theresa's mother at her job in Woolworth's. I try to be casual. Mrs. Carmody, I always deliver the telegram to your, I think your daughter, Theresa?

Yes, she's in the hospital.

Is she in the sanatorium?

I said she's in the hospital.

She's like everyone else in Limerick, ashamed of the TB, and she doesn't give me a shilling or any kind of tip. I cycle out to the sanatorium to see Theresa. They say you have to be a relation and you have to be an adult. I tell them I'm her cousin and I'll be fifteen in August. They tell me go away. I cycle to the Franciscan church to pray for Theresa. St. Francis, would you please talk to God. Tell Him it wasn't Theresa's fault. I could have refused that telegram Saturday after Saturday. Tell God Theresa was not responsible for the excitement on the sofa because that's what the consumption does to you. It doesn't matter anyway, St. Francis, because I love Theresa. I love her as much as you love any bird or beast or fish and will you tell God take the consumption away and I promise I'll never go near her again.

The next Saturday they give me the Carmody telegram. From halfway up the street I can see the blinds are drawn. I can see the black crepe wreath on the door. I can see the white purple-lined mourning card. I can see beyond the door and walls where Theresa and I tumbled naked and wild on the green sofa and I know now she is in hell and all because of me.

I slip the telegram under the door and cycle back down to the Franciscan church to beg for the repose of Theresa's soul. I pray to every statue, to the stained glass windows, the Stations of the Cross. I swear I'll lead a life of faith, hope and charity, poverty, chastity and obedience.

Next day, Sunday, I go to four Masses. I do the Stations of the Cross three times. I say rosaries all day. I go without food and drink, and wherever I find a quiet place I cry and beg God and the Virgin Mary to have mercy on the soul of Theresa Carmody.

On Monday I follow the funeral to the graveyard on my post office bicycle. I stand behind a tree a distance from the grave. Mrs. Carmody weeps and moans. Mr. Carmody snuffles and looks puzzled. The priest recites the Latin prayers and sprinkles the coffin with holy water.

I want to go to the priest, to Mr. and Mrs. Carmody. I want to tell them how I'm the one who sent Theresa to hell. They can do whatever they like with me. Abuse me. Revile me. Throw grave dirt at me. But I stay behind the tree till the mourners leave and the grave diggers fill in the grave.

Frost is already whitening the fresh earth on the grave and I think of Theresa cold in the coffin, the red hair, the green eyes. I can't understand the feelings going through me, but I know that with all the people who died in my family and all the people who died in the lanes around me and all the people who left, I never had a pain like this in my heart, and I hope I never will again.

It's getting dark. I walk my bicycle out of the graveyard. I have telegrams to deliver.

Frank McCourt was for many years a writing teacher at Stuyvesant High School, and performer with his brother Malachy in A Couple of Blaguards, *a musical review about their Irish youth. He is the author of the bestseller* Angela's Ashes: A Memoir, *from which this story was excerpted. He lives in New York City.*

Fire Beneath the Skin

Born of stars, how can we not burn?

Smoke hung over the city as we rode toward the ghats. In the distance over the river, we saw fireworks flash, bringing the jagged outlines of temples into dark relief, followed by thudding like artillery shells. Our rickshaw driver tried to avoid the crowds by following side roads. Off the main avenues, instead of electric lights, dozens of small oil lamps and candles had been planted in rows along the ledges of the homes. Strings of firecrackers burst like machine-gun fire from the city centre. The explosions came with greater and greater frequency as we neared the river. A young boy stepped out from between two buildings and hurled a banger into the middle of the road. It detonated in the path of our rickshaw, frightening the driver. He swerved, rocked on two wheels, and narrowly avoided a head-to-horn collision with a wandering cow. Roman candles flared across the sky, fizzling gold above us. The sacred city could well have been at war.

"I *am* a *Dis*-co *Dan*-cer," the current hit song from a popular Hindi movie, blared out from loudspeakers set up along the main market streets. Young men gyrated to the beat in front of garishly painted plaster idols of the God-King Rama and Queen Sita, spotlit and strung round with coloured lights. A mass of dancing worshippers, all clapping hands above their heads, jammed the next intersection, making further rickshaw travel impossible. I paid the driver and we dismounted into the crowd. Clutching each other's hands, Sabina and I pressed our way through the frenzy into the back streets at the centre of the city, trying to find a way to the river.

Wet, dung-filled paths, too narrow for cars or even oxcarts, covered the heart of Varanasi like a skein of dogged veins. They twisted and turned, dead-ended and looped back upon themselves. Through one doorway, I spotted a flash of red and the glitter of candles; a rear window into a shrine room was filled with praying, white-robed devotees. In the next alleyway, a water buffalo munched softly on a pile of dried grass. All the shops were still open, their wares spilling out onto the street: silver bangles, pewter pots and water jars, row upon row of small golden idols. Candles and coloured lights covered every ledge. Young boys huddled in small groups, daring each other to hold the tips of red bangers in their hands. The explosions made Sabina jump, and her skittishness attracted the boys' attention. They threw their tiny bombs directly at her sandalled feet, laughing as she shrieked, and giving chase as we tried to escape through the winding alleyways.

The boys fell back when we joined a train of well-to-do women in white saris. The procession led through the inner-city maze to the shore of the holy river, just upstream from the burning *ghats*. We had inadvertently joined the final steps of a funeral march. The cremation fires seemed muted under a hundred bright electric lamps, each hanging on the end of a long bamboo pole. Lamps for the dead, Sabina explained.

A second power failure struck, dousing the city once more in darkness. But the momentary blackness soon gave way to the yellow glow of cremation fires. Orange embers flickered upwards to the sky. Looking over the Ganges, we saw hundreds of small oil lamps set afloat as offerings to Rama. Moisture rose up from the river and drifted inland, swirling warm and fishy around us. A dog barked near the water's edge, then growled. We stepped down the dark stairs of the *ghats* and heard a voice call to us from the river.

"Hello, Mister, you want go boat ride?"

We heard the gentle slap of oars. We could not see the hull against the black water, just the boatman's glowing white turban as he slid towards shore. He held out a near-invisible hand to steady us as we boarded. We sat close together on the wooden planks in the bow, and the boat surged slowly upstream away from shore, into the current of tiny river lamps. Sabina urged the oarsman to be careful not to overturn any of the fragile offerings. He allowed the current to take us farther out until a thousand dancing lights bobbed between us and the shore. Beyond the banks, the city's darkened profile was shot through with dots of candlelight.

"Oh, so beautiful," said Sabina. "It's as if the stars have settled on the city."

Where was the rational Indologist now? I thought with a grin. But it vanished the next moment as I felt her fingers touch my cheek, slide down my neck, press lightly against my chest and rest there. The sudden intimacy of her touch inflamed me. I placed my hand on her thigh, felt her muscles tighten and relax. After a minute, she placed a hand over mine, holding it still.

"I have an idea," she whispered. "Another secret. I'll show you, back on shore."

When we reached the *ghats,* she took me by the hand and

led the way once more through the city's inner maze until we arrived at the gates of an ancient observatory. She quickly coaxed the watchman into opening the iron door for us, then drew me in after her through a confusing network of walkways and walls to a spiral staircase. It had charted the course of the sky. As we looked down on the city spread out beneath us, the power failure ended. Varanasi flashed out of the darkness with a million multicoloured lights. A spontaneous cry from thousands of voices rose up from the streets. "Disco Dancer" surged through the loudspeakers. A sudden volley of Roman candles filled the sky with luminous pinks and greens. The smoke that followed covered the city with a misty glow. Sabina leaned against my side and put her arms around my waist. She pressed against my chest, her breasts warm beneath her *kurta*. "I give you Varanasi for Diwali, Tim," she said, holding me close.

It was past one by the time we made our way back through the combat zones of the old city and the still-crowded market streets to the Maharajah Hotel. The moon-faced manager sat outside on the steps, keys in hand. When we entered, he drew an iron gate shut behind us and locked it with a chain. "Ah, Diwali!" he said dreamily as he climbed the stairs behind us.

"Good night!"

Sabina's eyes slowly surveyed the room. She smiled at the sight of the pomegranate, guava, and red bananas I had piled in a bowl in the centre of the wide blue bed. On one of the night tables, the small white elephant she had given me raised its trunk playfully. I lit four candles around the bed, then turned off the light. Bicycle bells rang in the street below. A burst of firecrackers popped dully in the distance, and the occasional Roman candle sent bars of light in through the cracks in the shutters.

"This is our room," I said, glad for how she lingered over the small details I had prepared.

I left her briefly for the sink, quickly sprinkling droplets of water to scare away the ants. They scurried in panic all across the porcelain bowl and back into the cracked ridges in the plaster. I returned to the room and sat on the bed, legs crossed, eyes closed in a final moment of meditation, listening to her brushing her teeth, peeing, flushing the toilet. Even such earthy sounds filled me with bliss. I felt exhausted and exhilarated, drugged by Diwali, one corner of my mind still wondering if she was going to come back out and announce she had to leave for an important meeting with some Buddhist monks.

She returned and lay on the bed beside me, her head propped on one arm, looking straight into my face. I sank into her gaze. I couldn't speak. We didn't move. After a few minutes, she reached out and touched my cheek.

We caressed, easing each other out of our long Indian shirts. She touched me like an accomplished ballroom dancer leading a novice through his steps, sweeping me along in her grace. She guided my hands, my lips, to where she wanted me, pulled my head to her breast, drew my fingers between her thighs. I felt her muscles tense with pleasure. Her hands stroked my back, my neck, nails scratching lightly across my shoulder blades, her eyes watching me closely in the candle-light, as if learning how my body moved and taking delight in mastering it. Her touch felt cool and I trembled. I clutched at her shoulder, panting. She smiled, inscrutable, shifted her hips and pulled me from my side to lie on top of her.

I rolled between her legs, felt her wet heat and pressed into her, gasping for air, blood roaring in my ears. It was too intense, too fast. I wanted to thrust wildly, claw her flesh, but instead dug my fingers into the bedclothes. I froze, afraid to move in case I burst, and an old spectre of shame rose up. Her eyes tried to catch mine, but I averted them. She too was breathing heavily, but stilled her hips. We hung together motionless for a while. Then slowly she began to rock, sliding me in a little deeper with each gentle movement, and the intensity held, did not spill over prematurely as it had done all too often in the past. She wrapped her ankles around the insides of my calves and strained to pull me tighter into her, increasing her rhythm. I opened my eyes and this time met her gaze, the blue sparking dark, honey hair tumbled all about. She threw back her head, and I kissed her neck, breathless with the quickening roll of our hips. Our breathing came together now, shorter, faster, her body quivering beneath me. She groaned, and I felt it through to my belly, triggering a shudder, a brief second of bliss, spasms of pleasure coursing outward as I rocked hard against her, and then lay still.

We made love once more in the late Diwali night, and again at dawn as the ringing of bicycle bells filled the alleyway below our room. After we made the great bed rattle one final time, she kissed my belly and slid off towards the bathroom.

"Where are you going?" I asked dreamily.

"Oh, I have a breakfast meeting with Strauss. He has—"

"I know, a Buddhist monk or scholar he wants you to meet for your research."

She grinned at me and closed the bathroom door.

"Ack—ants!"

I hated to let her go, marvelled that she could separate herself so easily. I pitied Strauss, so infatuated with her, but denied the pleasure of her touch. Yet I felt no pride. Rather, a sense of awe that someone so beautiful, so sexually accomplished had chosen to be with me. It was almost religious. After she left, I lay in the blue bed, thoughtfully munched a guava and picked up my journal. My skin still tingled from her touch. A lazy, drugged warmth ran through my muscles, as if I was drunk on mulled wine.

"Technically," I wrote, "this has been the most intense, longest, most exhilarating night I have ever spent with a woman. I think I have a blister."

Technically.

I stared at the word in my notebook and pondered how it had flowed from my pen. Sabina was certainly a master in the arts of love, but I wondered if I and all men were for her just canvases on which she expressed her art. We had made love passionately and energetically, and I felt an acceptance of my sexuality—even desire for it—that I had never felt with pre-vious lovers. Yet we hardly knew each other. This acceptance was exactly what I had longed for all my life; better, in fact, than I had ever imagined it to be. But somehow dissatisfaction was creeping in already. I picked up my pen again.

"Somehow it feels 'surface,'" I wrote. "Passion, but not real intimacy. I suppose that's not surprising on a first night. It just feels as if somewhere underneath there ought to be a lot more."

"If Strauss insists on coming to the station, can you just meet me on the platform?" she said after our second night in the blue bed. She was on her way out for a final goodbye breakfast, and I had agreed to meet her at the ticket office for our trip to Patna later in the day.

"No, I'll jump up and kiss you."

She laughed nervously and bit her lower lip.

At the station, she was late. Ten minutes before departure, I decided to leave our meeting place for a minute to confirm that our train was on time. As I passed through the gate lead-ing to the inquiry desk, a heavyset white man with a goatee came through the other way. He didn't recognize me, but the blonde woman at his side in the dark-blue, Punjabi-style pantsuit certainly did. She blanched, eyes pleading for silence. I brushed past her, not saying a word.

I inquired about the train, found that it was on time, and turned to see Sabina behind me.

"Meet me at the platform, please," she asked, out of breath from running.

I nodded. She turned and ran back through the gate.

"He wanted me to stay another day," she told me when we at last pulled out from the station, leaving the luckless professor behind. "But I told him I sacrifice myself for scholarship."

"Did he try to seduce you?" I asked.

The jealous tone of my own question annoyed me. I wasn't so much as uncomfortable at the apparently lighthearted way she had used his desire to accomplish her own ends. Of course, Strauss seemed a willing enough volunteer. Still, I could all too easily picture myself in his shoes, and was glad I could not be used to further her career.

"No, he didn't try," she replied, "except in a very academic way. We were discussing Mara's daughters, and he told me he didn't think their temptation of the Buddha was really about sex. He said he thought it symbolized the attraction of the world in general, and that it would be a misinterpretation to infer from the story that the Buddha was anti-sex."

"Quite a come-on. But it is a good question. What do you think about it? It seems pretty central to your work."

"I told you," she said, irritated, "my research is to catalogue and describe. It's science. You Western Buddhists, so concerned about whether or not Buddha thought sex was dirty! But I don't care."

"I'm not a Buddhist," I grumbled uneasily.

"Then tell me, what were you doing meditating in the mountains?"

"It's difficult to explain," I said awkwardly. "But let me try.

When I became a Christian at eighteen, my perspective on the world changed radically. Suddenly God was everywhere. The devil, too. There were new spiritual meanings for things that I previously didn't think of questioning. Everything from events in the state of Israel to my sex life, or rather, sudden lack of one, had a place in God's plan. My nonreligious friends thought I had lost my mind. Don't smile. Evangelical Christianity was just a different world, with its own quite-consistent internal logic. After I started studying philosophy and travelling in Europe, it hit me there were lots of different worlds, each valid from its own particular point of view. By becoming Christian, I had changed viewpoints, but not necessarily come any closer to the truth. And the Western cultural background in which I grew up was still determining how I saw things. I wanted to experience something radically different in order to really shake up my perspective. I went to a monastery not to become Buddhist, not to get enlightened, but to see how the world looks to a Buddhist, and in doing so, loosen the grip my own culture has on my mind. Ideally, just to get more free."

"You would have liked my father," she replied, surprisingly softly, for I suppose I had expected her to dismiss my philosophizing with an impatient wave of the hand. "He was an atheist, but very drawn to Zen. I remember he used to tell a story about being captured by the Russians during the war. He was a doctor in the German army. They sent him to a prisoner-of-war camp. He thought he would never see anyone he knew again. When he arrived, they stripped him of everything, down to his skin. They left him with absolutely nothing. 'This was the happiest moment of my life,' my father used to say. But he said as soon as they put him in prison, he started searching for a pencil to write a letter to his family to tell them he was still alive."

★

We stayed in Patna for five days, wandering through its museums and ruins, sketching and photographing Buddha statues of Mara and his seductive daughters. In the third century BC, Patna was the site of the imperial city of the Buddhist king Ashoka, and it remains the capital of modern Bihar State. Bihar comes from *vihar*, the word for a Buddhist temple. For some 1,500 years, the region was the heartland of a thriving Buddhist culture, rich in monasteries, temples, and universities, all of them wiped out by successive waves of invading Muslims who dispatched those unwilling to convert. It was now predominantly Hindu once again. For Sabina, Bihar was a treasure-house of research material, although by any economic standard, the state ranked among India's poorest.

One unique feature of the city made its most dismal streetside slums seem festive. Slum dwellers spray-painted their wandering goats and cows with bright Day-Glo patterns: hot pink, electric blue, lime green. Some streets looked like living, mooing, art exhibits. Presumably the markings identified the animals and kept them from being stolen; and in a land where the cow is sacred, paint struck me as a lot more humane than branding. The animals excited Sabina. Sometimes as we rode, she would call to our rickshaw driver to stop just so she could take a picture of a passing neon cow.

"You should be doing your thesis on cow art," I teased her.

"Oh, wouldn't that be wonderful!" she replied in earnest. "I love the cows of India. They are so beautiful, so gentle. No wonder they are sacred to the people. They give only good things: milk, dung for cooking fuel, and urine, which used to be taken as a medicine for certain sicknesses. I have often thought about doing a photo book, you know, a coffee-table book, *The Cows of India*."

We stayed at the Patna Tourist Guest House through the hot and humid nights. Our bed was covered with a white cotton mosquito net, which looked to me like a silken desert tent, closing out India and the world, or so we hoped. The wooden bed frame squeaked. I told Sabina I imagined the janitor sweeping one spot outside our door for fifteen minutes every morning, gradually being joined by other workers until the entire hotel staff congregated at our doorstep, hand brooms whisking in time to the rhythm of the bed, straining to hear the sounds coming from underneath the foreigners' door. We could shut India out, but could not prevent it listening in.

In Varanasi I had been forced to play the stranger for the sake of her reputation. In Patna, that same concession to Hindu morality demanded that we pretend to be husband and wife. Eyebrows were raised at front desk over our respective Austrian and Canadian passports, but provoked no objections. One elderly Brahmin, a visiting Congress party politician who spent his days chewing betel nut in a plush chair in the lobby, quizzed us thoroughly on our international marriage. For his sake, we quickly created three young daughters and a family home near Vienna.

Sabina's public persona changed as radically as her marital status. She kept her hair pulled straight back, the blonde ponytail usually knotted into a bun, and carried not a single sari in her heavy duffle bag, just pantaloons and long-sleeved pullover *kurtas*. In Delhi and Varanasi she had always seemed soft and feminine, relying on her charms to get what she wanted. In Patna she displayed a hard edge I had never seen before in public. She was blunt, imperious, almost sneering toward rickshaw drivers, porters, even peons at the museums. She bestowed not a single smile, except to museum curators, and her instructions in Hindi to those required to serve her sounded harsh, even to my uncomprehending ears.

"You sound so sharp," I told her once after she had snapped out our destination to a rickshaw driver.

"Yes, I have become a real *memsahib* in India, like the wife of some British general," she said as the three-wheeler jerked us out into traffic. "If I show any softness at all, then they are cheating me and grabbing at me. Men here are not used to taking orders from a woman. Especially a blonde European. They see me, and all they think of is American movie sex scenes. But they understand a *memsahib's* voice, a *memsahib's* scorn. If I keep my head high, never look at them, and yell orders, then they don't bother me."

Until that moment I had not fully appreciated what it took for her to negotiate India. Her yellow hair was a candle for over two hundred million sexually repressed male moths. Beating them off would be an exhausting task for anybody, yet she managed not only to deflect them but to conduct research at the same time. I respected her for her daily battle, and had a new understanding of my role as her assistant. Having a "husband" along helped with much of the deflecting, and that, far more than lugging her bag or searching with her for statues, sped up her work. It felt good to be useful to her, after all, and quite wonderful to be the one man in all Bihar with whom, in the privacy of our room, she dropped her defences and smiled upon.

At dinner our fourth night in Patna, we sat side by side at a table for four so that we could hold hands beneath the white tablecloth without attracting too much attention, although the waiters grinned widely with every visit to our table. Sabina asked if I had ever been in love. I told her about my years of celibacy, about trying to love Tina, my sense of inadequacy, both emotionally and sexually, and then leaving her to go to India. Sabina gazed at me.

"Is it such a long way to you?" she said.

"Yes. For you, maybe not so long. What you would find there, I don't know. Some of it scares me."

"I love you," she whispered to me as a waiter approached, then turned to him, "And now I would like the milk sweets for dessert."

I wanted to speak the words back to her, surprised at how quickly they were forming on my lips, but ordered a bowl of mango ice cream instead.

That night as we slid out of our clothing and under our gossamer netting, I caught something fragile in her mood, a sense of something slipping away. The way she held me when we embraced seemed almost mechanical, as if after several days of warming intimacy she had reverted once more to plain technique. It felt to me as if she was marking out a safe distance in the field of our loveplay. I wondered for the first time if she paid a price for her sexual freedom with men. I wondered if another kind of protective shield, far different from the *memsahib* act, had formed inside of her. Somehow it seemed her sexual expertise permitted her to embrace without being vulnerable enough to get hurt, as if she kept a divider between sex and love—almost like a man. Almost like me. Now the divider was sliding down once more, right in the midst of her caresses.

I thought I knew all too clearly what caused it. I had held back from her at the table. But not out of lack of loving, for now that the field was clear of rivals, I had abandoned my futile attempts at Buddhist detachment. Indeed, our sex was the best I had ever experienced, and she was a confident, informative, and intriguing travelling companion. As far as watchful India was concerned, we were a happily married couple, and I found it rather to my liking. But to say the words was difficult, more so because if I was going to really love her, I felt first I had to confess something that I was afraid to say. She might conclude I was crazy and just leave. But if she was going to love me, it was only right that she should know. I held her firmly in my arms, stopped her stroking fingers, and put a stilling hand on her shoulder.

"There's something I have to tell you," I said, cursing the tremor in my voice. "It's going to sound strange, and I don't know what you are going to make of it."

"All right," she said, uncertainly propping herself up on her elbow, eyes intent.

"It's not like I'm about to confess a murder or anything. You can relax. It's something that happened to me during my meditation in Ladakh, perhaps the most revolting and disturbing experience of my life. It takes a little time to explain. Do you mind?"

She shook her head, encouraging me to go on.

"You see, the text I was working with started out with a section on freeing yourself from desire by meditating on the composite nature of all being. Basically, the instructions were to visualize a beautiful woman—or a man for a woman student—someone who fills you with desire, and then focus the meditation to find out where the desire is located. So, for example, say I feel desire for my lover's beautiful long hair. Then I examine the hair through each of the five senses: do I desire the sight of it, smell, touch, taste, or sound it makes maybe when she swishes it back and forth? Wherever you find desire, you look more closely, as if through a microscope with a zoom lens. If I desire the sight of my lover's head of hair, do I desire a lock of it? A strand? Well, perhaps a strand? A four-inch piece? Two inches? There comes a point where there's no more desire for the speck that remains. Then you build it back up, strand by strand, back to the lock, to the full head. If desire returns, you go back to where it disappears once more, until you realize no feature of a woman is desirable in itself. Desirableness is something the observer superimposes on the object of his desire. This may seem like a fancy way of saying beauty is in the eye of the beholder, but discovering it for myself, it no longer seemed a cliché."

"And you wonder why I have no time for this spiritual foolishness?" she said angrily. "So, you're telling me you have mastered desire?"

"Oh, God, you, better than anyone else, know that isn't so." I gripped her arm for a second to make sure she wouldn't leave. "In fact, it took me a few days just to get started on the exercise, because I didn't really want desire rooted out so viciously. The text said to look on the body as a 'dirty machine, a frothing scum, or heap of sticks, stones, and pus.' And I couldn't do it. It seemed to me intent on fostering aversion. I didn't want to do that, but I did want to get into the rest of the text. It was my whole purpose for being in Ladakh. So I decided to do the meditation without bias. If disgust arose, I would just accept it. And if desire stayed, I would just accept that, too. At least in the end, if desire persisted, I would have a much clearer idea of what turned me on.

"Slowly I worked my way down from hair, forehead, ears, eyes, nose, mouth, through chin, neck, shoulder blades, armpits, nipples, elbows, wrists, each finger and the navel. It was exhausting work. Each single part took at least an hour's meditation. Some parts much more than others. But feeling all this desire every time I sat down to meditate proved good incentive for the work. It was amazing how clear the image grew, as if I could really see a woman in front of me, and could then get close-ups almost to the cellular level. It was working, too. In most cases, I could observe how I was adding the component of desire to the image, and then watch it disappear, but with some exceptions. For example, no matter how much I analysed my imaginary lover's eyes, I couldn't shake the feeling that this was more than looking into little black holes. Even in certain photographs or paintings, it's just ingrained in me that there's someone in there, someone I desire.

"After about two weeks of meditating four or so hours per day, I made it to the waist. From there on down, it was really slow going. Cutting through desire was as much work as clearing a rain forest with a pocketknife. Fortunately, by this point the process was moving almost automatically. Focus. Zoom. Analyse for desire. Repeat. Finally I got past the mons veneris. The genitalia were hell. They took forever to get through, and kept me in a pretty constant state of horniness that just wouldn't go away. In the next session, I turned my attention to the buttocks.

"When I zoomed in close on the buttocks, I felt desire take on a new quality, something dark. I tried to focus on it and suddenly it ballooned in intensity. It was as if a carefully controlled experiment was going into meltdown. From inside my chest, a creature sprang out with a yell, leapt into my meditation, and grabbed violently at the imaginary buttocks with long, bushy arms. It thrust itself fiercely, sexually into the image—a dirty, hairy, apelike little creature, hunched over, furtive. It reminded me of Gollum, you know, the obsessed, repulsive cave creature from *The Lord of the Rings*.

"It realized it had been lured into the light, and the beast froze. It cowered like a thing long used to caves and subterranean passages. It appeared as distant and real as if it was physically standing in front of me. I knew perfectly well it was a hallucination. But it was a real hallucination. It had come out of me. Luckily, I kept calm. I didn't break from my focused, meditative state, just noted the extreme aversion the vision aroused. It revolted me, this stinking, filthy animal. It chilled my flesh.

"'Stop,' I said, forbidding the beast from slinking back into my chest. It trembled, rooted to the spot by my voice, and obeyed. 'If you are my lust, my dark nature, whatever, all right,' I said out loud. 'I don't want to kill you. I won't deny you exist. Not any more. You are a part of me I—I never knew—did I do this to you? Did you have to be this way? Now I know what you are, and I will accept you. You do not lunge in real life. You are under my control. I just want to look at you, see if those sick emotions can be lost without denying or repressing you.'

"The creature glared at me, frightened and malevolent, while I looked it over.

"'Now go,' I said.

"In a flicker, the beast leapt back inside my chest. I felt it lurking there, prowling, angry at being tricked into the light. I fell back on my cot, completely exhausted. I never dreamed this part of me existed, so twisted and ashamed. I almost quit the meditation, Sabina, because I wasn't sure how to guard against the beast returning. But I had come to Ladakh to study Buddhism. To break free of my culture, get another perspective—you remember what I told you? I had to laugh. What I had wanted was so abstract, so analytical; instead I hallucinated a personal demon that feels more real than any philosophical truth I've known. I couldn't deny it. So I continued with the meditation, staying on my guard, without incident, right down to the toes.

"What I need to tell you, Sabina, is that it's still in here, this creature. It's a part of me. But I think I feel him changing since I've met you. Maybe it's possible for it to grow into something healthy? I don't really know."

I looked at her, eyes barely visible in the darkness. She said nothing. I knew how she scorned metaphysics, and this one was right over the top. But I continued.

"You said to me at dinner that you loved me, and I didn't say anything back, and you must wonder: Did he hear it? Is it making him afraid? Does he love me too? Yes, yes, yes. I do love you, without even knowing what the words mean. Here and now, I do. Does any of this make sense to you at all?"

"No, it sounds pretty confused," she said gently, stretching her arms around my neck, and pressing her breasts against my side. "But it doesn't matter. The last part is sounding better. Keep talking."

She crouched over me and kissed my shoulders, my nipples, ran her fingers through the hair of my chest, then bit my stomach. Her hands ran down my legs, and she slid down to take me in her mouth. I stopped talking. The feeling of impending orgasm grew in the centre of my belly. But instead of driving outward towards her body, the energy began to burn within. Heat seared up and down my limbs from inside. My nerves tingled like pins and needles, as in a leg that has gone to sleep and when the feeling returns it's so painful at first you can't walk. I began breathing fast and deep, hyperventilating, trying to absorb the strange sensation so that it would pass quickly, but its intensity kept growing. Bursts of white light flashed behind my eyes. It scared me. I felt I was losing control of my body. I pulled Sabina up, then rolled over to lay on top of her, anxious to have an orgasm and get rid of the sensations. My head, hands, feet, and belly felt on fire, the nerves incredibly sensitive to touch. The rush was weirdly ecstatic, electrifying, almost unbearable in its intensity. My body shuddered like paper before it ignites. The image of a curling corpse aflame in the burning *ghats* flickered through my mind. My hips thrust down at her, desperate for release. Suddenly I realized my erection was gone. My penis lay limply against her while the sensations inside my skin seared white hot. I felt I was losing consciousness. Beneath me, Sabina moaned and clutched. I could barely feel her, but held on, frightened and amazed as everything began to whirl around, and she was all that there was I could cling to.

I don't know how long it lasted, but gradually the burning ecstasy faded from my twitching nerves. It took perhaps another half hour for me to slow my breathing. Exhausted, slick with sweat, I turned to her and stroked her hair. Her eyes met mine uncertainly.

"This has never happened to me before," she said, her voice quavering, "that I have orgasm without penetration, without you…touching me." She felt my belly and the shaft of my penis. "You're still hot, but no sperm. It's very strange."

I nodded. For a while I could not speak. My mind searched for some frame of reference to connect this to, and an image surfaced from a visit to a remote mountain monastery in Ladakh. A lama friend had taken me to the special red chamber where the guardian deities dwelled. He permitted me to draw back the curtain to gaze on the wrathful aspect of the deity drawn on the temple wall. The ancient being radiated rings of flame. Its blue head was that of a snarling, fanged bull. Four of his arms bore tantric objects of power: a sword, a bell, a sceptre, a human skull filled with blood. The other two pair of hands caressed a green-skinned female goddess pressed against him in sexual embrace. She gripped him, standing, one leg wrapped around his waist. Their red tongues met, and in graphic detail the icon showed the thick blue shaft of the bull-god's penis entering her.

Such graphic sexual depictions of celestial and demonic beings were metaphors, so my Western commentaries on Tibetan Buddhism had said, for the spiritual union of the female and male poles of existence: yin and yang, darkness and light, potency and fertility. Yet I had also read that some tantric

Buddhists and Hindus lived out their metaphor in their own secret practices, transforming sex into a spiritual force so blinding, so powerful, it consumes all pleasure, all lust, all personality in its purifying fire.

I shook my head and sat up in bed, wondering if we had inadvertently touched that power together. It scared the hell out of me. What if we had been sexually united, had carried it through to orgasm? It felt as if I would have exploded, unable to contain the energy. My body would have broken open and shattered like a shell. But from that shell what would have emerged? I wondered with a brief laugh if Sabina did this to all her lovers, like some goddess in disguise. God, she'd laugh at me for that, I thought. I'm enthralled enough with her as it is.

"You give me so much," Sabina murmured, placing a hand on my back.

The remark caught me totally by surprise, for in all honesty, I had hardly been aware of her. Her gaze, her stroking, her subtle movements and sounds of passion that usually delighted me in our lovemaking, they were all lost in the storm. All I remembered was gripping her and once hearing her groan. She reached up and clasped my waist from behind, drawing me back down into her embrace. I realized it must have been late into the night.

"Sabina, I think we may have touched something here," I said, reluctant to lie down, but unable to resist her arms, "some kind of tantric energy. What was it like for you?"

"You were wonderful."

"That's not what I mean!"

"Hush, let's sleep a bit."

She put her fingers over my mouth and curled against me, one leg sliding up on top of my stomach. Metaphysics loses another argument, I sighed, and, suddenly feeling very weary, went to sleep.

Tim Ward is an ordained lay monk who spent six years in the Orient. He is the author of What the Buddha Never Taught, The Great Dragon's Fleas, *and* Arousing the Goddess, *from which this story was excerpted. He lives in Washington, D.C.*

TIM CAHILL

In Chief Yali's Shoes

A promise is a promise, a brother is a brother.

"Wabintok Mabel," Chief Yali Mabel whispered, by way of reverent introduction.

He held a lit candle under Wabintok's black and desiccated face. Flickering yellow light illuminated the mouth, which was open wide in a soundless, twisted scream. It was, I understood, a privilege to view Wabintok here, in the sanctity of the men's hut.

"*Wah*," I said. The Dani expression is, in my opinion, the finest word for "thank you" in the human vocabulary.

"*Wah*," Chief Yali replied politely.

"*Wah*," a number of the other men said.

The small, circular wooden hut smelled of straw, of countless fires, of singed pig fat. Wabintok himself smelled·of smoke, and, yes, singed fat. He was, by some village estimates, 400 years old. I'd never slept in the same hut with a smoked mummy before.

Chief Yali spoke with some awe about Wabintok, who was

his ancestor and a great hero of the Mabel family. "*Bintok*," Yali explained, is the Dani word for bamboo knife. Wabintok means "Thank you, Bamboo Knife." Chief Yali's ancestor had been a great warrior, a master of the bamboo knife, in the time of ritual war, before the first outsiders came to the valley of the Dani four generations ago.

The valley, the Grand Beliem Valley, is located in the highlands of New Guinea, specifically in the Indonesian western half of the island, called Irian Jaya. The valley is a mile high, almost 50 miles long, and is home to an estimated 100,000 Dani people, short sturdy Papuans who, according to one guidebook "are just now emerging from the Stone Age."

I suppose that's so. Dani women wear grass skirts. The men often wear nasal ornaments made of bone. They sometimes wear feathered headdresses and paint their bodies with special-colored clay. The Dani men are phallocrypts, which means that aside from feathers and bones, they wear penis sheaths. And nothing else.

In the men's hut, where Chief Yali invited me to spend the night, the Mabel family men all said that the time of ritual war was past. It was forbidden by the government, illegal. And yet, Yali, a handsome, powerful man who looked to be in his late thirties, sported at least five small circular scars.

If there was no war, I asked in a roundabout manner, who had fired all those arrows into Yali's chest and back? Well, it seemed that while there was no war, there were battles now and again.

And so I spent the night around a smoky fire, gnawing the charred remnants of what had been a piglet a few hours before. We laughed and sang and pounded on logs and talked of glorious battles. We pledged a kind of brotherhood and spoke of the spirit each man feels in his belly and in his heart.

It seemed to me that Yali could make a hell of a living in America leading "wild man" weekends. He made me promise that I'd come back and visit him, with at least one of my wives.

Just last month, I mailed Yali a present he had desperately wanted, and I had solemnly promised to send him. Certain culturally aware friends thought the gift insensitive. Such goods would "spoil" the naked Dani. Well, a promise is a promise, a brother is a brother, and screw the culturally aware. I like to think of the chief in his feathered headdress, his body paint, and his penis gourd: Yali Mabel, standing proud, wearing his new leather Redwing boots. I know what Yali said when he got the package.

He said, "Wah!"

Tim Cahill is editor-at-large of Outside *magazine and is the author of six books including* Jaguars Ripped My Flesh *and* Pass the Butterworms: Remote Journeys Oddly Rendered, *from which this story was excerpted. He also cowrote the IMAX film* Everest. *He lives in Montana with Linnea Larson, a couple of cats, and a dog.*

GEORGE VINCENT WRIGHT

Applause in Calcutta

Being a star takes on a different meaning.

I HAD HEARD ABOUT URINE THERAPY WHEN I WAS IN INDIA. It was part of traditional Indian Ayurvedic medicine, and I was curious about it. I was in Calcutta; a friend of mine told me of a small bookstore where I might find such a book. I went to the bookstore *et voila!,* there it was, *The Waters of Life: A Treatise on Urine Therapy,* paperbound with an appropriate yellow cover.

It felt so good to handle this nifty, slender, cute little book, exciting even, like a little hamster crawling from hand to hand, tickling the hands to almost unbearable sensation. With this book in hand, I went out to the odor of a Calcutta mid-afternoon.

This part of Calcutta had narrow streets with few cars, there were people, but it was not teeming; in a way, it was tranquil. After walking a short distance, I came to an intersection. At the corner, a group of younger men in a line were talking among themselves in animation. I caught their eyes, flashed a smile which instantaneously flashed back to me from them, a smile open-mouthed (the whiteness of the teeth and the pinkness of the gums made more vivid by the darkness of the skin), and a light, delighted, skipping laughter with it. My browsing eyes alighted on each of them, beelike, for a few seconds, downloading intensity. I was in the Seventh Heaven of The Twelfth Night. This Bengali eye intensity (I intensity) has to be seen to be believed. There is nothing like it in the West; it does not exist here. It is an intensity that doesn't need to be smiling, although in this case it was smiling. It is penetrating, like a fire in the deep belly which periscopes out through the eyes. It is fiery but it doesn't produce physical sensations of heat, perhaps because it is a fire of the soul. In my experience in India, this is something that happens between men; the relations with men toward women is more respectful and reserved. But what is very unique, from a Western viewpoint, is that there is no confrontation or challenge in the look, like a what-the-hell-are-you-looking-at-me-for-buddy look. It is being in a pure plasma of energy beyond personality.

I made a left turn and walked down the middle of this small street. There were no cars; the line of men was very long, stretching down a very long block to the corner. By now I realized that I had approached one of those very large Indian movie theaters, a square block in size, and that these men were in line for the next show. I bumble bee-d my way down the line a bit farther, eyes connecting, more plasma, when applause broke out. I didn't know what was happening, so I turned around to see what was going on, but I didn't see anything unusual; the applause continued and still not understanding, I kept turning around, and then I realized that they were applauding *me.* It was such an astounding revelation that I couldn't let the reality of it fully sink into my body. I was half numb in overwhelm. Walking down the block, I made a few more eye contacts as the applause continued. Not only was there applause but they were so clearly directing it to me, facing me with big, open-hearted smiles, joyful and excited. I didn't know how to handle it. This was the kind of reception received by popular heads of state and movie stars—however, it was not raucous but deep and abiding. So I became very shy and withdrawn as I traversed the remaining length of the street with my head bowed, studying the cobblestone pattern in the street. Despite this inward drawing of myself, the applause continued. I turned left at the end of the block; a right turn would mean following the line, but I had all the applause I could take at this moment. I slowly recovered. I was reminded of stories of people coming into contact with a divine presence, not being ready for it, and becoming very scared and "freaked."

Over the intervening years, I have always been charmed and flattered by the memory. Sometimes I thought they mistook me for a movie star, but that didn't seem quite right. Then I met a wise woman, to whom I told the story. Without hesitation she said: "Oh, in that part of the world they love people who can connect freely and easily to an inner place, and you did that in ample measure and that is why they reacted how they did." This is the view I now hold of that event.

George Vincent Wright grew up in Bayside, Queens (New York) and graduated from the Yale School of Architecture. In addition to designing, renovating, and building houses for more than twenty years in Maine, San Francisco, and the Bay Area, he's traveled the world, ever curious about water culture, bathhouses, history, music, and cuisine sauvage. *He has also harbored a long interest in being president. He now lives in the family home where he writes and gardens.*

PART TWO

WHEN THEY HEAR
A DIFFERENT DRUMMER

✦ ✦ ✦

Trail Mix

Hiking the Appalachian Trail,
the author and his buddy face
an unexpected challenge.

ON THE FOURTH EVENING, WE MADE A FRIEND. WE WERE
sitting in a nice little clearing beside the trail, our tents pitched,
eating our noodles, savoring the exquisite pleasure of just sitting, when a plumpish, bespectacled young woman in a red
jacket and the customary outsized pack came along. She regarded us with the crinkled squint of someone who is either
chronically confused or can't see very well. We exchanged
hellos and the usual banalities about the weather and where
we were. Then she squinted at the gathering gloom and announced she would camp with us.

Her name was Mary Ellen. She was from Florida, and she
was, as Katz forever after termed her in a special tone of awe, a
piece of work. She talked nonstop, except when she was clearing out her eustachian tubes (which she did frequently) by
pinching her nose and blowing out with a series of violent and
alarming snorts of a sort that would make a dog leave the sofa
and get under a table in the next room. I have long known that
it is part of God's plan for me to spend a little time with each

of the most stupid people on earth, and Mary Ellen was proof that even in the Appalachian woods I would not be spared. It became evident from the first moment that she was a rarity.

"So what are you guys eating?" she said, plonking herself down on a spare log and lifting her head to peer into our bowls. "Noodles? Big mistake. Noodles have got like no energy. I mean like zero." She unblocked her ears. "Is that a Starship tent?'

I looked at my tent. "I don't know."

"Big mistake. They must have seen you coming at the camping store. What did you pay for it?"

"I don't know."

"Too much, that's how much. You should have got a three-season tent."

"It is a three-season tent."

"Pardon me saying so, but it is like seriously dumb to come out here in March without a three-season tent." She unblocked her ears.

"It is a three-season tent."

"You're lucky you haven't froze yet. You should go back and like punch out the guy that sold it to you because he's been like, you know, negligible selling you that."

"Believe me, it is a three-season tent."

She unblocked her ears and shook her head impatiently. "*That's* a three-season tent." She indicated Katz's tent.

"That's exactly the same tent."

She glanced at it again. "Whatever. How many miles did you do today?"

"About ten." Actually we had done eight point four, but this had included several formidable escarpments, including a notable wall of hell called Preaching Rock, the highest eminence since Springer Mountain, for which we had awarded ourselves bonus miles, for purposes of morale.

"Ten miles? Is that all? You guys must be like *really* out of shape. I did fourteen-two."

"How many have your lips done?" said Katz, looking up from his noodles.

She fixed him with one of her more severe squints. "Same as the rest of me, of course." She gave me a private look as if to say, "Is your friend like seriously weird or something?" She cleared her ears. "I started at Gooch Gap."

"So did we. That's only eight point four miles."

She shook her head sharply, as if shooing a particularly tenacious fly. "Fourteen-two."

"No, really, it's only eight point four."

"Excuse me, but I just *walked* it. I think I ought to know." And then suddenly: "God, are those Timberland boots? *Mega* mistake. How much did you pay for them?"

And so it went. Eventually I went off to swill out the bowls and hang the food bag. When I came back, she was fixing her own dinner but still talking away at Katz.

"You know what your problem is?" she was saying. "Pardon my French, but you're too fat."

Katz looked at her in quiet wonder. "Excuse me?"

"You're too fat. You should have lost weight before you came out here. Shoulda done some training, 'cause you could have like a serious, you know, heart thing out here."

"Heart thing?"

"You know, when your heart stops and you like, you know, die."

"Do you mean a heart attack?"

"That's it."

Mary Ellen, it should be noted, was not short on flesh her-self, and unwisely at that moment she leaned over to get something from her pack, displaying an expanse of backside on which you could have projected motion pictures for, let us

say, an army base. It was an interesting test for Katz's forbearance. He said nothing but rose to go for a pee, and out of the
side of his mouth as he passed me he rendered a certain con-
venient expletive as three low, dismayed syllables, like the call
of a freight train in the night....

"So what's your star sign?" said Mary Ellen.

"Cunnilingus," Katz answered and looked profoundly
unhappy.

She looked at him. "I don't know that one." She made an
I'll-be-darned frown and said, "I thought I knew them all.
Mine's Libra." She turned to me. "What's yours?"

"I don't know." I tried to think of something. "Necrophilia."

"I don't know that one either. Say, are you guys putting
me on?"

"Yeah."

It was two nights later. We were camped at a lofty spot
called Indian Grave Gap, between two brooding summits—
the one tiring to recollect, the other dispiriting to behold. We
had hiked 22 miles in two days—a highly respectable distance
for us—but a distinct listlessness and sense of anticlimax, a
kind of midmountain lassitude, had set in. We spent our days
doing precisely what we had done on previous days and
would continue to do on future days, over the same sort of
hills, along the same wandering track through the same endless woods. The trees were so thick that we hardly ever got
views, and when we did get views it was of infinite hills covered in more trees. I was discouraged to note that I was
grubby again already and barking for white bread. And then
of course there was the constant, prattling, awesomely brain-
less presence of Mary Ellen.

"When's your birthday?" she said to me.

"December 8."

"That's Virgo."

"No, actually it's Sagittarius."

"Whatever." And then abruptly: "Jeez, you guys stink."

"Well, uh, we've been walking."

"Me, I don't sweat. Never have. Don't dream either."

"Everybody dreams," Katz said.

"Well, I don't."

"Except people of extremely low intelligence. It's a scientific fact."

Mary Ellen regarded him expressionlessly for a moment, then said abruptly, to neither of us in particular: "Do you ever have that dream where you're like at school and you look down and like you haven't got any clothes on?" She shuddered. "I hate that one."

"I thought you didn't dream," said Katz.

She stared at him for a very long moment, as if trying to remember where she had encountered him before. "And falling," she went on, unperturbed. "I hate that one, too. Like when you fall into a hole and just fall and fall." She gave a brief shiver and then noisily unblocked her ears.

Katz watched her with idle interest. "I know a guy who did that once," he said, "and one of his eyes popped out."

She looked at him doubtfully.

"It rolled right across the living room floor and his dog ate it. Isn't that right, Bryson?"

I nodded.

"You're making that up."

"I'm not. It rolled right across the floor and before anybody could do anything, the dog gobbled it down in one bite."

I confirmed it for her with another nod.

She considered this for a minute. "So what'd your friend do about his eye hole? Did he have to get a glass eye or something?"

"Well, he wanted to, but his family was kind of poor, you

know, so what he did was he got a Ping-Pong ball and painted an eye on it, and he used that."

"Ugh," said Mary Ellen softly.

"So I wouldn't go blowing out your ear holes any more."

She considered again. "Yeah, maybe you're right," she said at length, and blew out her ear holes.

In our few private moments, when Mary Ellen went off to tinkle in distant shrubs, Katz and I had formed a secret pact that we would hike fourteen miles on the morrow to a place called Dicks Creek Gap, where there was a highway to the town of Hiawassee, eleven miles to the north. We would hike to the gap if it killed us, and then try to hitchhike into Hiawassee for dinner and a night in a motel. Plan B was that we would kill Mary Ellen and take her Pop Tarts.

And so the next day we hiked, really hiked, startling Mary Ellen with our thrusting strides. There was a motel in Hiawassee—clean sheets! shower! color TV!—and a reputed choice of restaurants. We needed no more incentive than that to perk our step. Katz flagged in the first hour, and I felt tired too by afternoon, but we pushed determinedly on. Mary Ellen fell farther and farther off the pace, until she was behind even Katz. It was a kind of miracle in the hills.

At about four o'clock, tired and overheated and streaked about the face with rivulets of gritty sweat, I stepped from the woods onto the broad shoulder of U.S. Highway 76, an asphalt river through the woods, pleased to note that the road was wide and reasonably important looking. A half mile down the road there was a clearing in the trees and a drive—a hint of civilization—before the road curved away invitingly. Several cars passed as I stood there.

Katz tumbled from the woods a few minutes later, looking wild of hair and eye, and I hustled him across the road against his voluble protests that he needed to sit down *immediately*. I wanted to try to get a lift before Mary Ellen came along and screwed things up. I couldn't think how she might, but I knew she would.

"Have you seen her?" I asked anxiously.

"Miles back, sitting on a rock with her boots off rubbing her feet. She looked real tired."

"Good."

Katz sagged onto his pack, grubby and spent, and I stood beside him on the shoulder with my thumb out, trying to project an image of wholesomeness and respectability, making private irked tutting noises at every car and pickup that passed. I had not hitch-hiked in 25 years, and it was a vaguely humbling experience. Cars shot past very fast—unbelievably fast to us who now resided in Foot World—and gave us scarcely a glance. A very few approached more slowly, always occupied by elderly people—little white heads, just above the window line—who stared at us without sympathy or expression, as they would at a field of cows. It seemed unlikely that anyone would stop for us. I wouldn't have stopped for us.

"We're never going to get picked up," Katz announced despondently after cars had forsaken us for fifteen minutes.

He was right, of course, but it always exasperated me how easily he gave up on things. "Can't you try to be a little more positive?" I said.

"OK, I'm positive we're never going to get picked up. I mean, look at us." He smelled his armpits with disgust. "Jesus, I smell like Jeffrey Dahmer's refrigerator."

There is a phenomenon called Trail Magic, known and spoken of with reverence by everyone who hikes the trail, which holds that often when things look darkest some little piece of serendipity comes along to put you back on a heavenly plane. Ours was a baby-blue Pontiac Trans Am, which flew past, then screeched to a stop on the shoulder a hundred yards or so down the road, in a cloud of gravelly dust. It was so far beyond where we stood that we didn't think it could possibly be for us, but then it jerked into reverse and came at us, half on the shoulder and half off, moving very fast and a little wildly. I stood transfixed. The day before, we had been told by a pair of seasoned hikers that sometimes in the South drivers will swerve at hitchhikers, or run over their packs, for purposes of hilarity, and I supposed this was one of those moments. I was about to fly for cover, and even Katz was halfway to his feet, when it stopped just before us, with a rock and another cloud of dust, and a youthful female head popped out the passenger side window.

"Yew boys wunna rod?" she called.

"Yes, ma'am, we sure do," we said, putting on our best behavior.

We hastened to the car with our packs and bowed down at the window to find a very handsome, very happy, very drunk young couple, who didn't look to be more than eighteen or nineteen years old. The woman was carefully topping up two plastic cups from a three-quarters empty bottle of Wild Turkey. "Hi!" she said. "Hop in."

We hesitated. The car was packed nearly solid with stuff— suitcases, boxes, assorted black plastic bags, hangerloads of clothes. It was a small car to begin with and there was barely room for them.

"Darren, why'nt you make some room for these gentle-men," the young woman ordered and then added for us: "This yere's Darren."

Darren got out, grinned a hello, opened the trunk, and stared blankly at it while the perception slowly spread through his brain that it was also packed solid. He was so drunk that I thought for a moment he might fall asleep on his feet, but he snapped to and found some rope and quite deftly tied our packs on the roof. Then, ignoring the vigorous advice and instructions of his partner, he tossed stuff around in the back until he had somehow created a small cavity into which Katz and I climbed, puffing out apologies and expressions of the sincerest gratitude.

Her name was Donna, and they were on their way to some desperate-sounding community—Turkey Balls Falls or Coon Slick or someplace—another 50 miles up the road, but they were pleased to drop us in Hiawassee, if they didn't kill us all first. Darren drove at 127 miles an hour with one finger on the wheel, his head bouncing to the rhythm of some internal song, while Donna twirled in her seat to talk to us. She was stunningly pretty, entrancingly pretty.

"Y'all have to excuse us. We're celebrating." She held up her plastic cup as if in toast.

"What're you celebrating?" asked Katz.

"We're gittin married tomorrah," she announced proudly.

"No, kidding," said Katz. "Congratulations."

"Yup. Darren yere's gonna make a honest woman outta me." She tousled his hair, then impulsively lunged over and gave the side of his head a kiss, which became lingering, then probing, then frankly lascivious, and concluded, as a kind of bonus, by shooting her hand into a surprising place—or at least so we surmised because Darren abruptly banged his head on the ceiling and took us on a brief but exciting detour into a lane of oncoming traffic. Then she turned to us with a dreamy, unabashed leer, as if to say, "Who's next?" It looked, we reflected later, as if Darren might have his hands full, though we additionally concluded that it would probably be worth it.

"Hey, have a drink," she offered suddenly, seizing the bottle round the neck and looking for spare cups on the floor.

"Oh, no thanks," Katz said, but looked tempted.

"*G'won*," she encouraged.

Katz held up a palm. "I'm reformed."

"Yew *are*? Well, good for you. Have a drink then."

"No, really."

"How 'bout yew?" she said to me.

"Oh, no thanks. "I couldn't have freed my pinned arms even if I had wanted a drink. They dangled before me like tyrannosaur limbs.

"*Yer* not reformed, are ya?"

"Well, kind of." I had decided, for purposes of solidarity, to forswear alcohol for the duration.

She looked at us. "You guys like Mormons or something?"

"No, just hikers."

She nodded thoughtfully, satisfied with that, and had a drink. Then she made Darren jump again.

They dropped us at Mull's Motel in Hiawassee, an old–fashioned, nondescript, patently nonchain establishment on a bend in the road near the center of town. We thanked them profusely, went through a little song-and-dance of trying to give them gas money, which they stoutly refused, and watched as Darren returned to the busy road as if fired from a rocket launcher. I believe I saw him bang his head again as they disappeared over a small rise.

And then we were alone with our packs in an empty motel parking lot in a dusty, forgotten, queer-looking little town in northern Georgia. The word that clings to every hiker's thoughts in north Georgia is *Deliverance*, the 1970 novel by James Dickey that was made into a Hollywood movie. It concerns, as you may recall, four middle-aged men from Atlanta who go on a weekend canoeing trip down the fictional Cahulawasee River (but based on the real, nearby Chattooga) and find themselves severely out of their element. "Every family I've ever met up here has at least one relative in the penitentiary," a character in the book remarks forebodingly as they drive up. "Some of them are in for making liquor or running it, but most of them are in for murder. They don't think a whole lot about killing people up here." And so, of course, it proves, as our urban foursome find themselves variously buggered, murdered, and hunted by a brace of demented backwoodsmen.

Early in the book Dickey has his characters stop for directions in some "sleepy and hookwormy and ugly" town, which for all I know could have been Hiawassee. What is certainly true is that the book was set in this part of the state, and the movie was filmed in the area. The famous banjo-plucking albino who played "Dueling Banjos" in the movie still apparently lives in Clayton, just down the road.

Dickey's book, as you might expect, attracted heated criticism in the state when it was published (one observer called it "the most demeaning characterization of southern highlanders in modern literature," which, if anything, was an understatement), but in fact it must be said that people have been appalled by northern Georgians for 150 years. One nineteenth-century chronicler described the region's inhabitants as "tall, thin, cadaverous-looking animals, as melancholy and lazy as boiled cod-fish," and others freely employed words like "depraved," "rude," "uncivilized," and "backward" to describe the reclusive, underbred folk of Georgia's deep, dark woods and desperate townships. Dickey, who was himself a Georgian and knew the area well, swore that his book was a faithful description.

Perhaps it was the lingering influence of the book, perhaps simply the time of day, or maybe nothing more than the unaccustomedness of being in a town, but Hiawassee did feel palpably weird and unsettling—the kind of place where it wouldn't altogether surprise you to find your gasoline being pumped by a cyclops. We went into the motel reception area, which was more like a small, untidy living room than a place of business, and found an aged woman with lively white hair and a bright cotton dress sitting on a sofa by the door. She looked happy to see us.

"Hi," I said. "We're looking for a room."

The woman grinned and nodded.

"Actually, two rooms if you've got them."

The woman grinned and nodded again. I waited for her to get up, but she didn't move.

"For tonight," I said encouragingly. "You do have rooms?" Her grin became a kind of beam and she grasped my hand, and held on tight; her fingers felt cold and bony. She just looked at me intently and eagerly, as if she thought—hoped—that I would throw a stick for her to fetch.

"Tell her we come from Reality Land," Katz whispered in my ear.

At that moment, a door swung open and a grey-haired woman swept in, wiping her hands on an apron.

"Oh, ain't no good talking to her," she said in a friendly manner. "She don't know nothing, don't say nothing. Mother, let go the man's hand." Her mother beamed at her. "Mother, let *go* the man's hand."

My hand was released and we booked into two rooms. We went off with our keys and agreed to meet in half an hour. My room was basic and battered—there were cigarette burns on every possible surface, including the toilet seat and door lintels, and the walls and ceiling were covered in big stains that suggested a strange fight to the death involving lots of hot coffee—but it was heaven to me. I called Katz, for the novelty of using a telephone, and learned that his room was even worse. We were very happy.

We showered, put on such clean clothes as we could

muster, and eagerly repaired to a popular nearby bistro called the Georgia Mountain Restaurant. The parking lot was crowded with pickup trucks, and inside it was busy with meaty people in baseball caps. I had a feeling that if I'd said, "phone call for you, Bubba," every man in the room would have risen. I won't say the Georgia Mountain had food I would travel for, even within Hiawassee, but it was certainly reasonably prices. For $5.50 each, we got "meat and three," a trip to the salad bar, and dessert. I ordered fried chicken, black-eyed peas, roast potatoes, and "ruterbeggars," as the menu had it—I had never had them before, and can't say I will again. We ate noisily and with gusto, and ordered many refills of iced tea.

Dessert was, of course, the highlight. Everyone on the trail dreams of something, usually sweet and gooey, and my sustaining vision had been an outsized slab of pie. It had occupied my thoughts for days, and when the waitress came to take our order I asked her, with beseeching eyes and a hand on her forearm, to bring me the largest piece she could slice without losing her job. She brought me a vast, viscous, canary-yellow wedge of lemon pie. It was a monument to food technology, yellow enough to give you a headache, sweet enough to make your eyeballs roll up into your head—everything, in short, you could want in a pie so long as taste and quality didn't enter into your requirements. I was just plunging into it when Katz broke a long silence by saying, with a strange kind of nervousness. "You know what I keep doing? I keep looking up to see if Mary Ellen's coming through the door."

I paused, a forkful of shimmering goo halfway to my mouth, and noticed with passing disbelief that his dessert plate was already empty. "You're not going to tell me you miss her, Stephen?" I said dryly and pushed the food home.

"No," he responded tartly, not taking this as a joke at all. He took on a frustrated look from trying to find words to express his complex emotions. "We did kind of ditch her, you know," he finally blurted.

I considered the charge. "Actually, we didn't kind of ditch her. We ditched her." I wasn't with him at all on this. "So?"

"Well, I just, I just feel kind of bad—just *kind* of bad—that we left her out in the woods on her own." Then he crossed his arms as if to say: "There. I've said it."

I put my fork down and considered the point. "She came into the woods on her own," I said. "We're not actually responsible for her, you know. I mean, it's not as if we signed a contract to look after her."

Even as I said these things, I realized with a kind of horrible, seeping awareness that he was right. We had ditched her, left her to the bears and wolves and chortling mountain men. I had been so completely preoccupied with my own savage lust for food and a real bed that I had not paused to consider what our abrupt departure would mean for her—a night alone among the whispering trees, swaddled in darkness, listening with involuntary keenness for the telltale crack of branch or stick under a heavy foot or paw. It wasn't something I would wish on anyone. My gaze fell on my pie, and I realized I didn't want it any longer. "Maybe she'll have found somebody else to camp with," I suggested lamely, and pushed the pie away.

"Did *you* see anybody today?"

He was right. We had seen hardly a soul.

"She's probably still walking right now," Katz said with a hint of sudden heat. "Wondering where the hell we got to. Scared out of her chubby little wits."

"Oh, don't," I half pleaded, and distractedly pushed the pie a half inch farther away.

He nodded an emphatic, busy, righteous little nod and looked at me with a strange, glowing, accusatory expression that said, "And if she dies, let it be on *your* conscience." And he was right; I was the ringleader here. This was my fault.

Then he leaned closer and said in a completely different tone of voice, "If you're not going to eat that pie, can I have it?"

In the morning we breakfasted at a Hardees across the street and paid for a taxi to take us back to the trail. We didn't speak about Mary Ellen or much of anything else. Returning to the trail after a night's comforts in a town always left us disinclined to talk.

We were greeted with an immediate steep climb and walked slowly, almost gingerly. I always felt terrible on the trail the first day after a break. Katz, on the other hand, just always felt terrible. Whatever restorative effects a town visit offered always vanished with astounding swiftness on the trail. Within two minutes it was as if we had never been away—actually worse, because on a normal day I would not be laboring up a steep hill with a greasy, leaden Hardees breakfast threatening at every moment to come up for air.

We had been walking for about half an hour when another hiker—a fit-looking, middle-aged guy—came along from the other direction. We asked him if he had seen a girl named Mary Ellen in a red jacket with kind of a loud voice.

He made an expression of possible recognition and said: "Does she—I'm not being rude here or anything—but does she do this a lot?" and he pinched his nose and made a series of horrible honking noises.

We nodded vigorously.

"Yeah, I stayed with her and two other guys in Plum-orchard Gap Shelter last night." He gave us a dubious, sideways look. "She a friend of yours?"

"Oh, no," we said, disavowing her entirely, as any sensible person would. "She just sort of latched on to us for a couple of days."

He nodded in understanding, then grinned. "She's a piece of work, isn't she?"

We grinned, too. "Was it bad?" I said.

He made a look that showed genuine pain, then abruptly, as if putting two and two together, said, "So you must be the guys she was talking about."

"Really?" Katz said "What'd she say?"

"Oh, nothing," he said, but he was suppressing a small smile in that way that makes you say: "What?"

"Nothing. It was nothing." But he was smiling.

"*What?*"

He wavered. "Oh, all right. She said you guys were a couple of overweight wimps who didn't know the first thing about hiking and that she was tired of carrying you."

"She said *that?*" Katz said, scandalized.

"Actually I think she called you pussies."

"She called us *pussies?*" Katz said. "Now I will kill her."

"Well, I don't suppose you'll have any trouble finding people to hold her down for you," the man said absently, scanning the sky, and added: "Supposed to snow."

I made a crestfallen noise. This was the last thing we wanted. "Really? Bad?"

He nodded. "Six to eight inches. More on the higher elevations."

He lifted his eyebrows stoically, agreeing with my dismayed expression. Snow wasn't just discouraging, it was dangerous.

He let the prospect hang there for a moment, then said, "Well, better keep moving." I nodded in understanding, for that was what we did in these hills. I watched him go, then turned to Katz, who was shaking his head.

"Imagine her saying that after all we did for her," he said, then noticed me staring at him, and said in a kind of squirmy way, "What?" and then, more squirmily, "*What?*"

"Don't you ever, *ever*, spoil a piece of pie for me again. Do you understand?"

Two days later we heard that Mary Ellen had dropped out with blisters after trying to do 35 miles in two days. Big mistake.

Bill Bryson was born in Des Moines, Iowa, and lived for twenty years in England where he worked for the Times *and the* Independent *and wrote for most major British and American publications. His travel books include* Neither Here Nor There, The Lost Continent, Notes from a Small Island, I'm a Stranger Here Myself, *and* A Walk in the Woods: Rediscovering America on the Appalachian Trail *from which this story was excerpted. He now lives in Hanover, New Hampshire, with his wife and four children.*

★ ✶ ★

Turn the Tables

This game is not for sissies.

SAIGON HAS ALWAYS BEEN A LADY, AND A BEAUTIFUL ONE, BUT a lady with a touch of sin. There is a game you can play here, when you are tired of more mundane pastimes and hanker after a contest of wits and nerve. It is not inherently dangerous, but neither is it a game for the faint of heart. Much is at stake. For in this game the hunted becomes the hunter, and the predator turns prey. I should say that there is currently an Englishwoman residing at the 333 Hotel with her left leg in a cast for a torn ligament. But hers is the only injury I have ever heard of. And she played at three o'clock in the morning after an evening of drinking. And she played rough. Many beginners do. I did.

So you must not play this game when you have been drinking, or ill, or in a bad mood. Your senses and your reflexes, and your powers of observation and decision must be in top form, because you, the visitor, the amateur will be going up against the pros. But you can win at this game. If you follow my advice and learn from me you can win almost every time. In fact, I haven't lost yet. Although in fairness I'd have to say that the outcome of my most recent encounter was very dodgy and too close for comfort. And I had put too much at stake. But I won. The game is called Trolling for Pickpockets.

Trolling for pickpockets, as a Saigonese contact sport, was invented during the Tet new year celebrations of 1992 by Bruce and Paul Harmon and myself. We were wandering the Ben Thanh market on Le Thanh Ton boulevard one fine morning. The holiday crowd was dense and there was much rubbing of shoulders. Two unsavory looking guys walking side by side approached me head on. I knew I was their mark. Their appearance alone tipped me off. The best players look like the woodwork. Just before contact they parted like waters and went to both sides of me, bracketing me hard. I felt hands as they slid by.

I am very aware of hands in this country. In Vietnam it is impolite and unseemly to touch strangers. Most people don't even observe the Western custom of shaking hands. Children will sometimes touch you as you walk by, out of childish curiosity at some one who looks nothing like them or theirs. Or they will run up from behind, touch you and flee. But they're just playing a game of "counting coup." They know it's naughty, but the fascination of foreigners overcomes their good manners. Or they might be pickpockets in training. But certainly an adult who touches you on the street is at least being disrespectful, and could be trying to get your goods.

So that morning in the market when I felt hands, my own right hand went instinctively to the small bag I carry on my hip, slung to my belt like a holster. My hand brushed a strange hand that instantly snapped away. At the same time my left hand, almost of its own accord, shot through an undulating press of bodies and grabbed a fistful of shirt front. The guy on my right melted into the crowd. But on my left I gave a tug and jerked the wearer of the shirt to front and center. I relieved him of my sunglasses. Maintaining my grip on his shirt I told him in no uncertain looks and tone that I would eat him without salt if he should make me his mark again.

At this point Bruce and Paul, having seen what happened in the brief encounter, came rushing to my aid, ready to help me pound the culprit into the dirt like a railroad spike. But I let the lad go, sent him back to school to study his lessons a little harder. After all, he had nothing of mine. And I had one of his shirt buttons. To my amazement, I wasn't even angry at him. I felt no sense of outrage at the attempt on my person and property. I had no desire to haul the bad guy off to the pokey and demand justice. I didn't thirst for his blood. Rather, I was jazzed. Yessss! I was pumped. I was mighty. I had won.

"Richard," Paul said. "That was beautiful. You caught that guy like a fly ball!"

And Bruce said, "Damn it! I want to catch one too!"

And so the sport of trolling for pickpockets came into being. We immediately set our hooks with bait: sunglasses, bank notes, pens, etc. hanging provocatively from our pockets. And then we went watchfully on patrol. Bruce was the first to bag one. He was a solo operator who foolishly went for Bruce's front pocket, the most easily defensible. Obviously a rank beginner, and Bruce should take no undue pride in hooking him. (You hear me, Bruce?) Bruce's response to the guy? No shirt grabbing or nasty looks of intimidation. Just an openhanded straight right to the chest. Doesn't sound like much, but Bruce is a powerful man. It sent the cutpurse three or four steps back and almost onto his ass. A troupe of cyclo (SEEK-low, a Vietnamese pedicab) drivers lounging nearby saw the encounter and nearly rolled on the ground laughing. Cyclo drivers are poor, and nightclub entertainments are beyond their means. But Bruce had amused them mightily. So much so that they wanted more. Knowing who some of the local pickpockets were, they encouraged them to try their wiles on us. We all bagged our limit, and by midafternoon the Ben Thanh market was cleansed of pickpockets, and the people were secure.

Paul had the most dramatic capture. As we were new to the game, we didn't know that skillful players can get through even the strongest lines of defense in the forms of buttons, zippers, locks, etc. Only the most alert vigilance is proof against a good player. The brotherhood of cutpurses and pickpockets even has a saying on the subject: "You can't steal a man's goods when he's thinking about them."

Paul carries his expensive camera in a holster with Velcro, buttons, and a zipper to secure it. Seems safe. But a senior member of the opposing team actually got through the defenses, grabbed the camera, and was on the lam by the time Paul realized what was up. He gave chase with a hue and cry. Bruce and I followed about 20 paces behind. We ran passed the cyclo drivers, who cheered us on. We ran passed the fabric merchants who cursed us for the disruption. Rounding a corner into the food stalls Paul was closing in when the thief lost his breath, or heart for the chase, or just slipped on a banana peel. He went crashing into a stall selling deep-fried spring rolls. His impact knocked over a huge wok full of bubbling hot oil which spilled down his back, across his ass, and down his thighs. In an instant he was airborne. Almost before his feet touched the ground he was gone in a flash, leaving behind Paul's camera, the echoes of his screams, and a curious odor reminiscent of deep-fried pork skins.

Crowned with many victories we repaired to our digs at the Prince Hotel, at that time a favorite of backpackers and other budget travelers such as we were on that occasion. We told everyone then gathered in the bar of our exploits. But they were not amused or impressed. A pious Swede even scolded us. "You shouldn't do that," he complained. "These people are poor!"

"And they're gonna stay that way if they try to make a living out of our pockets," Bruce said.

"But they're socialists!" the Swede cried.

"Huh? What? Socialist thieves?" Paul wondered aloud.

"Socialists!" the man reiterated, trying to get it through to us why it was a bad thing to toy with commie crooks.

"Hey," I asked him, "with that kind of individual initiative and free enterprise spirit, wouldn't that make them capitalists?"

The Swede shook his head in despair. The backpackers shifted uncomfortably in their printed t-shirts and Indian-made cotton, pajama-style trousers. They tugged at their blond dreadlocks and stared into their watery budget beer and thin herbal teas.

Note to players: Don't share this game with backpackers or Swedes. They have no fire in the belly. Australians make good players. Any nation that has an annual dwarf tossing contest will make good players. Texans and Yorkshiremen are good for trolling. As are Nepalis, especially if they have a bit of Ghurka background. I spent a pleasant afternoon last week with a guy from Ghana. He told me that he plays the game at home! (I guess it's like the wheel: been invented many times.) I suppose it's not so much where people come from that counts the most. It's that gleam in their eye that tells you who will make a player.

Now I don't want you to get the idea that Saigon is a dangerous place. In fact it's one of the safest cities you can visit. Far safer than SF, LA, or NY. It is almost devoid of violent crime. I can nearly guarantee that you won't get shot in Saigon (unless it's by the authorities); that you will not get raped (unless you pay some one to do it); that you will not be hit on the head and your poke pinched; you won't be kid-napped, murdered, stabbed, gassed, poisoned or fed bad food. This is generally a nonviolent society. The criminal urge is expressed in the con, the counterfeit, the card sharp, the stock swindle, the pickpocket and the cutpurse.

Now there are exceptions to every rule, and one of them hangs out near my hotel. I've recognized him as a player and a mean sort, too. We've never spoken, but we have exchanged some hostile glances as I've passed by his station. We know each other, and we both know we know. A few days ago, he made an attempt on me as I made my way home.

I was hot and tired and in no mood to play. For the first time in all my encounters, I got angry. As soon as I felt him make his move, I wheeled around and threw up my fists in a proper boxing stance and challenged him to "try it again if you dare, you SOB!" At the same instant he assumed a kung fu–type pose, curled up with one foot off the ground, ready to release a kick. We had a standoff for about two or three seconds, and we had begun to draw attention when I decided that he had just rendered a good performance. Most pick-pockets would have slunk away at the prospect of a punch in the nose. I laughed and offered him my hand, and we shook. Then I turned to go, and the creep tried me again! I swung around to backhand him, but by then he was gone. Fast man. Dangerous player. But I still won.

In playing this game, the ideal conclusion to any encounter is so subtle that only you and your fish know that it happened. You troll through a market or fair or promenade where you know that they school. Your baited hook is out, not too obviously but temptingly. (And, of course, you're not carrying anything you can't afford to lose.) Your senses are heightened. You see, hear, even smell with intense acuity. You are very much alive to all around you. You watch for any unusual or sudden movement, especially at the periphery of your vision. You listen for sounds of breathing and the rustle of clothing or bags, or the soft footfalls that tell you it's about to happen. But most of all your sense of touch is so acute that you can feel odors afloat on the air. You're aware of the slightest change in temperature. You know the texture, weight, and fit of your clothing. For it's your tactile faculties that will most likely tell you that the hand is at your pocket and you've just hooked your fish.

You now have one, maybe two seconds at most, to win the game. That's not much time, but it's you that have the advantage of surprise. Your quarry doesn't know that you've been lying in wait for him. He thinks you're easy pickings. So now! Wheel around! Make you move small and without show, but make it sudden and swift, for the fright it will give him. Grab for the wrist whose hand has your bait and hold firmly because he may try to bolt. The trick is not to wrestle with him, but to make eye contact as soon as possible. Nine times out of ten it will make him freeze. He knows the jig is up, might even realize he's been had. And being the nonviolent, nonconfrontational sort that he is, he submits. You hold him for a second or two, just for emphasis. And just to appreciate his racing pulse. Then you quietly let him go. Just catch and release. He'll scurry off to hide somewhere, or perhaps to be cuffed and scolded by his master who was watching from a fair vantage point. Score one for the visitors. Yesss!

There is one class of pickpocket that bears warning of. He is the same type that provided the Englishwoman in the 333 Hotel with her leg cast. He is known as a "cowboy." He rides a motorbike with an accomplice passenger behind known as "the snatch." They ride up alongside you, usually from behind, and grab whatever protrudes, then they're off across town. Because of their speed, power, and clever tactics, they are the worst you'll ever go up against. The trick with them is simply to step aside as they pass and let the snatch grab nothing but air.

But when a cowboy and his snatch made their move upon the Englishwoman she was feeling cocky and thought she could drop the snatch to the ground by hanging on tight to her boodle. But at 3:00 a.m. and full of drink, she was in no shape for combat. They dragged her for a few yards until she let go and slammed into a tree. She cursed them loudly, and if their feelings were hurt thereby, it would be a good thing. Now she plots a better game, while the cowboy and his snatch live well.

In all my years in Southeast Asia, I never once personally encountered a cowboy. Until last week. I was in a cyclo driven by a guy I hire often. He's a good guy with a sense of humor, and we get along well. I can't pronounce his name, nor he mine, so I call him Joe. He calls me Kieu. I don't know if my spelling is correct, and he can't tell me because he's illiterate, but I'm sure it's close enough.

We had stopped at an intersection for a traffic light. The light was just about to turn green, and I could feel Joe taking a strain on the pedals of his cyclo, preparing for the mad free-for-all that Saigon traffic is. Cars, motorbikes, and cyclos lined up behind us were doing the same.

I am blessed with good vision. It's 20/10, which means that I can see twice as far as most people. I'm also just an observant sort of guy. Most writers are. I saw to my right on the cross street, and heading into the intersection, a red-and-white motorbike driven by a t-shirt-clad man, and another riding pillion. The one on the rear was looking straight at me and hollering something to the driver. No alarms tripped until I saw him suddenly bank left and accelerate into the turn. The computer in my head that does idle geometry and lead computations as I observe moving objects ran a quick calculation on the bike's curve. It wasn't heading for the middle of the opposite lane. It was heading for a close encounter with *moi*. A cowboy and his snatch, at last! My time, rate, and distance computer were now running millisecond updates. I had three seconds till impact.

One Mississippi…

The snatch's eyes are locked on me, watching intently for dangers and opportunities. I know if I make any move of preparation or defense, he will abort his run. I keep my face forward, watching from behind dark lenses. Joe's cyclo lurches into movement. I have to know what the snatch is going to go for. I have to know ahead of time in order to make my move quickly enough.

Two Mississippi…

I've got a shopping bag at my feet, some miscellaneous stuff hanging out of my shirt pocket, a leather folder on my lap. Wearing no jewelry. So he's got three options. But I can't tell where his focus is. Damn! This is going to be close. Look to his grab hand. It's open and ready, waist level and rising. So it won't be the shopping bag. I'm holding stone still. He's closing fast and on schedule. There! I can see his eyes. I can see the whites of them.

Three…

He seems to be looking me in the eyes. Is he going for my shades? They'll steal anything, if only just for practice. I can hear the cowboy's engine, he's still winding up, accelerating. They'll make the grab and be gone in a heartbeat.

Miss…

There! I see it: the vector of the snatch's hand and eye. He's going for my hat! The bastard! My $80 handwoven-in-Ecuador genuine Panama hat! That changes the whole game. It's one thing to nick a man's briefcase, but his hat is just too damned personal. He who steals my purse steals trash; but he who messes with my hat gets punished.

issi...

So now I want to hurt him. But how? I could stiff-arm the driver and spill them both onto the pavement. But they're coming too fast, I could dislocate my shoulder. His hand is up for the grab, and I've got to decide. I could spit in his eye. But I might miss. Never been a good spitter. I could have tossed the shopping bag at their heads, but there's no time now. Head butt them? Scratch at their eyes? Call 'em names?

POW!

I high fived the snatch as hard as I could. I know it was solid because it stung my own hand like frenzy. The force and surprise rotated the snatch's body counterclockwise around the axis of his spine more than 90 degrees. The motion translated the speeding vehicle's forward momentum into one wild and crazy ride. The driver almost lost it to the right, overcompensated to the left and straight into oncoming traffic. He slalomed back and forth across both lanes for 100 yards, the snatch screaming and cursing like a jilted Latina.

Both Joe and I laughed our heads off. "How do you like that, you SOBs?" I hollered after them, waving my hat. "I win, you bastards! I win!"

"You win, Kieu! You win!" Joe shouted and laughed.

Joe didn't know precisely what game I had been playing, but it was abundantly clear to him that I had won. Hands down.

Richard Sterling also contributed "The Perfect Punch in the Face" in Part One.

Original Sin

A father reveals a few things to his adult son
as they trek the Grand Canyon.

THOUGH WE HAD BEEN IN THE CANYON FOUR DAYS, THE HIKE along Shinumo Creek was the first time we had experienced the natural rhythm of time unfolding—slow, steady, inevitable. No clouds or light show distracted from the impending certainty of night in the deepening hues of the darkening sky.

After what seemed a long time of hard hiking up and down ledges, back and forth across the creek, Brandon moved as if we'd just started out. Or so it seemed as I struggled to keep up. "Hold up, Tchombiano," I finally called to his ever-retreating back. "I'm dragging ass. We'll make better time if I stop a minute to recharge."

"No prob. There's a flat spot on an outcropping up ahead."

"I don't dare close my eyes," I said as I spread out, "so I'd better talk to stay awake. Besides, something's rattling around in my head like a tune that won't go away. As you undoubtedly noticed, Malcolm and I curse like pig-boaters down here. It's part of the freedom of the canyon. You've joined in with an occasional 'shit,' 'damn,' or 'goddammit,' but I realized back

there I'd never before heard you say 'fuck.' Given the circumstances, it made a big impression and reminded me of a —"

"You have a story about fucking?!" Brandon interrupted,
laughing.

"I have a question. Do you remember the very first time
you said 'fuck'?"

"You're kidding."

"Just checking. I didn't think you'd remember. But my first
time came back to me in a flash when I heard you say it."

"You mean your life started passing in front of your eyes
just before you jumped?"

"Not my whole life, just one incident. It's a good illustration
of how our coming-of-age experiences have been different."

"Like how?"

"Cursing was absolutely forbidden to me. Mouth washed
out with soap for 'crap.' Sent to my room without dinner for
'darn.' Grounded for a week for 'dang.' And a full-scale belt-
whipping when 'goldarn' once slipped out. Major sin. Risking-
hell kind of sin. Given all that, as you might imagine, the
forbidden language took on gargantuan significance."

"Actually, I can't imagine," he said.

"Satan's lurking presence, trying to tempt me, felt very real.
He exposed me daily to the kind of gross, mean, taunting, and
hurtful profanity that male seventh- and eighth-graders spe-
cialize in. I knew Jesus had put me in that school on purpose
to test me, I prayed that it would be said of me as Saint Paul
wished it said of him, 'I have fought a good fight, I have finished my course, I have kept the faith: henceforth there is laid
up for me a crown of righteousness.'"

Brandon whispered something under his breath, as if utter-
ing an incantation against evil.

"Amen," I smiled, "I believed everything I experienced was
for some reason, that God had a purpose for my life, and I had

to set an example for others, witnessing for Jesus through my behavior. That's why I remember as one of the vivid memories of childhood the day I fell into Satan's grasp. I skipped 'damn,' 'bitch,' and 'shit,' and plunged right into the bottom of the abyss."

"You scored an F," Brandon laughed.

"Big time," I confirmed. "It happened on one of the first spring afternoons too warm for jackets, so I had tied mine around my waist. All the way down the long hill from school, three eighth-grade 'colored' girls—that's how we referred to African-Americans in those days—followed teasing about my 'skirt.' I was a mere sixth grader. In addition to being older and bolder, their sexual taunting played on my vulnerability as a proudly nonsexual Christian, meaning I was ignorant about sex and easily embarrassed as only a shy, pure, school-smart, street-dumb, and evangelical white boy could be at the advanced age of eleven.

"The ring leader, Felicia, was already quite buxom, a fact that had not escaped my Christian notice. 'That boy sure nuf is dressed like a girl,' she taunted. 'I wonder what's under his skirt. I wonder if any little ole white thing is under there.'

"The other two giggled. 'Felicia, you too mean, girl. You gonna plum embarrass that pore white boy to death,' they warned, urging her on.

"She didn't need any encouragement. 'I seen you watching my titties,' she said to my honor. 'Hey white boy, take off that skirt and we'll see what you got, then you can feel my titties.'

"I prayed: Jesus, I know you are testing me. Forgive them their impure thoughts. Let my body be the temple of God and my mind worthy of your purpose. The more they taunted and the louder they giggled, the faster I walked and the harder I prayed.

"I never looked back, never gave them the pleasure of

knowing how my flesh was mortified. At the bottom of the hill, as I turned to cross the railroad tracks, Felicia snuck up and grabbed me in the crotch. 'He's got a hard-on,' she yelled to the whole world. 'My titties done made his little white thing grow up under that there skirt.' And the three of them ran off screaming and laughing.

"'FUCK YOU!' I screamed.

"It just came out. Had a train been coming down the tracks, I could not have moved. I was planted there listening with fascination and horror at this sound that Satan had emitted through me. My first impulse was to ask God's forgiveness. What stopped me, I suspect, was how good it felt. Having entered the firegates of hell, I stood there trying to imitate the boys who daily, hourly, used this magical oath with deftness and authority. 'FUCK YOU, Felicia! FUCK YOU.'

"It would take many more years and lots of railroad tracks before I could curse with nary a twinge of guilt. But that's how it started, how your father lost his linguistic virginity." So saying, I jumped up exclaiming, "I'm rejuvenated. Let's truck."

"I've been trying to remember my first time, but I'm afraid it's lost," Brandon lamented.

"That's the point," I replied, pulling him up. "You'll never have my affection for or overindulgence in profanity because it's never been absolutely forbidden to you. You still have the capacity to reserve your oaths for special occasions, which is as it should be. I say that because I learned anew from you today the awesome effect of discretion and precise timing. It rivets the attention of the listener." With that I pushed Brandon ahead. "We've got places to go and people to see. Move the fuck out!"

After that the trek to base camp is a blur. The horror of impending darkness having been my companion all afternoon, I cursed myself for not bringing along a flashlight. After all we'd been through that day, I thought, it would be an absurd tragi-comedy to get hurt tripping over a stone on the path. I admit to being susceptible to a sense of irrational karmic justice where good and bad ultimately balance each other out. It had been an amazing day—a wonderful four days. My joy was tempered only by the sense that, at some point, we'd have to pay for all that wonderfulness. But as the first stars appeared, I found myself laughing at the absurd notion that I was important enough to be running a karmic balance sheet—the lingering, hard-to-wash-away residues of years of fear-inducing Sunday school. The feeling of cosmic insignificance so often reported in wilderness experiences engulfed and comforted me. Contrary to everything I knew about myself, I found solace in the impending darkness. I can't say why. But the fear I had been expecting, the terror I knew was just under the surface, never materialized.

The dim light heightened my senses and awareness. I found I was noticing more about the terrain in the contrasts of the shadows that I had seen in the light. The distinct outline of a tree or bush against the purple sky highlighted every branch and leaf. I could see the texture of a boulder in such detail that it felt like my eyes suddenly had the capacity to touch. My heightened senses were attuned like radar, giving me detailed information about everything around me, scanning for any possible danger. Being forced by the darkness to really look at the path, I saw each stone, twig, hole, thorn, or exposed root—details that typically escaped my attention in daylight. I experienced what I suspect the mystically inclined would describe as a sixth sense, but I interpreted it not as an added, new, or different sense, but as greater use of, perhaps even the seamless integration of the ordinary five, making the darkness palpable.

Climbing up and down crags, jumping back and forth across the creek and bushwhacking through waterside vegetation suddenly felt like walking on a wide, open highway. That morning I had tested the stability of each midstream boulder to avoid slipping into the water or twisting an ankle. Now, returning, I danced across the rocks that marked the intersection with White Creek just above base camp. I turned back, looked at where I had crossed, and was stunned by the contrast with the morning's cautious and calculated crossing. I was jolted out of this reverie by Malcolm's greeting to Brandon: "Decided to stay out late, I see. Any trouble? Where's your dad?"

His words seemed suspended in the air, as did Brandon's reply, each word drawn out, deep, like the sound on a tape recorder when the battery is low. "he's...right...be...hind... me...No...trou...ble...Mer...lin...was...awe...some.... Aaanddd...I'mmm...starvveedd."

Brandon went on talking, but I didn't track his words. The reference to hunger brought me crashing back onto ordinary consciousness. I presume I had been working off an adrenaline high or infusion of endorphins. Whatever it was left instantly with the awareness that we had made it back. I was drained. My body felt heavy, my legs so dead I had to will myself to take each step in the sand to make it the twenty yards up the beach to Brandon and Malcolm, like a marathoner stumbling across the finish line and disintegrating. I collapsed near the cookstove, aware in seeing the blue flame that it was totally dark. Malcolm was using a flashlight to cook. "The old man looks like shit," he laughed. "What've you boys been up to?"

Michael Quinn Patton is a social science professor with The Union Institute, a former Peace Corps volunteer, and the author of Grand Canyon Celebration: A Father-Son Journey of Discovery, *from which this story was excerpted. He lives in Minnesota.*

MICHAEL PATERNITI

⋆ ⋆ ⋆

An American Hero

You never know how you're going
to act in a crisis.

So wake now in Lorton, Virginia, invisible. Wake in this 45-year-old body with a walrus mustache, your waist thickening, skin loosening, the whole fleshy ornament of you beginning to schlump earthward. Rise in this cramped, brick two-bedroom among other cemented-together brick houses in a perfectly bland brick subdivision on a busy thoroughfare. Feel your way down the dark halls of your cramped brick house, past the photographs of your family—your wife, the teacher's aide; your teenage son with the blinding fast-ball—to the kitchen with flowered wallpaper and linoleum floor. Drink coffee at the oak table you refinished yourself, sitting in a pool of 100-watt light, and then head out the door for the one-hour bus ride to Washington, D.C., to the old Annex II building and your job in the congressional Budget Office. Like every day. Like every day before and every day after.

This the grind, your nine-to-five-thirty as a low-level government bureaucrat. Your life of put-on-the-same-old-clothes and take-the-same-bus and drink-the-same-bad-coffee and unjam-the-same-damn-Xerox-machine. Like, Do we have enough Bic pens around here? See, you're nobody. Or you're everybody—but either way, you're invisible. Just another guy. The anonymous Joe up in the grandstand, hot dog in mouth, proudly watching his son pitch goose eggs into the seventh inning. Invisible—which is why sometimes January 13,1982, feels like a dream, as if it all happened to another Lenny Skutnik who wasn't you. That day, like every day, you woke, rose, and stumbled down the dark hall. You drank coffee. On the radio, clouds, some snow in the forecast. You were thinking: Snow? C'mon, this is D.C. You carpooled with your father Marty and some coworkers. At the office, you did the usual. Checked the copy machines, delivered the mail. Ate lunch in the cafeteria, a club sandwich, and every once in a while stole a look out the window.

By early afternoon, the snow was so thick it seemed as if the moon itself had blown up, was coming down in woolly clumps, like Armageddon. Everything falling out of the sky but car fenders. Seemed impossible, but all federal workers were let out early. Freedom! And suddenly you were heading back to the brick subdivision to shovel the walk. Some warm soup and television on the couch. Home sweet home.

But no. The interstate was snarled, a bumper-to-bumper crawl. Took one hour to get one mile. High drifts on the ground. Then, around 4 p.m., just as the light began to drain from the sky, you came to a full stop before the Fourteenth Street Bridge, just off the main runway of National Airport. There was a commotion; people were out of their cars, out in the snow, looking over the guardrail at the frozen Potomac. People began working their way down the embankment by the bridge, slipping and sliding—something urgent—and you followed them in that silver light, with bits of the moon falling on your head. You weren't sure why, but you followed them down with your father and the other guys in your car. Your understanding of this came retroactively—all these people in the snow, running—as if you were speed-reading a story.

In the river were six people—splashing, fighting for air, trying to hang on to the tail of Air Florida flight 90, scheduled from Washington to Tampa. The plane had lumbered slowly down the tarmac on takeoff, banked hard left, and just couldn't raise itself up in the air, fighting all that icy downfall. Skimmed the Fourteenth Street Bridge, took off several car roofs, decapitated a few drivers, knocked over a truck, then crashed through the ice and vanished. About 70 people were already on the river bottom, buckled fast to their seats. Never had a chance, those people. Never got the flight magazine out of the seat pocket or moved on to the peanuts-and-soft-drinks portion of this beautiful, sad life. Swallowed whole by the Potomac.

You saw this big gash in the ice, smelled the sickening smell of jet fuel, and you—you, Lenny Skutnik, government clerk—could see bodies floating around, human hands and legs trying to hang on to the wrecked tail of the plane like toddlers without water wings, one moment hurtling down a runway, then suddenly thrown tumbling into this slushy water. It didn't compute: your life, then these bodies. A bystander, a sheet-metal worker, was already down by the water's edge, and people were trying to tie a makeshift line around him. One woman was taking off her nylons to add to some jumper cables—her naked legs gooseflesh in that silver light. The sheet-metal worker had his coat and boots still on, and he began to wade into the river, 33-degree water, sucked in hard, walked up to his knees, thighs, waist, walking as if he'd suddenly become the Tin Man, but that's as far as he got before a helicopter appeared and you all pulled him back in.

Now everything moved in horrible slow motion. More

people were slipping and sliding down the embankment, maybe 50 on the shore, watching the helicopter hover over the dazed, iced bodies in the river. Up on the bridge, there were more people, throwing rope to yet another survivor, who was trapped beneath the ice, trying to punch up through it. Over the open water, near the plane's tail, the helicopter dangled a lifeline with an open-noosed strap. There were three men and three women there. One of the men just seemed to disappear beneath the surface—gone. Another struggled to shore, and then another made it, too. But one of the women— you could tell she was in trouble. Somewhere on the river's bottom were her husband and her newborn baby, and somehow she had popped up on the surface, completely lost and pale, with a broken leg and some dim understanding that she needed to keep her mouth above the waterline, though the rest of her, that broken body of hers, just seemed to want to sink back down to her family.

The helicopter lowered itself, blowing everything sideways, bossing everything silver. Rotor blades shot wind under the skin of the wreckage and flipped the woman over with a piece of metal from the tail, flicked her like an insect. Flailing in that open water, wearing red, she reached for the lifeline from the helicopter, grabbed it, but then didn't have the strength to hold on when the helicopter rose. Again and again, same thing. The pale woman somehow struggled up onto a slab of ice, wobbling, and the lifeline came down, and you saw her grabbing it in slow motion, excruciating, and her whole body dragged back in the water, her lame leg dragged behind her. But then she couldn't hold on, let go with one hand, then two, and fell back in the water, in one pathetic, stonelike splash, washed under by the deafening sound of the chopper, which itself had become some kind of demented bird in this slow torture.

And suddenly, impossibly, out of nowhere—you! Her head was underwater, 50 people gawking from shore, fixed in place, the sky spitting moon, and you just went. Like, outta here! Boots off! Reached down and yanked them off and tore off the puff jacket, just ripped loose of that thing, down to short-sleeves—the same shirt as other days—and just leaped from the bank. Didn't think, didn't care. Just out of nowhere, roaring, skipping minutes, slicing between them, speeding time in order to get to this woman before she vanished, too. Out of nowhere, you, in the drink, in that slushie, windmilling like a sicko, a slashing fury of strokes. A blur. Fifty people standing there—Yo, who is this madman? Mark Spitz?—and you, like, That's it! Enough! She's coming with *me*.

You powered to her, six ferocious strokes through elec-trocutingly cold water, got to her at the give-up point, the *sayonara*-this-life split second, her eyes rolling back in her head. She was gone, unconscious and sinking, and you just grabbed her. You didn't feel anything. Not cold—nothing. Claimed her, took her back from the river. Pulled her head up, then pushed her to shore, like water polo. Handed her off to a fire-man who'd waded in. Dragged yourself to shore on your own. Stood up, soaking wet, breathing—yes, breathing!—looked back at the wreckage, and, once you knew everyone would get out, started up the embankment, picking up your puff jacket, looking around for your car pool, thinking: Time to go home. Let's go.

But then some cops corralled you. Led you to an ambu-lance. You said, Is this gonna cost me anything? I don't make no money. Free, they said. Someone put a hand on your back, and you got in. Noticed for the first time that your feet were cold. Missing your watch and a pack of cigarettes.

That's when it began, that's when the other Lenny Skutnik was born, when you realized what you'd actually done. Then found out it had been captured by a camera crew on the bank. At the hospital, they gave you a warm bath and some food, and as you were getting ready to go, they asked if you would answer some questions from the reporters. The story was out, the lead already written: In the nation's capital today, a blizzard and a plane crash. Seventy-eight dead. A gaping hole in the ice, and debris floating in the water. Helicopters circling, looking for survivors. Rescue crews waiting on the shore to rush the victims to the hospital. The media already had that part down, had their victim, too: Priscilla Tirado, the woman in the water. Now they needed their hero.

So you answered a few questions: Why'd you do it? Something just told me, Go in after her. Would you do it again? Yes, I'd do it again. Simple stuff. Obvious. Time to get home.

But no one would let you go. There was just this great, gaping need for you—not the Lenny you, the brick-subdivision guy, the government functionary; no, they wanted the Hero you, the part of you in them that they most needed to see and touch and believe in. The part of them that went diving in that icy water with you. On *Nightline,* Ted Koppel told you, It's not only courage—there has to be a certain kind of magnificent insanity about it all. You said, Something just told me to go in after her.

The morning shows, newspapers, magazines paraded into your living room. They made you into a soap-opera star. Lenny and Priscilla, Priscilla, and Lenny. Hero and victim, victim and hero. They hauled Priscilla's father-in-law, father of her dead husband, into your living room and tried to film him crying in front of you. You said, Wait a minute! Wait! Took him away from that camera, back into the bedroom. You wanted to beat the hell out of that network guy.

When people heard you lost your watch, you were offered a hundred new ones—then trips to Hawaii, Canada, Puerto

Rico. President Ronald Reagan invited you to his State of the Union address, seated you and your wife up there in the balcony with his beautiful wife Nancy—nice, nice woman. President went drifting off on some yabble about American heroes, suddenly mentioned your name, and the whole place erupted, Democrats and Republicans leaped to their feet. Hear them! Lenny!

You got 2,000 letters, some running deep with emotion. People wrote and said they were jumping up and down in their living rooms in front of their televisions, crying, screaming, watching that girl drown, saying, Do something! Do something! Some told you they had always been terrified to express their true feelings about anything in their real lives. Then suddenly they were jumping up and down in their living rooms, screaming, blubbering at the television. You came out of nowhere, dove into that dark river for them, pulled them out, too.

So that was it—you became public property, a character in your own life. Without wanting any of it, you were shot from a cannon, along the Icarus arc of American hero-hood. Didn't matter that every day, today even, there are people out there pulling bodies from some wreckage. That there's someone taking a bullet right now on some school playground. Seventy-eight people died in that crash. Hard to think of heroes when an image plays in your mind of that one survivor who surfaced in the wrong place, couldn't break through; people on the bridge saw his face pressed against that ice, alive, guppy-mouthed. And then he was gone.

No, the sweetest thing about that day wasn't the name they gave you—no, that seemed more like a joke—but when the day actually ended, when you got back to Lorton at about 2 a.m. Nearly seventeen years later, you remember it as if it were last night. Awesome tired. A little stiff. Everything in your brick subdivision was absolutely still and glittering with ice, strung yet with some Christmas lights, just solidly, beautifully *there*, and you started up the walk. Shoes crunching on the snow.

Never forget that: the clean smell of winter, the mysterious dark in all of those houses, and, inside, these men and women, your neighbors, drawn together, wrapped in each other, in their bedrooms sleeping—these mothers and fathers having begotten children who would one day beget their own children, and all of you wrapped together. Cemented together like these brick buildings. A light was on in your brick house, you remember that. A woman in the kitchen and a newborn kid. Your family, Lenny Skutnik. And the moon—it just kept falling, kept swirling down on you. It was suddenly as if you were drawn by a fast-moving current, reaching for a lifeline, moving toward some deeper place. And then you were up the steps, through the door, lost in that 100-watt light. Home.

Michael Paterniti writes for Esquire *and other publications.*

✦ ✦ ✦

The Pilot and the Elements

The author of The Little Prince
fights for his life.

WHEN JOSEPH CONRAD DESCRIBED A TYPHOON, HE SAID very little about towering waves, or darkness, or the whistling of the wind in the shrouds. He knew better. Instead, he took his reader down into the hold of the vessel, packed with emigrant coolies, where the rolling and the pitching of the ship had ripped up and scattered their bags and bundles, burst open their boxes, and flung their humble belongings into a crazy heap. Family treasures painfully collected in a lifetime of poverty, pitiful mementoes so alike that nobody but their owners could have told them apart, had lost their identity and lapsed into chaos, into anonymity, into an amorphous magma. It was this human drama that Conrad described when he painted a typhoon.

Every airline pilot has flown through tornados, has returned out of them to the fold—to the little restaurant in Toulouse where we sit in peace under the watchful eye of the waitress—and there, recognizing his powerlessness to convey what he has been through, has given up the idea of describing hell. His descriptions, his gestures, his big words would have made the rest of us smile as if we were listening to a little boy bragging. And necessarily so. The cyclone of which I am about to speak was, physically, much the most brutal and overwhelming experience I ever underwent; and yet beyond a certain point, I do not know how to convey its violence except by piling one adjective on another, so that in the end I should convey no impression at all—unless that of an embarrassing taste for exaggeration.

It took me some time to grasp the fundamental reason for this powerlessness, which is simply that I should be trying to describe a catastrophe that never took place. The reason why writers fail when they attempt to evoke horror is that horror is something invented after the fact, when one is re-creating the experience over again in memory. Horror does not manifest itself in the world of reality. And so, in beginning my story of a revolt of the elements which I myself lived through I have no feeling that I shall write something which you will find dramatic.

I had taken off from the field at Trelew and was flying down to Comodoro Rivadavia, in the Patagonian Argentine. Here the crust of the earth is as dented as an old boiler. The high-pressure regions over the Pacific send the winds past a gap in the Andes into a corridor 50 miles wide through which they rush to the Atlantic in a strangled and accelerated buffeting that scrapes the surface of everything in their path. The sole vegetation visible in this barren landscape is a plantation of oil derricks looking like the after-effects of a forest fire. Towering over the round hills on which the winds have left a residue of stony gravel, there rises a chain of prow-shaped, saw-toothed, razor-edged mountains stripped by the elements down to the bare rock.

For three months of the year, the speed of these winds at

ground level is up to 100 miles an hour. We who flew the route knew that once we had crossed the marshes of Trelew and had reached the threshold of the zone they swept, we should recognize the winds from afar by a gray-blue tint in the atmosphere at the sight of which we would tighten our belts and shoulder straps in preparation for what was coming. From then on, we had an hour of stiff fighting and of stumbling again and again into invisible ditches of air. This was manual labor, and our muscles felt it pretty much as if we had been carrying a longshoreman's load. But it lasted only an hour. Our machines stood up under it. We had no fear of wings suddenly dropping off. Visibility was generally good, and not a problem. This section of the line was a stint, yes. It was certainly not a drama.

But on this particular day, I did not like the color of the sky.

The sky was blue. Pure blue. Too pure. A hard blue sky that shone over the scraped and barren world while the fleshless vertebrae of the mountain chain flashed in the sunlight. Not a cloud. The blue sky glittered like a new-honed knife. I felt in advance the vague distaste that accompanies the prospect of physical exertion. The purity of the sky upset me. Give me a good black storm in which the enemy is plainly visible. I can measure its extent and prepare myself for its attack. I can get my hands on my adversary. But when you are flying very high in clear weather the shock of a blue storm is as disturbing as if something collapsed that had been holding up your ship in the air. It is the only time when a pilot feels that there is a gulf beneath his ship.

Another thing bothered me. I could see on a level with the mountain peaks not a haze, not a mist, not a sandy fog, but a sort of ash-colored streamer in the sky. I did not like the look of that scarf of filings scraped off the surface of the earth and borne out to sea by the wind. I tightened my leather harness as far as it would go, and I steered the ship with one hand while with the other I hung on to the longeron that ran alongside my seat. I was still flying in remarkably calm air.

Very soon came a slight tremor. As every pilot knows, there are secret little quiverings that foretell your real storm. No rolling, no pitching. No swing to speak of. The flight continues horizontal and rectilinear. But you have felt a warning drum on the wings of your plane, little intermittent rappings scarcely audible and infinitely brief, little cracklings from time to time as if there were traces of gunpowder in the air.

And then everything round me blew up.

Concerning the next couple of minutes I have nothing to say. All that I can find in my memory is a few rudimentary notions, fragments of thoughts, direct observations. I cannot compose them into a dramatic recital because there was no drama. The best I can do is to line them up in a kind of chronological order.

In the first place, I was standing still. Having banked right in order to correct a sudden drift, I saw the landscape freeze abruptly where it was and remain jiggling on the same spot. I was making no headway. My wings had ceased to nibble into the outline of the earth. I could see the earth buckle, pivot—but it stayed put. The plane was skidding as if on a toothless cogwheel.

Meanwhile I had the absurd feeling that I had exposed myself completely to the enemy. All those peaks, those crests, those teeth that were cutting into the wind and unleashing its gusts in my direction, seemed to me so many guns pointed straight at my defenseless person. I was slow to think, but the thought did come to me that I ought to give up altitude and make for one of the neighboring valleys where I might take shelter against a mountainside. As a matter of fact, whether I liked it or not, I was being helplessly sucked down toward the earth.

Trapped this way in the first breaking waves of a cyclone about which I learned, twenty minutes later, that at sea level it was blowing at the fantastic rate of 150 miles an hour, I certainly had no impression of tragedy. Now, as I write, if I shut my eyes, if I forget the plane and the flight and try to express the plain truth about what was happening to me, I find that I felt weighed down, I felt like a porter carrying a slippery load, grabbing one object in a jerky movement that sent another slithering down, so that, overcome by exasperation, the porter is tempted to let the whole load drop. There is a kind of law of the shortest distance to the image, a psychological law by which the event to which one is subjected is visualized in a symbol that represents its swiftest summing up: I was a man who, carrying a pile of plates, had slipped on a wax floor and let his scaffolding of porcelain crash.

I found myself imprisoned in a valley. My discomfort was not less, it was greater. I grant you that a down current has never killed anybody, that the expression "flattened out by a down current" belongs to journalism and not to the language of fliers. How could air possibly pierce the ground? But here I was in a valley at the wheel of a ship that was three-quarters out of my control. Ahead of me a rocky prow swung to left and right, rose suddenly high in the air for a second like a wave over my head, and then plunged down below my horizon.

Horizon. There was no longer a horizon. I was in the wings of a theater cluttered up with bits of scenery. Vertical, oblique, horizontal, all of plane geometry was awhirl. A hundred transversal valleys were muddled in a jumble of perspectives. Whenever I seemed about to take my bearings, a new eruption would swing me round in a circle or send me tumbling wing over wing, and I would have to try all over again to get clear of all this rubbish. Two ideas came into my mind. One was a discovery: for the first time I understood the cause of certain accidents in the mountains when no fog was present to explain them. For a single second, in a waltzing landscape like this, the flyer had been unable to distinguish between vertical mountainsides and horizontal planes. The other idea was a fixation: the sea is flat; I shall not hook anything out at sea.

I banked—or should I use that word to indicate a vague and stubborn jockeying through the east-west valleys? Still nothing pathetic to report. I was wrestling with chaos, was wearing myself out in a battle with chaos, struggling to keep in the air a gigantic house of cards that kept collapsing despite all I could do. Scarcely the faintest twinge of fear went through me when one of the walls of my prison rose suddenly like a tidal wave over my head. My heart scarcely skipped a beat when I was tripped up by one of the whirling eddies of air that the sharp ridge darted into my ship. If I felt anything unmistakably in the haze of confused feelings and notions that came over me each time one of these powder magazines blew up, it was a feeling of respect. I respected that sharp-toothed ridge. I respected that peak. I respected that dome. I respected that transversal valley opening out into my valley and about to toss me God knew how violently as soon as its torrent of wind flowed into the one on which I was being borne along.

What I was struggling against, I discovered, was not the wind but the ridge itself, the crest, the rocky peak. Despite my distance from it, it was the wall of rock I was fighting with. By some trick of invisible prolongation, by the play of a secret set of muscles, this was what was pummeling me. It was against this that I was butting my head. Before me on the right I recognized the peak of Salamanca, a perfect cone which, I knew, dominated the sea. It cheered me to think I was about to escape out to sea. But first I should have to wrestle with the gale off that peak, try to avoid its down-crushing blow. The peak of Salamanca was a giant. I was filled with respect for the peak of Salamanca.

There had been granted me one second of respite. Two seconds. Something was collecting itself into a knot, coiling itself up, growing taut. I sat amazed. I opened astonished eyes. My whole plane seemed to be shivering, spreading outward, swelling up. Horizontal and stationary it was, yet lifted before I knew it 1,500 feet straight into the air in a kind of apotheosis. I who for 40 minutes had not been able to climb higher than 200 feet off the ground was suddenly able to look down on the enemy. The plane quivered as if in boiling water. I could see the wide waters of the ocean. The valley opened out into this ocean, this salvation, and at that very moment, without any warning whatever, half a mile from Salamanca, I was suddenly struck straight in the midriff by the gale off that peak and sent hurtling out to sea.

There I was, throttle wide open, facing the coast. At right angles to the coast and facing it. A lot had happened in a single minute. In the first place, I had not flown out to sea. I had been spat out to sea by a monstrous cough, vomited out of my valley as from the mouth of a howitzer. When, what seemed to me instantly, I banked in order to put myself where I wanted to be in respect of the coastline, I saw that the coastline was a mere blur, a characterless strip of blue; and I was five miles out to sea. The mountain range stood up like a crenelated fortress against the pure sky while the cyclone crushed me down to the surface of the waters. How hard that wind was blowing I found out as soon as I tried to climb, as soon as I became conscious of my disastrous mistake: throttle wide open, engines running at my maximum, which was 150 miles an hour, my plane hanging 60 feet over the water, I was unable to budge. When a wind like this one attacks a tropical forest, it swirls through the branches like a flame, twists them into corkscrews, and uproots giant trees as if they were radishes. Here, bounding off the mountain range, it was leveling out the sea.

Hanging on with all the power in my engines, face to the coast, face to that wind where each gap in the teeth of the range sent forth a stream of air like a long reptile, I felt as if I were clinging to the tip of a monstrous whip that was cracking over the sea.

In this latitude, the South American continent is narrow and the Andes are not far from the Atlantic. I was struggling not merely against the whirling winds that blew off the east coast range, but more likely also against a whole sky blown down upon me off the peaks of the Andean chain. For the first time in four years of airline flying, I began to worry about the strength of my wings. Also, I was fearful of bumping the sea—not because of the down currents which, at sea level, would necessarily provide me with a horizontal air mattress, but because of the helplessly acrobatic positions in which this wind was buffeting me. Each time that I was tossed I became afraid that I might be unable to straighten out. Besides, there was a chance that I should find myself out of fuel and simply drown. I kept expecting the gasoline pumps to stop priming, and indeed the plane was so violently shaken up that in the half-filled tanks as well as in the gas lines the gasoline was sloshing round, not coming through, and the engines, instead of their steady roar, were sputtering in a sort of dot-and-dash series of uncertain growls.

I hung on, meanwhile, to the controls of my heavy transport plane, my attention monopolized by the physical struggle and my mind occupied by the very simplest thoughts. I was feeling practically nothing as I stared down at the imprint made by the wind on the sea. I saw a series of great white puddles, each perhaps 800 yards in extent. They were running toward me at a speed of 150 miles an hour where the down-surging wind-spouts broke against the surface of the sea in a succession of horizontal explosions. The sea was white and it was green—white with the whiteness of crushed sugar and green in puddles the color of emeralds. In this tumult, one wave was indistinguishable from another. Torrents of air were pouring down upon the sea. The winds were sweeping past in giant gusts as when, before the autumn harvests, they blow a great flowing change of color over a wheatfield. Now and again the water went incongruously transparent between the white pools, and I could see a green and black sea-bottom. And then the great glass of the sea would be shattered anew into a thousand glittering fragments.

It seemed hopeless. In twenty minutes of struggle I had not moved forward 100 yards. What was more, with flying as hard as it was out here five miles from the coast, I wondered how I could possibly buck the winds along the shore, assuming I was able to fight my way in. I was a perfect target for the enemy there on shore. Fear, however, was out of the question. I was incapable of thinking. I was emptied of everything except the vision of a very simple act. I must straighten out. Straighten out. Straighten out.

There were moments of respite, nevertheless. I dare say those moments themselves were equal to the worst storms I had hitherto met, but by comparison with the cyclone they were moments of relaxation. The urgency of fighting off the wind was not quite so great. And I could tell when these intervals were coming. It was not I who moved toward those zones of relative calm, those almost green oases clearly painted on the sea, but they that flowed toward me. I could read clearly in the waters the advertisement of a habitable province. And with each interval of repose the power to feel and to think was restored to me. Then, in those moments, I began to feel I was doomed. Then was the time that little by little I began to tremble for myself. So much so that each time I saw the unfurling of a new wave of the white offensive I was seized by a brief spasm of panic which lasted until the exact instant when, on the edge of that bubbling cauldron, I bumped into the invisible wall of wind. That restored me to numbness again.

Up! I wanted to be higher up. The next time I saw one of those green zones of calm it seemed to me deeper than before and I began to be hopeful of getting out. If I could climb high enough, I thought, I would find other currents in which I could make some headway. I took advantage of the truce to essay a swift climb. It was hard. The enemy had not weakened. Three hundred feet. Six hundred feet. If I could get up to 3,000 feet, I was safe, I said to myself. But there on the horizon I saw again that white pack unleashed in my direction. I gave it up. I did not want them at my throat again; I did not want to be caught off balance. But it was too late. The first blow sent me rolling over and over, and the sky became a slippery dome on which I could not find a footing.

One has a pair of hands and they obey. How are one's orders transmitted to one's hands?

I had made a discovery that horrified me: my hands were numb. My hands were dead. They sent me no message. Probably they had been numb a long time and I had not noticed it. The pity was that I had noticed it, had raised the question.

That was serious.

Lashed by the wind, the wings of the plane had been dragging and jerking at the cables by which they were controlled from the wheel, and the wheel in my hands had not ceased jerking a single second. I had been gripping the wheel with all my might for 40 minutes, fearful lest the strain snap the cables. So desperate had been my grip that now I could not feel my hands.

What a discovery! My hands were not my own. I looked at them and decided to lift a finger. It obeyed me. I looked away and issued the same order. Now I could not feel whether the finger had obeyed or not. No message had reached me. I thought, "Suppose my hands were to open; how would I know it?" I swung my head round and looked again. My hands were still locked round the wheel. Nevertheless, I was afraid. How can a man tell the difference between the sight of a hand opening and the decision to open that hand, when there is no longer an exchange of sensations between the hand and the brain? How can one tell the difference between an image and an act of the will? Better stop thinking of the picture of open hands. Hands live a life of their own. Better not offer them this monstrous temptation. And I began to chant a silly litany which went on uninterruptedly until this flight was over. A single thought. A single image. A single phrase tirelessly chanted over and over again: "I shut my hands. I shut my hands. I shut my hands." All of me was condensed into that phrase and for me the white sea, the whirling eddies, the saw-toothed range ceased to exist. There was only "I shut my hands." There was no danger, no cyclone, no land unattained. Somewhere there was a pair of rubber hands which, once they let go the wheel, could not possibly come alive in time to recover from the tumbling drop into the sea.

I had no thoughts. I had no feelings except the feeling of being emptied out. My strength was draining out of me and so was my impulse to go on fighting. The engines continued their dot-and-dash sputterings, their little crashing noises that were like the intermittent cracklings of a ripping canvas. Whenever they were silent longer than a second I felt as if a heart had stopped beating. There! That's the end. No, they've started up again.

The thermometer on the wing, I happened to see, stood at twenty below zero, but I was bathed in sweat from head to foot. My face was running with perspiration. What a dance! Later I was to discover that my storage batteries had been jerked out of their steel flanges and hurtled up through the roof of the plane. I did not know then, either, that the ribs on my wings had come unglued and that certain of my steel cables had been sawed down to the last thread. And I continued to feel strength and will oozing out of me. Any minute now I should be overcome by the indifference born of utter weariness and by the mortal yearning to take my rest.

What can I say about this? Nothing. My shoulders ached. Very painfully. As if I had been carrying too many sacks too heavy for me. I leaned forward. Through a green transparency, I saw sea-bottom so close that I could make out all the details. Then the wind's hand brushed the picture away.

In an hour and twenty minutes I had succeeded in climbing to 900 feet. A little to the south—that is, on my left—I could see a long trail on the surface of the sea, a sort of blue stream. I decided to let myself drift as far down as that stream. Here where I was, facing west, I was as good as motionless, unable either to advance or retreat. If I could reach that blue pathway, which must be lying in the shelter of something not the cyclone, I might be able to move in slowly to the coast. So I let myself drift to the left. I had the feeling, meanwhile, that the wind's violence had perhaps slackened.

It took me an hour to cover the five miles to shore. There in the shelter of a long cliff, I was able to finish my journey south. Thereafter I succeeded in keeping enough altitude to fly inland to the field that was my destination. I was able to stay up at 900 feet. It was very stormy, but nothing like the cyclone I had come out of. That was over.

On the ground I saw a platoon of soldiers. They had been sent down to watch for me. I landed nearby and we were a whole hour getting the plane into the hangar. I climbed out of the cockpit and walked off. There was nothing to say. I was very sleepy. I kept moving my fingers, but they stayed numb. I could not collect my thoughts enough to decide whether or not I had been afraid. Had I been afraid? I couldn't say. I had witnessed a strange sight. What strange sight? I couldn't say. The sky was blue and the sea was white. I felt I ought to tell someone about it since I was back from so far away! But I had no grip on what I had been through. "Imagine a very white sea...very white...whiter still." You cannot convey things to people by piling up adjectives, by stammering.

You cannot convey anything because there is nothing to convey. My shoulders were aching. My insides felt as if they had been crushed in by a terrible weight. You cannot make drama out of that, or out of the cone-shaped peak of Salamanca. That peak was charged like a powder magazine; but if I said so, people would laugh. I would myself. I respected the peak of Salamanca. That is my story. And it is not a story.

There is nothing dramatic in the world, nothing pathetic except in human relations. The day after I landed I might get emotional, might dress up my adventure by imagining that I who was alive and walking on earth was living through the hell of a cyclone. But that would be cheating, for the man who fought tooth and nail against that cyclone had nothing in common with the fortunate man alive the next day. He was far too busy.

I came away with very little booty indeed, with no more than this meager discovery, this contribution: how can one tell an act of the will from a simple image when there is no transmission of the senses?

I could perhaps succeed in upsetting you if I told you some story of a child unjustly punished. As it is, I have involved you in a cyclone, probably without upsetting you in the least. This is no novel experience for any of us. Every week men sit comfortably at the cinema and look on at the bombardment of some Shanghai or other, some Guernica, and marvel without a trace of horror at the long fringes of ash and soot that twist their slow way into the sky from those man-made volcanoes. Yet we all know that together with the grain in the granaries, with the heritage of generations of men, with the treasures of families, it is the burning flesh of children and their elders that, dissipated in smoke, is slowly fertilizing those black cumuli.

The physical drama itself cannot touch us until someone points out its spiritual sense.

Antoine de Saint-Exupéry, best known for his children's book, The Little Prince, *was also a pilot. He was assigned the responsibility of plotting the last section of Aeropostal Argentina's air routes from Comodoro Rivadavia to Punta Arenas. He flew the reconnaissance missions himself and established the bases at Comodoro Rivadavia–San Julián, and Punta Arenas. After inspecting the airport installations at Pacheco, he took off in a Laté-26 on his first exploratory flight in the extreme south. This story came out of that experience and was excerpted from his book* A Sense of Life. *He disappeared over the Mediterranean in 1944 while flying a mission for France.*

The Longing

*Two brothers explore the center
of the universe.*

TOGETHER WITH MY BROTHER PAUL, I TOOK THE LONG BOAT
ride up the Mekong River in Cambodia to see one of the great
riddles of the ancient world, the sacred sprawl of ruined temples and palaces that a twelfth-century traveler said "housed numerous marvels."

On our first morning at the walled city of Angkor Wat, we
witnessed a glorious sunrise over its lotus-crowned towers,
then began the ritual walk up the long bridgeway toward the
sanctuary. Our arms were draped across each other's shoulders. Our heads shook at the impossibly beautiful sight of the
"marvelous enigma" that early European chroniclers regarded as one of the Wonders of the World, and later colo-
nialists described as rivaling the divinely inspired architecture
of Solomon.

We walked as if in a fever-dream. Halfway down the cause-
way, we paused to take in the beauty of the shifting light. We
snapped a few photographs of the *nagas*, the five-headed stone
serpents that undulated along the moat, and of the chiseled

lacework in the colossal gateway looming before us, then grinned at each other and took a deep breath of the morning air. At that moment, we noticed a gray-robed Buddhist nun limping by us on her way to the temple. Her head was shaved and bronzed. When she drew even with us, I held out an offering, which she calmly accepted with stumps where once had been hands. Stunned, I then realized why she had been walking as if on stilts. Her feet had been severed at the ankle, and she was hobbling on the knobs of her ankles. I was stricken with images of her mutilation by the demonic Khmer Rouge, then wondered if she'd been a victim of one of the eleven million landmines forgotten in the forests, fields, and roads of Cambodia.

Her eyes met mine with a gaze of almost surreal serenity. Utterly moved, we offered a few dollars for the shrine in the temple. She calmly accepted the donation in a small woven bag, bowed, and limped away, like a thin-legged crane moving stiffly through the mud of one of the nearby ponds.

The encounter with the Cambodian nun was an ominous way to begin our visit, a gift briefly disguised as a disturbance. Her enigmatic smile eerily anticipated the expression on the sculptured faces of the 54 giant bodhisattvas that loomed in the Holy of Holies above the nearby pyramid temples of the Bayon. Each time I met their timeless gaze, my heart leapt. As the lotus ponds and pools throughout the complex were created to reflect each work of religious art, the faces of the bodhisattvas and the nun mirrored each other. I began to think of the nun as the embodiment of the Bodhisattvas Avalokiteshvara, the god of inexhaustible compassion, who has come to symbolize the miracle of Angkor for millions of pilgrims.

How far does your forgiveness reach? the sculpted faces ask from a thousand statues.

As far as prayers allow, the nun's eyes seemed to respond.

I rambled through the ruins with my brother for the next several hours, stunned by our sheer good fortune of being there. The Angkor complex was destroyed in the fifteenth century, then forgotten for 400 years and overrun with the stone-strangling vines of the jungle. Marveling at the beauty laced with terror in the stories of our young Cambodian guide (who told us the local villagers believed that Angkor was built by angels and giants), time seemed poised on the still-point of the world. This was more than an architectural curiosity, a pious parable of fleeting glory; it was a microcosm of the universe itself. According to scholars, the walls, moats, and soaring terraces represented the different levels of existence itself. The five towers of Angkor symbolized the five peaks of Mount Meru, the center of the world in Hindu cosmology. This was the world mountain in stone, a monumental mandala encompassed by moats that evoked the oceans. A visit was an accomplishment demanding the rigorous climbing of precipitously steep staircases, built that way not without reason.

"It is clear," wrote Vice Admiral Bonard, an early colonialist, "that the worshiper penetrating the temple was intended to have a tangible sense of moving to higher and higher levels of initiation." Our three days stretched on. The hours seemed to contain days, the days held weeks, as in all dreamtime adventures. We were graced with one strangely moving encounter after another. Silently, we mingled with saffron-robed monks who had walked hundreds of miles in the footsteps of their ancestors from Cambodia, Thailand, India, and Japan to pray in the sanctuary of a place believed for a thousand years to be the center of the world. Gratefully, we traded road stories with travelers who'd been through Burma, Vietnam, and China. After dark, we read the accounts of fellow pilgrims who had been making the arduous trek here by foot for centuries, from China and Japan in ancient times, then by car from France and England, and by boat from America.

Though neither Buddhist nor Hindu, wandering through the site I was more than smitten by the romancing of old stones. In the uncanny way of spiritually magnetized centers of pilgrimage, I felt a wonderful calm exploring the derelict pavilions, abandoned libraries, and looted monasteries. My imagination was animated by the strange and wonderful challenge to fill in what time had destroyed, thrilling to the knowledge that tigers, panthers, and elephants still roamed over the flagstones of these shrines when Angkor was rediscovered in the 1860s.

But through our visit the dark thread ran.

With every step through the ghostly glory of the ancient temple grounds, it was impossible not to be reminded of the scourge of Pol Pot, the ever-present threat of historical chaos. The maimed children and fierce soldiers we encountered everywhere were grim evidence of a never-ending war. Once upon a time, foreigners were spared the horrors of remote revolutions, but no more. In a local English-language newspaper, we read that Pol Pot had ordered the executions of three Australian tourists, saying only, "Crush them."

Overshadowing even this were the twinges of guilt I felt for having undertaken the journey—Jo, my partner back in San Francisco, was seven months pregnant with our baby. Though she was selflessly supportive, I was uneasy. So why make such a risky journey?

To fulfill a vow.

Twice in the previous fifteen years, my plans to make the long trek to the ruins of Angkor had been thwarted at the Thai-Cambodia border. Dreading that war might break out again and the borders clamp shut for another twenty years, I believed that the research trip my brother and I were on in the Philippines serendipitously offered a last chance to fulfill a promise to my father.

On my eleventh birthday, he had presented me with a book, not a Zane Grey Western or the biography of my hometown baseball hero, Al Kaline, that I had asked for, but a book with a bronze-tinted cover depicting sculptures of fabulous creatures from a distant world. These creatures were not from a phantasmagorical planet out of science fiction, but the long-forgotten world of the Khmers, the ancient civilization that had built Angkor.

From that moment on, the book came to symbolize for me the hidden beauty of the world. With the transportive magic that only books possess, it offered a vision of the vast world outside of my small hometown in Michigan; it set a fire in my heart and through the years inspired in me the pilgrim's desire to see this wondrous place for myself.

When my father became ill in the fall of 1984, I drove cross-country from San Francisco to Detroit to see him and, in an effort to lift his spirits, promised him that when he recovered we would travel together. I tried to convince him that after years of unfulfilled plans to see Europe, we would travel together to Amsterdam and visit van Gogh's nephew, whom he had once guided on a personal tour through Ford's River Rouge complex in Dearborn. After Holland, I suggested, we could take the train to Périgueux in southern France and track down the story of our ancestors who had left there in 1678. Then, I said haltingly, we could take a direct flight from Paris to Phnom Penh and visit Angkor Wat. He seemed pleased by the former, puzzled by the latter.

"Don't you remember the book you gave me as a boy?" I asked him, disappointed in his response to my cue. "The one on the excavations at Angkor?" He riffled through the memory of a lifetime of books he had bestowed on friends and family. Then his face lit up, and he harrumphed, "Oh, yes. *Angkor*, the Malcolm MacDonald book, the one with the sculptures of the Temple of the Leper King on the cover." He paused to consider the possibilities of our traveling together, then painfully read-justed himself in his old leather reading chair.

"I just wish I were as confident as you that I was going to recover," he said with the first note of despair I'd ever heard from him. "Of course, I'd like to see these places with you. It would be *wonderful*."

Then his voice broke. "But I don't know, son, if I'm going to make it."

No one I've ever met has pronounced the word "wonder-ful" like my father. He stressed the first syllable, "won," as if the adjective did indeed have its roots in victory and triumph. He so rarely used upbeat words, so when he did I knew he meant it. Hearing it there and then, watching this once-ferocious and formidable man sit in a chair, unable to move his hands and feet because of a crippling nerve disease, I was shaken. Still, I feigned confidence and courage and promised we would hit the road together as soon as he recovered.

He didn't. Four months later, on the very Ides of March which he had announced every year in our house as though it were the strangest day on the calendar, my father died in his sleep.

Shortly after the funeral, while packing up the books in his stilled apartment, I made one of the few vows in my life. I promised myself I would take the journey for both of us, make the pilgrimage to a place made holy by the play of light on stone and the devotion of pilgrims who had walked astonish-ing distances so that they might touch the sacred sculpture and offer their prayers on the wings of incense.

And, in so doing, perhaps restore my faith in life itself.

Phil Cousineau's peripatetic career has included stints as a sports-writer, playing basketball in Europe, harvesting date trees on an Israeli kibbutz, painting 44 Victorian houses in San Francisco, and leading adventure travel tours around the world. He is the author of several books, including The Art of Pilgrimage: The Seeker's Guide to Making Travel Sacred, *from which this story was excerpted. He grew up in Wayne, Michigan, and lives with his family in San Francisco.*

EDDY L. HARRIS

⋆ ✴ ⋆

On the Road

On a motorcycle journey through the American South,
a black man confronts his demons.

THE ROAD UNDER MY WHEELS SHINES AS AFTER A HEAVY RAIN, the smell of wet pavement rising with the morning mist and crowding the space inside my helmet. The sun has climbed into the southern Kentucky sky but not very high, the air is warming but not yet warm, the road to Somerset has not yet dried. Above the eastern horizon, a line of thick clouds waits to snare the rising sun and hide its shining, to cast the earth in shadow, to play tricks on the eye with shade and with shafts of light. Shapes form, faces and figures, a guessing game for children, a premonition for me. In the clouds looms something ominous and almost familiar, but something I can only vaguely make out, ever changing in the light wind, the clouds drifting in and out of one another. A new shape appears. A face, perhaps. Someone I know. Someone I have yet to meet.

Or perhaps only a storm advancing. Rain and winter on the way.

The air blows softly, crisp and fresh on my face and on my hands. Quickly, though, the bike gets up to speed and the wind whips past me at 80 miles an hour. Now suddenly the air is freezing, and so am I. Cold rushes by me, cold surrounds me, cold enters into me. Cold that has been transferred from the air to the metal of the bike's gas tank and the cold of the metal creeps into me there, settles around my legs and spreads down to my toes, up into my back and ripples all the way through my body. I find myself shivering. My teeth chatter. Soon the morning will shake away its chill, and the moisture that has settled during the night will shrink away like a distant memory, but for now the air remains very cool. I ride glove-less and the wind numbs my fingers.

As I come to the top of a high hill, the bike slows and stops itself in a patch of bright sunlight that soon fades away. A shadow washes over me. Clouds have come to block the sun and there is no warmth. I am shivering from the cold, yes, but shivering as well from a feeling of dread that suddenly has fallen down upon me. Call me a coward, but fear once more has its hands around my throat. I am at last, completely and utterly, in the South, in a southern state of mind, and fear of this evil place grips me still. I know what the South was once; I do not know what the South has become.

Nor can I tell which comes first, this fear or the anger that goes along with it, but there they are, side by side, and they never quite go away. Nor perhaps can they ever, for once you have experienced racism from the receiving end and have been made aware, once you have felt its sting, thought about the pain of it, the stupidity and the senselessness, brooded about it and obsessed about it, once you have known the shame and the degradation of racism, this fear and this anger both come alive, and they cannot be gotten rid of. Not easily. Nor ever completely.

Yes, I know what has been and I am angry.

I do not know what will come and I am afraid.

I stop to rest, to take a deep breath and to look down across the valley that spreads out before me. The hill I am on falls away abruptly and then flattens out before beginning the gentle undulations that recede like an endless sea rolling to the horizon and beyond. Like the sea, these hills seem eternal and unmoving, yet they are alive with ceaseless motion and music. Their shapes and their colors change with the shifting sun, with the coming and the going of light and shadow. The wind blows and the tall grass dances. The pines and the oak trees sway. And if you stand perfectly still holding your breath until silence surrounds you, you can hear the quiet whooshing of their leaves brushing together. The sound sails on the breeze and over the hills, caressing my ears and soothing my thoughts.

My gaze drifts lazily up one faraway hill and down the next until sight can see no more, but can only imagine what might lie over the last hill I can see, and the next one after that, and still the next.

The sunlight comes and goes. Clouds move with the wind, and shadows slide slowly across the landscape like a caravan of spirits creeping through the valley, following along after the creek that winds through a crease in the terrain. My mind follows after them, over these hills, along this valley, back in time. Suddenly I find myself nostalgic for a time I never knew, a time long ago when life was simpler and a man could change his life, change his luck, change even the way the world presented itself to his eye and to his mind; all these things simply by heading for the darkness of the unknown and setting out to see what lay on the other side of the hills.

As my mind begins to wander, my eye is snared by the brusque movement of horses that a moment ago were grazing placidly. Now they are galloping joyfully to music only they can hear, stopping suddenly and rearing, snorting, grazing again, oblivious to me, to my fears and to my angers, oblivious to the world. All in the valley below seems as peaceful and as perfect as God intended it to be and seems untouched, except for the fences, by the hand of man. I cannot help but wonder, the same as George Custer couldn't help but wonder in the predawn as his gaze drifted lazily across a western plain: how must it all have been before we came and impured not just the land, but the spirit of the land, when all was future and all was perfect with nothing but possibility?

The sun was just coming up and mist still hovered over the land. An encampment of Native Americans in the valley below was waking to the new day. Smoke was rising from their lodge fires. The dogs were barking the morning into day. Even Custer had to behold and wonder. The Seventh Cavalry was preparing to attack, ready and more than willing to slaughter the old men, the women, the children, even the dogs. And Custer paused. *"What was the(ir) world like,"* he asked himself, *"before we became part of it?"*

What indeed?

When Custer looked out across the plain all he could see was raw wilderness. The future and all its ripe promise. A Native American regarding the same view at the same time would not have seen the same thing. He would have been looking not so much and certainly not only at the future, but at the past as well. His history was there, the story of his people hidden in the tall grass and buried in the hills. The things that explained who he was lay in that prairie, in those forests, lay in the fields and in the mountains, in the streams and in all those things that were being stolen away from him. And as he looked out across his own valleys and plains, must he not have wondered what had happened? Must he not have said to himself in his native tongue, *"Something has gone horribly wrong. This is not the way the world is supposed to be."*

It is impossible to imagine what he felt, but not so hard at all to imagine that he felt it, for I find myself thinking the same thing: that something has gone horribly wrong, that the world is not supposed to be like this. No one, not man, not woman, not the tiniest child, ought to be afraid in his own home. And yet here I am, home at last and very much afraid.

Yes, this is my land. Here in this southern soil, my people were known. Long before I was a glimmer in my father's eye or a worry in my mother's womb, my roots were planted, fertilized by the living, perhaps the suffering, and the dying of my ancestors. Here in these hills my ancestors walked and toiled. They breathed this air, and tilled these fields. They lived and died to become these hills, these trees, this land. They became these things so that I might be. And their voices whisper in my ears.

I owe them this journey, if only to smell this soil and breathe this air and see these trees, if only to remember them and what they endured for my sake. This land is home to me, bought and paid for with the sweat, anguish, and joy of those who went before me and willed it to me. This air is familiar to me. This land is familiar to me. I could recognize the smells of this land, the sounds and the tastes of this place, with my eyes closed, for in my dreams I have visited this place a thousand times. This place haunts my nights and owns my reverie, created my childhood and the stories my father has told. I have not been here before, except in lightest passing, but indeed I have been here before. I may not stand where my ancestors stood, nor tread the same patches of earth that they once trod, but they were here, somewhere here. I can feel their presence.

And somewhere here, there is proof that they truly existed. Wouldn't it be wonderful, a miracle almost, if as I traveled this land I stumbled across concrete evidence of some long-ago ancestor of mine, some great-great-grandfather who perhaps had been—no, surely had been—a slave?

A thousand waves of fear and excitement surge over me.

This land is mine. I have come to reclaim it. My roots are here. This land is me. Fear or no fear, I cannot distance myself from these hills, from this soil, these smells, this past. Nor should I want to. I am these hills.

The wind grew stronger and howled for a moment and then settled down. The clouds swirled, formed new shapes. Quite suddenly the weather turned serene, and a warm peaceful wind drifted over the land. The sun found a large gap in the clouds and peeped through. The day began to warm. The warmth wrapped round me. A sense of quiet elation settled upon me and enveloped me like a cloak draped over my shoulders. A hand soothed my back and my arms. Sounds like voices whispered soft syllables in my ear. The words I could not make out, but the earth was talking to me—the earth or the past or some great ghosts hovering over the landscape and wandering in this valley. And their voices murmured, urging me on. It was, of course, only the wind whispering over the grass.

I was in the South. I was home at last.

I took a deep breath. And then I took another, and then another and another, each one like the Magi, bearing a different gift. The South was happy to have me home and showered me with the gentle scent of pine from the trees on the faraway hills, with the strong equine smells of sweat and manure, with the rich smells of earth and grass, and enveloping it all, holding it all together in the precious package it was, the soft sweet smell of moist tobacco.

The clouds formed a new face then, without hair or nose or chin, but only mouth and eyes. The mouth smiled briefly, then stretched long and emotionless before shifting once more and falling passively into the billows below. The eyes, though, were unmoving. They did not blink or flinch. For the longest time they hovered there like the eyes of angels, just waiting and watching, always watching, until finally I looked away. A hawk had soared on rising thermals and crossed the path of my staring. I followed its gliding, its swooping and its sudden dive until it had flown out of sight. When I looked back to the clouds, the sun had risen fully above them, warm and bright, erasing all from the sky but the blue and the haze. The eyes had disappeared.

I was ready to travel. But which way now—which way to go?

When a writer first puts pen to paper, he has before him the paralyzing problem of infinite possibilities. But once the first word is written, the writer loses his will and it is the story which dictates. The writer becomes merely the medium through whom the poetry passes. The muse sits on his shoulder and directs him with whispers.

Likewise the wanderer. The spirit that persuades him sits on his shoulder and directs him too with whispers, with soft nudges, warm winds, and rumors. The traveler merely goes where he is told.

The road before me was all mine, I thought, and I could follow any route I chose. But really I had no choice. There was only one path, only one right road. Everything that had already happened, everything yet to happen, were pebbles laid down to guide the way into the labyrinth and then out again. This journey had been preordained.

I hadn't pulled the bike very far off the road when I stopped to take my rest. I nudged the bike back on the road again. Coming over the hill and aiming straight for me with all the rumble of an earthquake was a gigantic rebel flag painted on the front of a huge semitrailer barreling so fast along the curves in the road that the truck seemed out of control. My mind said to get out of the way, but my body sat paralyzed on the bike for what seemed an eternity.

My gaze locked on the flag, the square red field crisscrossed with a great blue X bordered in white. Inside the X, thirteen white stars. The battle flag of the Confederacy. But much more than that to me. Symbol of racism, symbol of hate, a symbol that caused to rise in me all the rage I had ever felt and that splintered the fragile peace I had made with the South.

I hated this driver.

Perhaps this is what it is to be black in America, maybe to be black in any world of white men. To be black is to always be reminded that you are a stranger in your native land. To be black is to be surrounded by those who would remind you. To be black is having to be ever vigilant, never completely at ease.

I got off the bike and put one foot on the road. I wanted to startle the driver, not so much that he would swerve across the center line and possibly plow into anyone who might be coming round the bend, but I wanted to give him a scare. I wanted him to sit up and take notice of the crazy man in the middle of the road. I dared him to hit me.

The truck screamed. Its horn blared. The lumbering monster lurched and clattered as it passed. The driver made an angry face. I thought I heard him yell obscenities.

I put my helmet back on, my gloves and my jacket. I got back on the bike, started it up and gave chase. I wanted to catch the driver and challenge him. I wanted to know—and of course I knew—why he had that flag painted on the front of his truck. I wanted to fight him, hurt him, kick his truck, and puncture his tires. I wanted to make him pay.

But it had taken me too long to get the bike in gear and going. By the time I was in pursuit, he was long gone. The road was too windy and unfamiliar for me to do much over 80 and that truck must have been doing 85. But for twelve hot minutes I sped after him. Then I slowed down and laughed at myself.

What would I do if I caught up with him? Scream at him? Bite his ankle while he beat me over the head with a tire iron?

This being the South he probably carried a pistol in the cab of his truck.

Hmmm. Perhaps I had taken so long with the helmet and the gloves for a reason.

Yeah, call me a coward.

I gave up the chase at the top of a rise that looked down on a small town in Kentucky called London. A tangle of roads came together in the junction below. Maybe the driver of that truck was down there somewhere waiting for me in the confusion of roads and traffic and fast-food burger joints. Maybe he was waiting for me a little farther on. I slowed.

The road I was on widened into a four-lane expressway, crossed Interstate 75, and then slipped back into a two-lane road winding into the mountains one hour to the east. The Daniel Boone Expressway crossed nearby going into the mountains as well, but it was superhighway all the way to somewhere and probably a toll road to boot, the route for travelers in a hurry. I definitely was not in a hurry. I didn't even know the name of the somewhere I was going. Like that song Sylvester the Cat is always singing in the cartoons: you never know where you're going till you get there.

No, this was not a journey about going anywhere in particular, nor about keeping time. It was perhaps more about losing time, about blurring it, contracting it and elongating it, erasing it. What a miracle if we could somehow erase time, retrace our steps to where we went wrong, start all over again.

If we could do that, I would come back one of these days to the rise in this road. No, farther back to when the truck with the rebel flag painted on it came racing over the hill and spoiled my morning. I would go back to the dawn, back to the lake, and start this day once more. I would not look up when

I heard the truck coming this time. I would not allow him to harm the peace. I would get back on my bike after he had passed and I would come to this very spot. I would sift through the tangle until I found the road, the one that goes south before it goes east, the one that runs down through Corbin and Barbourville, Pineville and Harlan, up into the mountains and then down the other side. After that, who knows?

After that, who cares?

Eddy L. Harris graduated from Stanford University, studied in London, and has been a screenwriter and journalist. His first book was the critically acclaimed Mississippi Solo, *which was followed by* Native Stranger, Still Life in Harlem, *and* South of Haunted Dreams: A Ride Through Slavery's Old Back Yard, *from which this story was excerpted.*

EMILY JENKINS

✦ ✦ ✦

The Blue Man

*He has found an enduring canvas
for his life's work.*

ThEnigma (pronounced The Enigma) has made choices
that challenge almost everyone's ideas about self-decoration.
Even those of a tattoo fan like myself. Formerly—according to
Jim Rose of the Jim Rose Circus Sideshow—a "sweet-faced,
wholesome-looking kid" named Paul, Enigma is now a puzzle. Literally. His entire body is tattooed as if he were a jigsaw,
with pieces about an inch and a half in diameter. He's covered
on public skin and private: face, neck, arms, palms, ass. His
head is shaved, and marked likewise. He is gradually having
the puzzle pieces filled in blue, some plain and some with patterns. He works in Rose's sideshow, comporting himself as a
silent, nearly naked monster. He eats live bugs, swallows
swords, and moons the audience. On an episode of *The X-
Files*, he played The Conundrum, a circus freak who fishes
with his hands and mouth like an animal.

ThEnigma seems barely human. More than human. In
photos, only a few tiny details remind us of the man beneath
the ink—a pinch of flab around his waist as he bends over,

fingernails that look bitten to the quick, what is apparently a mosquito bite on his foot. The tattoo is the work of over a hundred artists, and he holds the world's record for being tattooed by the most people at one time: 22. But, he says, it felt like only 10. All the work is done free, by artists who want to contribute to his self-creation. Although ThEnigma is a collector of work by some of the most famous tattooists alive, he is the one who graces the cover of *Savage* and *International Tattoo Art* while they go uncredited, too numerous to mention. He is not only the canvas, but the collector and the artist as well.

Sitting across a table from him in a crowded Chelsea restaurant is one of the most intense physical experiences I have ever had: two hours with a blue man, a man whose history of pain is literally etched across his face, whose baby blue eyes match the color of his skin. His nose is bisected by a jigsaw line, half blue, half skin-tone. He is disturbingly sexy, exuding an incredible confidence in the power of his body to interest, shock, attract, repel. Next to him, no one else is worth looking at. He orders pasta.

ThEnigma's philosophy makes Rebecca's idea about the body reflecting the mind seem pretty limited. For him, self and art are completely merged. The young, white sword swallower of only a couple years ago has completely disappeared. When I ask if anyone calls him Paul, he hides his face in his hands. "Oh please! Paul?!...When I go to Safeway I'm still ThEnigma."

Well, what does his mother call him?

"By my real name," he says, reluctant to pronounce it.

On one hand, it seems as if he is realizing a vision that is at the core of his wacked-out mind; on the other, his body is threatening to obliterate any shreds of his mind that are not commensurate with being blue. "The self is sacrificed for the art," he tells me without a trace of regret. "When you do this to your body, you throw away everything that was. Or maybe you don't. Maybe you're already gone anyway. This isn't about me. All that matters is for some old housewife to see me, and maybe she'll let go a bit. Maybe she'll find some sort of freedom in herself that she didn't find before...One person came up to me and told me that I'd never have to say another word in my entire life. It's all said. Right here."

He married the woman who tattooed the puzzle outline on his body. She is The Kat, and her skin is striped like a tiger. "Head to tail," ThEnigma says proudly. I ask him if getting the tattoo was a romantic gesture, like having her name etched on his arm. "It was kinda like a piece for a piece, you know?" he laughs, winking. "A tit for a tat. I always figure it's like a perfume commercial: ThEnigma—made by a woman for a woman."

I tell him about my tattoo fantasies, which have been proliferating at an incredible rate since we sat down to lunch. ThEnigma is very encouraging, but it is clear he views my interest as amateurish. He claims alternately that it's a good idea for everyone ("I think everybody should tattoo their entire face. What a colorful world it would be!") and that I should think it over with care: "You really have to know yourself. You have to really want this to get it, because of how painful it is."

ThEnigma's own commitment is written in the lines on his face—commitment to his wife, to his creative vision, to the tattoo community he represents every time he leaves the house, to his daughter. "Having kids is a bigger commitment than tattooing your body," he argues. "And people do that all the time. Most people don't know who they are. I know who I am, so it's safe to make this choice (to be tattooed)."

He is emphatic about the suffering he has undergone to become blue. "People are always asking me if it hurt. Well, the skin is full of nerves. Nerves, when you get hit by a needle, send signals to the brain. You're constantly explaining this to people and they're just fucking stupid. It's like, "No, I'm completely numb from the head down." Jesus Christ! Of course it fucken' hurt. He shows me a little spot on the inside of his elbow that hasn't healed properly. He's got blue scabs.

I think the people asking don't realize ThEnigma's skin is ordinary—that if you prick him he will bleed, tickle him he will laugh. That his hair would grow back if he didn't shave it. It is easy to forget these things about him. As a representative of the tattoo community, ThEnigma always tries to be friendly, winking and smiling to remind others of his humanity. Yet it was hard for me, eating lunch with him, to remember that he has feelings, partly because he has chosen his strange identity, has deliberately made himself the ultimate other. I think that even for the most socially aware of us, tolerance and understanding of others in skins different from our own—whether because of color, illness, or disability—is based on the idea that people don't choose their bodies. They are born with them, or something happens to them, and remembering this fact allows us an empathy with a scarred face or another skin color. We have difficulty finding a similar empathy for a man who has turned himself blue, or for a man in a sequined dress and platform heels.

Being entirely blue is ThEnigma's ultimate goal, and he sees it as an escape from the dominant beliefs of mainstream white America. When he is all the way blue, he says, "I will have escaped that white man's guilt—being a colored person, a person of color."

As a teenager growing up outside Seattle, he watched The *Twilight Zone, Battlestar Galactica,* and *The Outer Limits* with intense fascination, only to be disappointed with reality as it was presented scientifically. "In chemistry class in high school, you find out about the laws of equilibrium. You learn that you can't just make something appear from nowhere, and that dashes your dreams of being a biochemist or an alchemist. There are no hidden doorways to different dimensions. It's all just on TV. So then you have to do what's second-best and make impossibility as possible as you can. Yes, there are monsters in the world."

He didn't become a monster until 1993, but did develop a sense of personal agency and creativity in those *Battlestar Galactica* years. "In high school it all fell apart. My dad was in Vietnam. He had shrapnel in his brain, so he kinda went religious cuckoo. And then divorce and then depression. Explosion, you know? I think everybody kind of goes through that at some period. And then a sense of total freedom, craziness—like you can do anything and everything. Move things"—he waves his glass of water and his spoon around— "woaah, there it goes! All of a sudden creation is everything. Art is everything...Then you can just be visionary. It has to do with the vision of 7-Eleven, and a blue guy there. Or McDonalds, in Europe, and a blue guy there...I look at the stage and I say, I want to see a blue person. He's blue at first, and then as you get closer you see all these images within it."

As the only blue person on the planet, ThEnigma can easily manipulate people's perceptions of him. "If I don't want people to notice me, then people won't, because they look to me for how they should respond. As a blue person you can get away with a lot more than you can as just a regular Joe...People accept that and expect it. They expect whatever you give them. I'm their first experience with a completely tattooed blue guy. They don't know how to judge a person like that...Whatever I do is typical behavior for me."

People proposition ThEnigma all the time. "Hey," he laughs, "they all want to do a puzzle!" He writes their advances off as interest in a novelty, evidence of the attraction people have for performers, but I think he misses the real reasons. His sex appeal goes beyond the standard erotic thrill of a tottooed guy with a good build, or the politically suspect but nonetheless powerful attraction of someone who is physically "other" to oneself. It is more, too, than his superhuman confidence in the specialness of his body. ThEnigma's particular tattoo invites a sort of voyeuristic interest because of his unfinished status. He is a work in progress. While most people with heavy tattooing have large areas of unmarked skin that await art, ThEnigma has created an unusual scenario in that his whole body is covered in such a way that its partially finished state is still always apparent. I want not only to get under his shorts (is it blue, or is it pink?), but to get under his tattoo. But I never can. I can only peek through the holes of the puzzle to his skin beneath.

He is also sexy for the same reason Miss Ash in the Florida dance club was sexy. Although ThEnigma's tattoos are hypermasculine, even frightening, and Miss Ash's drag is hyperfeminine, even silly—both are decorated men. They have the appeal of peacocks, strutting with tails extended around a barnyard full of lumpy gray beasts. Especially in the heterosexual circles I move in, men almost never show themselves off. If they do, it is almost always by removing their shirts, exposing what is (relatively speaking) naturally there, rather than enhancing it with cosmetics or decorating it with feathers, jewelry, or tattoo ink. A half-nude man is very nice—I'm not complaining—but he's not engaging with any of the subtle, overlapping, contradictory meanings that make self-decoration so interesting. He's too obedient to invisible rules about masculinity to be irresistible. Michael Stipe with his eyeliner and layers of clothes, is much spicier than some cute boy with his polo shirt wrapped around his waist. And I don't think Stipe is androgynous, or in drag. He's just decorated.

I want to know what's going on under Miss Ash's wet shirt, under Miss Coffy's painted face, under ThEnigma's blue bathing suit. I am pleased that they have adorned themselves, turned on by the mystery of the reinvented self, intrigued by a male body unhampered by the usual restrictions on masculinity.

What does it say about our culture that we understand the scraping and sucking away of tissues we perceive as shameful (hair, dead skin, excess fat), but resist overt decoration of like permanence? Why is decoration acceptable only if it is removable or disguised as natural, and repulsive if it announces itself as permanent? ThEnigma forces everyone he comes in contact with to reevaluate their understanding of art and the body, of the possibilities for otherness. His status as a self-made, eroticized other forces us to revise our unacknowledged definitions of humanity. Looking at him, we have to admit our anxieties about blatant self-decoration and our investment in maintaining an illusion of impermanence with regard to our artifice, hiding our interest in self-display under a disguise of naturalism. Our standard preferences are unsettled by ThEnigma's presence, so obviously constructed and artificial, so obviously painful to achieve.

Emily Jenkins is completing a Ph.D. in English at Columbia University, and lives in New York City. This story was excerpted from her book Tongue First: Adventures in Physical Culture.

PART THREE

IN THEIR OWN SHADOW

⋆ ⋆ ⋆

Crevasse

Sometimes the mountains exact a heavy toll.

WE MOVED DOWN THE PETERS GLACIER SLOWLY, A SLED between us loaded heavy with supplies. Twenty feet of rope linked us—too close, we knew, but required by the rough, undulating surface beneath our feet. A glacier is not a fixed, solid thing. It flows like a river, with currents, some parts smooth, others rough. Where it changes direction, or where the angle of its slope steepens, the surface will split, creating cracks as deep as a hundred feet. A thin layer of snow can make them invisible.

Chris walked in front. I walked behind, righting the sled each time it flipped. The afternoon sun beat down on us, softening the snow, casting long shadows. Moments after we had decided to head toward smoother ground, Chris broke through the crust and plunged headfirst into a crevasse. I was concentrating on the sled and did not see him fall. Just as I sensed trouble, the rope yanked me into the air, then down into an icy void. "This is it," I thought, "I'm about to die."

In an instant, the sled and I slammed on top of Chris.

Stunned but still conscious after the impact, I checked myself for injuries. My left shoulder felt numb and I could not raise my arm. (I later learned my shoulder had broken.) Suppressing an urge to panic, I glanced around and considered what I should do. Balanced awkwardly with one foot on the sled, the other against a slight bulge in the ice, I tried my best to reassure Chris as I took off my pack and squeezed it into an eighteen-inch space between the walls. Then, using my pack for support, I shoved the sled off Chris into an area just below us, where it lodged.

All I could see of my companion were his legs, still in snowshoes, dangling behind his large black pack, which had compressed to half its normal width between the crevasse walls. Suspended facedown, parallel to the crevasse bottom far below, he yelled, "I can't move, Wick, you've got to get me out!" Trapped under the pack, Chris's entire upper body was immobilized. When I noticed his left hand, twisted back, caught between his pack and the wall, I grabbed it and asked if he could feel the pressure. "No," he barked, "I can't feel anything! You've got to get me out, Wick!" I assured him, "I will, Chris, I promise." I tried lifting him by his pack, but hard as I pulled, he would not budge. Within a few minutes I realized I could do nothing more for him until I got myself out of the crevasse.

The tapered walls were as slick as a skating rink. The distant slit of daylight looked a hundred feet away. To make it to the surface, I needed to put on my crampons—steel spikes attached to each boot to prevent slipping. Luckily, they were on the back of my pack. In a space so tight, I could maneuver only by facing the wall. I awkwardly pulled off my snowshoes and strapped the crampons on. Then I retied our rope to the back of Chris's pack, clipped a three-foot aluminum picket and a pair of jumars—mechanical devices to move up and down a rope—to my waist sling, and prepared to climb out. When I tried kicking the front two points of a crampon into the wall, they bounced off. I tried using my ice hammer, but without room to swing my arm, I barely made a scratch. How could I get out if I couldn't penetrate the ice? I began to panic. Calm down, I told myself, think of something that will work.

I tried chipping out a little indentation, narrower than a finger width, and placed the front points of my crampon on the tiny ledge. I edged myself up, placing my back against the opposite wall as a counterforce. The front points held my weight. Using my good arm to wield the hammer, I slowly worked my way up the cold, glassy walls, chiseling a ladder of little ledges as I went. Three chips and a step up, again and again. I concentrated harder than I ever had before. The whole time Chris kept yelling from beneath his pack, "You've got to get me out, Wick! You've got to get me out!" Between puffs and grunts, I continued to reassure him, "It'll be okay, I'll get you out." And I felt sure I could.

Despite my impatience to reach the surface, I never let the distance between indentations exceed six inches. I knew that if I fell back down, I would probably get wedged, like Chris, between the walls or be hurt worse than I already was. This was my only chance. Near the top, where the shaft widened to about three feet, I twisted my upper torso, drove the ice hammer into the lip of the crevasse at my back, and pressed my feet against the opposite wall. With one rapid movement, I levered my body over the lip and onto the surface of the glacier. It had taken an hour to ascend what turned out to be a 25-foot shaft.

Nearly exhausted, relieved to be alive, I lay on the snow and gasped for breath. Raising my head to look around, I was startled by the quiet and the brightness of the sun on the broad, tilted glacier. Though tempted to rest a little longer, a sense of urgency made me struggle to my feet. I knew I must work fast. If I didn't get Chris out before nightfall, he would die from the cold.

From the crevasse edge, I took up the slack in the rope and pulled with all my might. He did not budge. I tried again— nothing. And again—still no movement. I would need to go back down. I tied the rope to the picket, which I pounded into the hard snow. Then I attached the rope to the jumars (with nylon slings for my feet), which allowed me to descend swiftly but safely into the crevasse.

It took me about five minutes to return to Chris. Hanging a few inches above him, I tried to hoist his pack with my hands and one good arm, but nothing budged. In the hope that changing the rope's position would make a difference, I tied it to each of the pack's accessible cross straps and pulled. But still the pack did not move. I tried to reassure Chris, but when I drove my ice hammer into the pack, all I did was move the top a few inches; then it settled back into place. I attempted to use the power of my legs to lift the pack by stepping upward in the slings. Nothing was working.

I thought that if I could open Chris's pack and empty its contents, enough pressure would be released to let him move, but when I tried tearing its tough fabric open with my ice hammer I could only make ineffectual punctures. The pack, like a block of wood in a vise, was simply too compressed. Lacking equipment with which to construct a pulley system, I could not dislodge Chris. So, after two hours of continuous effort, I stopped. "Sorry, this isn't working," I conceded. I'm going back up to try to get someone, *anyone,* on the radio."

After hauling up my pack, I retraced our tracks to a nearby knoll, where I desperately radioed for help: "This is an emergency. Can anyone hear me? If you can, I need your help." I repeated the message again and again, but no one answered; I never really expected a reply. In this valley, so far away from anyone who might have come, our line-of-sight radio was useless. We had set out to climb Mount McKinley by a remote, untraveled route, and this was the price we paid. No one would come to help. We were alone.

I went back down with little hope of freeing my friend and repeated the rescue maneuvers I feared would fail. Chris's incessant pleas subsided as he gradually realized I could *not* get him out. Having planned to climb Mount Everest with me the following year, he said, "Climb it for me, Wick. Remember me when you're on the summit." A classical trumpeter, Chris asked me to take his mouthpiece there. "I don't know about me," I replied, "but someone will. I promise." We spoke of his imminent death, but I could not believe that so young and vibrant a man was actually about to die right in front of me.

After asking me to relay messages to his family and closest friends, Chris entreated me to help him die with dignity. However, I could think of no way to ease his suffering or speed his death. I asked him whether he wanted his body left in the crevasse or brought out. He said his father could decide. At about nine-thirty, six hours after we fell into the crevasse, Chris conceded, "There's nothing more you can do, Wick. You should go up." I told him I loved him and said a tearful good-bye. As I began my ascent, Chris said simply, "Take care of yourself, Jim."

Back on the surface, physically spent, emotionally exhausted, and racked with guilt, I pulled on a parka and collapsed into my half-sleeping-bag and bivouac sack—an uninsulated nylon bag used in emergencies for protection against the wind. Lying at the edge of the crevasse, I listened to my friend grow delirious from the searing cold. He talked to himself, moaned, and, at around eleven, sang what sounded like a school song. At 2 a.m. I heard him for the last time. Chris Kerrebrock was 25. I was 40.

The next morning I wrote in my diary.

I feel indescribable guilt and failure for not getting him out and for leaving him to die alone. I don't know how I got myself out with my injured arm. I had to if I would see my precious wife and children again. I can't write more because of sobbing.

Chris and I had arrived on Mount McKinley the week before, eager to undertake a challenging route up the mountain's Wickersham Wall. No one had climbed it since 1963, eighteen years before, when first a group of Canadians and then the Harvard Mountaineering Club established the only routes up its treacherous face. Its reputation as an avalanche trap kept climbers away. We planned to take a new line up the massive wall between the two existing routes. Although I felt confident about our prospects, I left my wife Mary Lou with more than the usual trepidation. Why, I was not sure.

After a spectacular flight over Kahiltna Pass to check out our route, Doug Geeting, the bush pilot I'd used on several expeditions to Mount McKinley, dropped us at the mountain's main landing site. He said he would pick us up in about three weeks. In the interim he promised to fly over and check on us at least once. From the air, Wickersham Wall looked huge, but not particularly steep. While concerned about its ice cliffs and the prospect of avalanches, we saw nothing to deter us. Dangerous in places, yes, but climbable. Barring bad weather, we believed we could reach the summit.

Storms confined us to a camp close to the landing site. For the next three days, we ate bacon, eggs, steak, and fresh fruit as we planned our climb and became friends. Reading the Harvard Mountaineering Club's expedition summary reinforced our decision to climb by an entirely new route. Since we had elected to climb the mountain in a single push, with just four ice screws and two pickets between us, we could not take their more technical route.

Chris's easy company and good humor made me look forward to the next three weeks. A year earlier Chris had entered graduate school in philosophy at Columbia University, after earning a degree in classical music at Oberlin, and a reputation for exceptional strength and speed at Mount Rainier, where he had worked as a summer guide for Rainier Mountaineering, Inc. (RMI). Through his father's contacts with Chinese government officials, he had managed to obtain a coveted permit to climb Mount Everest from Tibet, then asked Lou Whittaker, one of RMI's owners, to organize and lead an expedition the following spring. During the months spent planning that climb, Chris and I came to know and like each other. Although we had never climbed together, we suspected we would be a compatible team.

We each approached Lou and asked him what he thought. He encouraged me to climb with Chris, describing him as one of the strongest members of the Everest expedition. While characterizing me as an expert climber, Lou cautioned Chris to go to McKinley prepared to look out for himself since I was not a trained guide.

Just as Chris and I finished the last of our fresh food, the weather cleared and other climbing parties began passing our camp on their way to more popular routes. On Tuesday, May 5, 1981, we set out, taking turns in the lead. To make it up Wickersham Wall, we would need to be a fast, strong, and well-coordinated team.

On Wednesday, I wrote:

Chris and I are getting along marvelously. Our personalities seem to mesh and thus far there isn't the slightest semblance of getting on each other's nerves. We make a good team and if this expedition is the trail run for Everest, we should do well there together.

The next day we left a route crowded with climbers and proceeded alone. We crossed over the pass separating the usual West Buttress climbing route on McKinley from the remote north side of the mountain where few, if any, climbers go each year. Descending 2,000 feet to the Peters Glacier, our route to the base of Wickersham Wall, we negotiated a tricky series of crevasses, ice cliffs, and a bergschrund—a large crevasse at the head of the glacier. There we discovered the most beautiful campsite either of us had ever seen. Surrounded on three sides by a ridge curved like an amphitheater, we were protected from the wind and restored by the silence. As the soft afternoon light swept gently over the cirque, we felt safe and at peace.

I could see that Chris, having come through the rigors of the day in excellent spirits, possessed not only the requisite energy and strength for this climb, but the good temper and patience to wait out the storms that would inevitably slow our progress. Refreshed, euphoric, and eager to set off the next morning for the base of Wickersham Wall, we talked late into the evening. Though we had not known each other long, we related remarkably well. In addition to shared interests in classical music, philosophy, and mountaineering, we laughed a lot, thanks mostly to Chris's warm, infectious wit. The force of Chris's personality and the gleam in his eyes moved me to photograph his face, made rosy by the fading northern light. As night fell, Chris commented philosophically, "When your number's up, it's up," to which I remarked, "I plan to do all I can to stay alive since I want to grow old with Mary Lou." I told myself that as a climber I might risk my life, but I would never consciously court death. Just where that line falls is a matter of opinion.

On Friday, May 8, we spent a leisurely morning enjoying the glacier's quiet beauty and reveling in our solitude. We talked about the National Park Service's policy against landings and airdrops in the area. Chris pointed out, "If the prohibition were lifted, masses of climbers and their attendant garbage would desecrate this wonderful place. How satisfying to know it can only be reached on foot."

Saturday, May 9:

Chris is dead. I am injured. My only hope is Doug Geeting. I pray he does a "flyby" before the next big storm.

I spent the day in my bivouac sack consumed with grief and guilt, impatient for Geeting to come. My miniweather radio predicted cold air from the northwest. Did that mean a storm, I wondered, or just colder weather? I kept imagining the sound of an airplane, but all I really heard was an occasional rock or chunk of ice falling in the distance. A setting that once seemed benign became ominous. As I gazed up at the huge ice cliffs that towered above me, I hoped I could escape an avalanche. In the distance, low hills completed the valley, blocking my radio signal.

Although Doug had said he would fly by to check on us, I realized he might not come for several days. With just a few pieces of beef jerky, a bottle of water, and a half-empty thermos of lukewarm soup, I knew I must conserve. Intense pain in my shoulders, upper arms, and chest made shifting position in my bivouac sack difficult. The adrenaline I had produced after the fall and in my frantic attempts to rescue Chris must have blocked the pain, but now I began to feel the full force of my injuries. I would need sleeping pills to get through the night.

All day long I tried to think of how I could have freed Chris. From where I lay, I could see the hole we had made when we broke through the snow roof and plunged into the crevasse. On each side of the hole, I saw a telltale dip we should have noticed. I kept asking myself, He noticed all the others, why not this one? Why didn't I tell him to slow down? I despaired that Chris, a young man with such a promising, adventurous future before him, had lost his life because of a single misstep. I hated being the only one who knew he was dead.

As I reeled from Chris's death and my own close call, thoughts of my wife overwhelmed me. From now on I planned to stay closer to home: I committed to quitting serious climbing. I promised myself that, if I survived, I would withdraw from the Everest expedition.

It snowed all night, but by Sunday morning the sky had cleared. Then a cloud descended, blotting out the surrounding valley, and I knew that if Geeting waited much longer, storms would keep him away for several days. I prayed he would remember to check on us, not wait for us to call him from the summit.

When I had left Chris as he was dying, it did not occur to me to dig through our sled for supplies. Now I needed them, but I could not face the prospect of going back down. In the two days since the accident, I had eaten just two sticks of beef jerky, a cup of soup, and a few sips of water. I felt light-headed from dehydration. Without my stove (tucked deep inside the sled), I knew melting snow would be difficult. To keep my bottle as full as possible, I started adding snow to the water and slowly melted it with the heat of my body. Though I grew desperately thirsty, I could never afford to drink enough.

I thought back to the hour before the accident when I told Chris I had lost a buckle from the waist belt of my pack. We dropped our gear and retraced our steps a quarter mile before I realized I hadn't lost my buckle after all. Returning to retrieve the sled, we discussed whether to change positions. We didn't. Chris remained in the lead, pulling while I braked. If we had switched positions, I would be the one dead in the crevasse. What wedged Chris between the walls was the weight of his body and pack plunging into the crevasse, compounded by the weight of the 85-pound sled, me, and my 50-pound pack.

Although I knew second-guessing would not bring Chris back or lessen my anguish, thoughts of the accident continued to haunt me. I kept thinking, Why couldn't I free him? I didn't, I simply didn't. I tried everything I could but it wasn't enough. The way Chris died seemed so much worse than if he had died instantly, as in a fall. It was not a particularly difficult part of the climb that got us but a crevasse on easy terrain, just like so many others we had encountered and crossed without mishap. Some people would say we were careless. Perhaps we were.

Why had I survived the accident? Doubting divine intervention, I wondered, Could it be my amulets? Since first attempting K2 in 1975, I had always carried a Zuni owl for protection. Some sixth sense had led me to bring a second amulet on this climb.

A year after I left a plastic, pink match case on the summit of K2, Reinhold Messner—the first person to climb all fourteen of the world's highest mountains—found it, protruding from where I'd buried it on the windswept, snowcapped peak. Ever since he returned it to me, I had kept it as a good-luck charm.

I had survived bivouacs on K2 and Mount Rainier, and now this. Why? Convinced there must be some reason, some higher purpose for me, I resolved to hold out until someone found me. I told myself, "I will not die here." Our tent, stove, pots, and most of our food remained in the crevasse. I wondered how far I would be able to stretch twelve sticks of beef jerky. Rationing one a day, my supply would last twelve days. I couldn't imagine Doug Geeting waiting any longer than that, but I steeled myself for the worst. As much as I wanted to get up and walk out of there, I knew my best hope was to sit tight and wait.

Thoughts of my wife both upset and sustained me. I longed to be with her, to hold her and cry. But it sickened me to realize that had I died in the crevasse, she and our five children would never have known what happened to me. I resolved never again to take so great a risk. For 21 years I had pursued mountain climbing with an intensity greater that I had devoted to either my family or my career. This was my tenth expedition in nine years. There was still time for me to become a better husband, a better father, a better son to my aging parents. I wrote:

Something good must come from this tragic expedition. I think of a photograph of an old Patagonian couple whose faces radiate serenity; after lives lived together in love. I don't want to drift apart from Mary Lou in our middle and later years, as so many couples do. I want us to grow closer, to become like the couple in the picture.

I told myself to heed the words of Maurice Herzog from his mountaineering classic, *Annapurna*: "There are other Annapurnas in the lives of men; a new life begins." It was time for me to stop serious mountain climbing and begin a new kind of life. From now on I would live differently, my priorities would change—I owed it to those I loved.

Sleeping pills let me get through the freezing night so I was only vaguely aware of the snow and wind bombarding my bivouac sack. I awoke to a brilliantly clear morning—a perfect time for Geeting to fly by. As I dried my soaked parka and halfbag, I heard the sound of aircraft engines. But they were only my imagination. "Please remember to check on us, Doug. You must remember." In my gut, I knew he would not come.

When I stood up for the first time since the accident three days before, I felt light-headed and my legs felt weak. I looked at the ice cliffs towering above me and wondered if they would crash down in the next storm. Should I move up the hill? Concerned about traveling alone over such dangerous terrain, I resolved to wait, at least until I felt stronger.

All day I tried to figure out how I could have rescued Chris and thought about the people who would suggest they could have freed him. Uphill where we encountered so many crevasses, Chris had led cautiously, detecting the slightest depressions where the snow sagged over them. Once we had passed through what seemed the most dangerous terrain, we mistakenly relaxed and picked up our pace. Had we approached the crevasse from more of an angle—instead of nearly parallel—Chris's momentum would have carried him across, but he hit the opening in such a way that he was propelled down the shaft.

Desperate for a temporary respite from my predicament, I read *The Snow Leopard* by Peter Matthiessen and was struck by his comment that "in high mountains, there is small room for mistake." After *The Snow Leopard*, I began *Pnin*, a short novel by my favorite author, Vladimir Nabokov. Nabokov's recurrent theme of deep marital love consoled me, but it also made my heart ache for home. Lying in my bivouac sack for hours, looking out over the lonely white landscape, I began to search my soul. When I returned to Seattle, I intended to visit one of the few priests I felt I could talk to. Perhaps he could help make sense of this tragedy.

Tuesday morning I dozed, waking briefly when two planes (the first I'd seen since before the accident) flew over around ten. Both were quite high and headed southwest, and I could reach neither on my radio. The wait seemed endless. Though the weather remained clear and cold, another storm would surely wipe out our tracks. Would Geeting find me without them? Perhaps he would wait until May 23, the day we planned to fly out. Could I survive eleven more days? When I left Chris for the last time, he warned, "Sit tight, Wick; don't try walking out alone. The risk of falling into another crevasse is too great." I knew he was right. Besides, I felt too hungry and weak.

All afternoon, I thought about the challenge and satisfaction Chris and I would have had climbing the Wickersham Wall and felt depressed. I had refused to contemplate going back into the crevasse, but now hunger convinced me to reconsider. To survive another eleven days, I'd need more than beef jerky. I reassured myself that Chris would not mind, that he would want me to survive. Though the prospect of confronting his corpse scared me, and my left arm and shoulder still caused me considerable pain, I realized I must go back down.

Early Wednesday morning I returned to the crevasse with my stomach in a knot. On the Friday before, the ice had echoed with Chris's pleas; now there was an eerie quiet. His legs, once shaking with agitation, stuck out stiff from beneath his snow-encrusted pack. Hanging in the slings, I could reach only one end of the sled and felt lucky to find pilot bread, margarine, honey, and raspberry jam. Stretching to retrieve the food, I accidentally touched Chris's body. I had dreaded going so close, but since the frozen corpse was no longer my friend, touching it did not upset me. I did not linger but grabbed what food I could quickly find and left. As I made my way up the crevasse walls, I looked down at Chris's pack and realized there was no way I could have freed him.

I ascended slowly and paused frequently to rest. With one arm useless, the other strained by my exertions, and my strength diminished by a week's starvation, I relied mainly on willpower to get myself out. After I got back to my bivouac sack, I prepared a meal of pilot crackers smeared with jam and honey. The taste was indescribable.

Even though an afternoon snowfall drenched everything, I

felt reasonably warm in my bivouac sack where I lay, listening for airplanes. None came, but the noises the mountain made often sounded like aircraft engines and raised my hopes. "Where is Geeting?" I lamented. "Why doesn't he come?" I wondered if I should retrace our steps and try heading out. I owed it to Chris to deliver his messages, but trying to walk out, only to fall into a crevasse and die myself, would mean failing him yet again.

Six days since the accident and Geeting still hadn't come. At moments I felt angry. "A plane could fly in this weather," I grumbled to myself. "Where is he!" In another week we would be overdue. In that case surely someone would undertake a search. But maybe they would conclude we died in an avalanche on Wickersham Wall. Maybe they wouldn't even look. I did not want to contemplate that alternative. I kept hearing planes, but they always sounded far away or around the other side of the mountain. They were probably my imagination.

On the seventh day, the mountain cleared and my spirits rose. Perhaps someone would fly over, notice a minute speck on the huge glacier, and rescue me. As a storm approached, my hope faded. Reluctant to get drenched again, I created a sort of lean-to by propping up two snowshoes, laced together with rope on which I rested my pack. This kept some of the wet snow off my head, but I still got cold enough to begin worrying about frostbite.

Nearby avalanches triggered by the storm increased my fears, so on Friday, May 15, I got up and moved with my equipment to a safer site higher on the hill. Before I left, I wrote a note, which I wrapped in a piece of cloth and attached to a rope on the picket two feet from the crevasse: "In the event I do not make it out, Chris Kerrebrock and I fell into this crevasse at 3 p.m. on Friday, May 8, 1981. He died early Saturday morning. God have mercy on his soul." After signing the note, I stood at the edge of the crevasse and prayed for us both. I thanked God for letting me survive and asked for help in getting safely home. With that, I turned and walked away.

My arms hurt so much I barely got my pack on. Weak from hunger, legs unsteady from lying in my bivouac sack for six days, I trudged uphill, stopping frequently. Once I lost my balance and fell over backward. By retracing our faint tracks I reached the crest of the hill—high enough to be out of the avalanche path. After testing the ground with my ice ax, I decided to stop. As I removed my snowshoes, I kicked through the crust of a crevasse. Spinning to one side, I quickly caught myself and managed to keep from falling in. Shaken, I stumbled a few feet away from the hole where, crawling into my bivouac sack, I felt safe. Farther up the glacier our tracks had disappeared; to continue without them as a guide would be too dangerous. I must stay put.

That afternoon the weather deteriorated, though I could glimpse the upper mountain through the clouds and falling snow. Despite my foray into the crevasse, my food supplies looked meager. I wondered how I could make them last if I had to survive another week. I decided to take each moment as it came. If I thought of everything that might interfere with my rescue, I feared I would go crazy. At times I turned to talk to someone, sensing I was not alone. Was it part of my personality disengaging from itself? Or Chris's spirit? Or was it just my fear and loneliness? Other times I got depressed, but most of the time I believed everything would work out. Doug Geeting would show up eventually.

After a crystal-clear morning, clouds came. Eight days and still no Geeting. Perhaps reading another selection from *The Portable Nabokov* would keep me from feeling so frustrated. Just as I settled down to read, an avalanche from high on McKinley's northwest wall crashed down above me with a deafening roar. I watched its cloud blast roll toward me with the speed of a hurricane. Afraid of being hit by heavy ice debris, I grabbed the top of my bivouac sack and hunched down. Luckily, a large crevasse between me and the slope above consumed most of the debris. Only a small storm of ice pellets made it far enough to pepper the back of my head and shoulders.

The absence of planes overhead made me think it might be difficult for small craft to get around to the mountain's north side. Despite the risk of falling into another crevasse, I decided that to survive I must move to a place where my radio could reach a pilot flying overhead—somewhere far from the threat of avalanches. With just an ice ax and an ice hammer, I carefully negotiated my way through a honeycomb of crevasses, most less than a foot wide. Crawling on all fours, punching my ice ax into the crust in front of me each time I moved, I avoided the few large crevasses and crossed the small ones. After I reached an isolated knoll, I returned to retrieve my pack and bivouac sack and moved on to my second temporary campsite.

I planned to probe my way across what remained of the most treacherous terrain. Then, if all seemed safe, I would move my camp again. By proceeding slowly and cautiously, I decided to try to make it to the other side of the mountain where there would be climbers who could help me. In spite of my sore arms and weakened body, I believed I would get there, eventually. That evening, I wrote in my diary:

It's Saturday evening in Seattle. Susie must be performing in her school play right about now. I wonder if the entire family is there? I wish I were home.

The next morning I traversed the worst part of the basin. Through my binoculars I spotted two crevasses higher on the glacier that I would need to cross on Monday. After that—assuming all went well—I could speed up. On the way to my next campsite, I managed to spill honey all over my meager food supply. Though I generally abhor sugary meats, I discovered that starvation made honey-coated beef jerky taste delicious. It took restraint to resist eating everything I had, and my will was weakening. After my tiny lunch, I settled down to read Nabokov. Resting in the sunshine, I felt cautiously hopeful, and looking over at the ice cliffs, that had produced Saturday's avalanche, I was glad I had moved.

My resolution to stop climbing, made in the wake of Chris's death, began to weaken. I no longer wanted to give up climbing completely. But the thought of going to Everest on an expedition Chris had conceived still bothered me. I decided to wait a few years, then do something smaller, maybe a joint Pakistani-American climb.

In the late afternoon, I realized that while making my way to the new campsite, my ice hammer had dropped off my pack. Relieved to find it just 30 feet away, I decided to stamp out an SOS before crawling back into the bivouac sack. As I did, I dropped my guard and kicked through the crust, nearly falling into another crevasse—I lunged to the side just in time. Early morning was obviously the only safe time to walk around on this treacherous terrain. The sun might feel good, but it was melting the glacier's crust.

Alone, so far from all the climbers on the other side of the mountain, I realized I might never be rescued. But barring another bad storm, I should reach the main trail by late the next morning. Just a few more hours of danger, just a few more crevasses to cross. I left early Monday, and walking straight up the glacier, sometimes staggering drunkenly from weakness, I made it past the last of the crevasses. As I approached the 2,000-foot slope I would need to climb to reach the other side of the mountain, the wind increased. I decided to stop and wait out what was fast becoming a ground blizzard.

With my food supply depleted, all I could afford to eat was one stick of beef jerky and three-quarters of a pilot cracker smeared with jam and margarine. Delicious, but not enough to keep me going long. My stomach ached, but I willed myself not to think of the food I craved: fresh fruit and vegetables, hot soup and meat, cocoa, hot tea, and bread. The hungrier I got, the lonelier I felt; I yearned to talk to someone about the accident. The storm raged on all day and through the night, freezing my feet. Hoping to forestall frostbite a little longer, I manager to clear a huge pile of snow pinning me down and changed my inner socks. I feared the violent storm might tear my bivouac sack; without it intact I knew I would die of hypothermia.

I began to dread the prospect of confronting the media back home. Although I planned to recommend leaving Chris's body where it was when the National Park Service asked me to prepare a report, the Kerrebrocks might feel the need to see his remains. Removing the frozen corpse would be difficult, but not impossible with enough people and equipment. I wondered what I would decide had Chris been my son.

With only a little food left, I began thinking more and more about the people on the other side of the pass. Perhaps one of the parties Chris and I had encountered before heading off toward Wickersham Wall would offer me something hot to drink. Oh, how I wanted a hot drink, more than almost anything else I wanted a hot drink. Increasingly discouraged, I wrote:

I'm so frustrated and so lonely. Why choose to put myself in this kind of danger? It makes no sense. I promise to change.

When I awoke Tuesday morning, I felt warmer and once again comforted by the sense I was not alone, that someone was there with me. The storm continued to rage. Drifting snow, hard-packed during the night, nearly covered my bivouac sack. My left arm and shoulder hurt so much I could hardly write in my diary—the main outlet for my anxiety and loneliness. Chris once said he relished our isolation but would never want to be here alone. My solitude had become almost unbearable. I wanted to be out of the sack, off the glacier, away from Mount McKinley, Now! But I knew I must be patient and stay calm—not waste the little energy I had left.

On the third day of the storm, the twelfth since the accident, I stayed huddled in my bivouac sack daydreaming about various projects I should do around the house. Maybe I would install some new bookshelves in the study, maybe a new fence in the backyard. In the afternoon, during a lull in the wind, I heard a large bird swoop by. Did I look like something to eat? Or was it simply investigating a strange, blue-and-red object in the middle of nowhere?

I worried that when I finally climbed the last 2,000 feet to the main route, all the new snow might trigger an avalanche. I prayed that once there, someone would make me a meal and a hot drink. Hot chocolate, chicken soup, hot tea, maybe even steak and bacon brought in by a recent arrival to the mountain. Craving food did nothing but distress me. I had to force myself to think of something else.

My miniweather radio estimated subzero temperatures and winds as high as 75 miles per hour. Throughout the storm, I had kept out the snow and wind by drawing together the top of my bivouac sack, then tying it with cord. Buffeted by wind, squeezed by mounting snow, I prayed the sack would not tear. At times I felt like an astronaut confined in a capsule without a smidgen of extra space. A benefit of my starvation diet was that my bowel movements had ceased—not a bad thing when one is living in a small nylon sack in the midst of a blizzard. And what would I have done without my pee bottle?

This experience convinced me that I must start reaching out to others, first and foremost to my family. I wanted to be more than simply "one of the first Americans to climb K2" or "the mountain climber." I was determined climbing must no longer dominate my life. As a climber I had remained in a kind of perpetual adolescence, often neglecting my primary responsibilities. It was time for me to reset my priorities and grow up.

Making up for a sleepless night, I dozed most of the morning. Other than for my sore arm and shoulder I felt pretty good, especially when the sky began to clear. My weather radio predicted sunny skies and my spirits soared. At four-thirty Thursday afternoon, thirteen days after the accident, I heard an airplane and flipped on my line-of-sight radio just in time to hear Doug Geeting notify someone of his plans to rescue an injured climber on the other side of the mountain. "A storm's coming," he explained. "I need to move fast." Though I frantically tried to break into the conversation, he did not hear me. Despite my disappointment, the sound of Doug's voice filled me with fresh energy and optimism. I was almost home.

Early the next morning, I once again heard the sound of a plane. Quickly turning on the radio, I called Doug and this time he answered, "Chris. Jim. Where are you? Are you on the summit?"

"No," I replied, "Chris is dead. I'm here, on the upper glacier. Can you see me? I'm just below the pass."

"I see you, Jim!" he exclaimed, and began circling his plane in search of a safe place to land. As I moved to pick up my pack, my foot punched through yet another crevasse. There weren't supposed to be any more crevasses. I lunged forward and rolled to safety. Then, scared and relieved, I sat on the snow and wept.

I watched Doug's plane approach me, a silver speck growing ever large until it skidded to a stop 30 feet away. When Geeting opened the door and helped me in, I weighed 25 pounds less than when he had dropped me off three weeks before. All my frustration about why he had not come sooner disappeared. Emotion and gratitude overwhelmed me, and as we flew over the crevasse where Chris had died, I told Doug what had happened. Beyond the base of the mountain, we flew over green trees; returning to all those things we take for granted, I felt profoundly grateful to be alive.

When I called Mary Lou, her compassion made me break down and cry. Although I did appreciate *receiving* phone calls—Lou Whittaker was particularly understanding—I found them difficult to make. Mary Lou knew this and took the burden on herself. When she called my parents, Dad told her he couldn't understand why Chris and I ever chose to go somewhere so isolated in the first place. She called her mother, who mentioned having had a troubling premonition about the expedition. Mary Lou reported that, while relieved I had survived, our relatives all expressed frustration that I continued to risk my life for reasons they could not understand. Yet, even as I affirmed my commitment to stop serious climbing, I could feel my resolve begin to fade.

A park ranger called Chris's father, Jack Kerrebrock. Hoping to notify Chris's brother and sister before they heard about his death on the news, Dr. Kerrebrock asked the ranger to wait a day before releasing his son's name to the media. He promised, but the *Anchorage Daily News* got hold of the story anyway, and the phone rang off the hook. Fortunately, the Kerrebrocks reached Chris's siblings in time.

Later, Dr. Kerrebrock asked the Park Service if they would

assess the feasibility of retrieving Chris's remains. So on the morning before I returned to Seattle, two climbing rangers and I boarded a helicopter and headed for the crevasse. When dense clouds forced us back short of the Peters Glacier, the others promised they would go back.

Flying home, I felt a deep sense of loss. Facing danger with another person creates a strong bond, transcending the limits of time and place—perhaps even death. I suspect that is one of the reasons I climb. My friendships are deeper in the mountains than in the city, where I tend to be more of a loner. In the mountains, awed by nature's beauty, thrilled by the risk and the physical challenge, my heart opens.

Jim Wickwire is a partner in the law firm of Wickwire, Greene, Crosby, Brewer & Seward. He lives in Seattle with his wife Mary Lou and has five children and twin granddaughters. Dorothy Bullitt is the author of Filling the Void: Six Steps from Loss to Fulfillment. *She lives with her husband in Seattle. This story was excerpted from their book,* Addicted to Danger: A Memoir.

MICHAEL HERR

⋆ ⋆ ⋆

Breathing In

*A war correspondent in Vietnam walks the line
between madness and sanity.*

THERE WERE TIMES DURING THE NIGHT WHEN ALL THE JUNGLE sounds would stop at once. There was no dwindling down or fading away, it was all gone in a single instant as though some signal had been transmitted out to the life: bats, birds, snakes, monkeys, insects, picking up on a frequency that a thousand years in the jungle might condition you to receive, but leaving you as it was to wonder what you weren't hearing now, straining for any sound, one piece of information. I had heard it before in other jungles, the Amazon and the Philippines, but those jungles were "secure," there wasn't much chance that hundreds of Viet Cong were coming and going, moving and waiting, living out there just to do you harm. The thought of that one could turn any sudden silence into a space that you'd fill with everything you thought was quiet in you, it could even put you on the approach to clairaudience. You thought you heard impossible things: damp roots breathing, fruit sweating, fervid bug action, the heartbeat of tiny animals.

You could sustain that sensitivity for a long time, either

until the babbling and chittering and shrieking of the jungle had started up again, or until something familiar brought you out of it, a helicopter flying around above your canopy or the strangely reassuring sound next to you of one going into the chamber. Once we heard a really frightening thing blaring down from a Psyops sound-ship broadcasting the sound of a baby crying. You wouldn't have wanted to hear that during daylight, let alone at night when the volume and distortion came down through two or three layers of cover and froze us all in place for a moment. And there wasn't much release in the pitched hysteria of the message that followed, hyper-Vietnamese like an icepick in the ear, something like, "Friendly Baby, GVN Baby, Don't Let This Happen to *Your* Baby, Resist the Viet Cong Today!"

Sometimes you'd get so tired that you'd forget where you were and sleep the way you hadn't slept since you were a child. I know that a lot of people there never got up from that kind of sleep; some called them lucky (Never knew what hit him), some called them fucked (If he'd been on the stick...), but that was worse than academic, everyone's death got talked about, it was a way of constantly touching and turning the odds, and real sleep was at a premium. (I met a ranger-recondo who could go to sleep just like that, say, "Guess I'll get some," close his eyes and be there, day or night, sitting or lying down, sleeping through some things but not others; a loud radio or a 105 firing outside the tent wouldn't wake him, but a rustle in the bushes 50 feet away would, or a stopped generator.) Mostly what you had was on the agitated side of half-sleep, you thought you were sleeping but you were really just waiting. Night sweats, harsh functionings of consciousness, drifting in and out of your head, pinned to a canvas cot somewhere, looking up at a strange ceiling or out through a tent flap at the glimmering night sky of a combat zone. Or dozing and waking under mosquito netting in a mess of slick sweat, gagging for air that wasn't 99 percent moisture, one clean breath to dry-sluice your anxiety and the backwater smell of your own body. But all you got and all there was was misty clots of air that corroded your appetite and burned your eyes and made your cigarettes taste like swollen insects rolled up and smoked alive, crackling and wet. There were spots in the jungle where you had to have a cigarette going all the time, whether you smoked or not, just to keep the mosquitoes from swarming into your mouth. War underwater, swamp fever and instant involuntary weight control, malarias that could burn you out and cave you in, put you into 23 hours of sleep a day without giving you a minute of rest, leaving you there to listen to the trance music that they said came in with terminal brain funk. ("Take your pills, baby," a medic in Can Tho told me. "Big orange ones every week, little white ones every day, and don't miss a day whatever you do. They got strains over here that could waste a heavyset fella like you in a week.") Sometimes you couldn't live with the terms any longer and headed for air conditioners in Danang and Saigon. And sometimes the only reason you didn't panic was that you didn't have the energy.

Every day people were dying there because of some small detail that they couldn't be bothered to observe. Imagine being too tired to snap a flak jacket closed, too tired to clean your rifle, too tired to guard a light, too tired to deal with the half-inch margins of safety that moving through the war often demanded, just too tired to give a fuck and then dying behind that exhaustion. There were times when the whole war itself seemed tapped of its vitality: epic enervation, the machine running half-assed and depressed, fueled on the watery residue of last year's war-making energy. Entire divisions would function in a bad dream state, acting out a weird set of moves without any connection to their source. Once I talked for maybe five minutes with a sergeant who had just brought his squad in from a long patrol before I realized that the dopey-dummy film over his eyes and the fly abstraction of his words were coming from deep sleep. He was standing there at the bar of the NCO club with his eyes open and a beer in his hand, responding to some dream conversation far inside his head. It really gave me the creeps—this was the second day of the Tet Offensive, our installation was more or less surrounded, the only secure road out of there was littered with dead Vietnamese, information was scarce, and I was pretty touchy and tired myself—and for a second I imagined that I was talking to a dead man. When I told him about it later, he just laughed and said, "Shit, that's nothing. I do that all the time."

One night I woke up and heard the sounds of a firefight going on kilometers away, a "skirmish" outside our perimeter, muffled by distance to sound like the noises we made playing guns as children, KSSSHH KSSHH; we knew it was more authentic than BANG BANG, it enriched the game, and this game was the same, only way out of hand at last, too rich for all but a few serious players. The rules now were tight and absolute, no arguing over who missed who and who was really dead; *No fair* was no good, *Why me?* the saddest question in the world.

Well, good luck, the Vietnam verbal tic, even Ocean Eyes, the third-tour Lurp, had remembered to at least say it to me that night before he went on the job. It came out dry and distant, I knew he didn't care one way or the other, maybe I admired his detachment. It was as though people couldn't stop themselves from saying it, even when they actually meant to express the opposite wish, like, "Die, motherfucker." Usually it was only an uninhabited passage of dead language, sometimes it came out five times in a sentence, like punctuation, often it was spoken flat side up to telegraph the belief that there wasn't any way out; tough shit, *sin loi*, smack it, good luck. Sometimes, though, it was said with such feeling and tenderness that it could crack your mask, that much love where there was so much war. Me too, every day, compulsively, good luck: to friends in the press corps going out on operations, to grunts I'd meet at firebases and airstrips, to the wounded, the dead and all the Vietnamese I ever saw getting fucked over by us and each other, less often but most passionately to myself, and though I meant it every time I said it, it was meaningless. It was like telling someone going out in a storm not to get any on him, it was the same as saying, "Gee, I hope you don't get killed or wounded or see anything that drives you insane." You could make all the ritual moves, carry your lucky piece, wear your magic jungle hat, kiss your thumb knuckle smooth as stones under running water, the Inscrutable Immutable was still out there, and you kept on or not at its pitiless discretion. All you could say that wasn't fundamentally lame was something like, "He who bites it this day is safe from the next," and that was exactly what nobody wanted to hear. After enough time passed and memory receded and settled, the name itself became a prayer, coded like all prayer to go past the extremes of petition and gratitude: Vietnam Vietnam Vietnam, say again, until the word lost all its old loads of pain, pleasure, horror, guilt, nostalgia. Then and there, everyone was just trying to get through it, existential crunch, no atheists in foxholes like you wouldn't believe. Even bitter refracted faith was better than none at all, like the black Marine I'd heard about during heavy shelling at Con Thien who said, "Don't worry, baby, God'll think of something."

Flip religion, it was so far out, you couldn't blame anybody for believing anything. Guys dressed up in Batman fetishes, I

saw a whole squad like that, it gave them a kind of dumb es-
prit. Guys stuck the ace of spades in their helmet bands, they
picked relics off of an enemy they'd killed, a little transfer of
power; they carried around five-pound Bibles from home,
crosses, Saint Christophers, mezuzahs, locks of hair, girlfriends'
underwear, snaps of their families, their wives, their dogs, their
cows, their cars, pictures of John Kennedy, Lyndon Johnson,
Martin Luther King, Huey Newton, the Pope, Che Guevara,
the Beatles, Jimi Hendrix, wiggier than cargo cultists. One
man was carrying an oatmeal cookie through his tour,
wrapped up in foil and plastic and three pairs of socks. He
took a lot of shit about it. ("When you go to sleep we're
gonna eat your fucking cookie"), but his wife had baked it and
mailed it to him, he wasn't kidding.

On operations you'd see men clustering around the
charmed grunt that many outfits created who would take
himself and whoever stayed close enough through a field of
safety, at least until he rotated home or got blown away, and
then the outfit would hand the charm to someone else. If a
bullet creased your head or you'd stepped on a dud mine or a
grenade rolled between your feet and just lay there, you were
magic enough. If you had any kind of extra-sense capacity, if
you could smell VC or their danger the way hunting guides
smelled the coming weather, if you had special night vision, or
great ears, you were magic too; anything bad that happened to
you could leave the men in your outfit pretty depressed. I met
a man in the Cav who'd been "fucking the duck" one afternoon, sound asleep in a huge tent with 30 cots inside, all
empty but his, when some mortar rounds came in, tore the
tent down to canvas slaw and put frags through every single
cot but his, he was still high out of his mind from it, speedy,
sure and lucky. The Soldier's Prayer came in two versions:
Standard, printed on a plastic-coated card by the Defense

Department, and Standard Revised, impossible to convey because it got translated outside of language, into chaos—screams, begging, promises, threats, sobs, repetitions of holy names until their throats were cracked and dry, until some men had bitten through their collar points and rifle straps and even their dog-tag chains.

Varieties of religious experience, good news and bad news; a lot of men found their compassion in the war, some found it and couldn't live with it, war-washed shutdown of feeling, like who gives a fuck. People retreated into positions of hard irony, cynicism, despair, some saw the action and declared for it, only heavy killing could make them feel so alive. And some just went insane, followed the black-light arrow around the bend and took possession of the madness that had been waiting there in trust for them for 18 or 25 or 50 years. Every time there was combat, you had a license to go maniac, everyone snapped over the line at least once there and nobody noticed, they hardly noticed if you forgot to snap back again.

One afternoon at Khe Sanh, a Marine opened the door of a latrine and was killed by a grenade that had been rigged on the door. The Command tried to blame it on a North Vietnamese infiltrator, but the grunts knew what had happened: "Like a gook is really gonna tunnel all the way in here to booby-trap a shithouse, right? Some guy just flipped out is all. And it became another one of those stories that moved across the DMZ, making people laugh and shake their heads and look knowingly at each other, but shocking no one. They'd talk about physical wounds in one way and psychic wounds in another, each man in a squad would tell you how crazy everyone else in the squad was, everyone knew grunts who'd gone crazy in the middle of a firefight, gone crazy on patrol, gone crazy back at camp, gone crazy on R&R, gone crazy during their first month home. Going crazy was built into the tour, the best you could hope for was that it didn't happen around you, the kind of crazy that made men empty clips into strangers or fix grenades on latrine doors. That was *really crazy*; anything less was almost standard, as standard as the vague prolonged stares and involuntary smiles, common as ponchos or 16s or any other piece of war issue. If you wanted someone to know you'd gone insane, you really had to sound off like you had a pair, "Scream a lot, and all the time."

Some people just wanted to blow it all to hell, animal vegetable and mineral. They wanted a Vietnam they could fit into their car ashtrays; the joke went, "What you do is, you load all the Friendlies onto ships and take them out to the South China Sea. Then you bomb the country flat. Then you sink the ships." A lot of people knew that the country could never be won, only destroyed, and they locked into that with breathtaking concentration, no quarter, laying down the seeds of the disease, round-eye fever, until it reached plague proportions, taking one from every family, a family from every hamlet, a hamlet from every province, until a million had died from it and millions more were left uncentered and lost in their flight from it.

Up on the roof of the Rex BOQ in Saigon, I walked into a scene more bellicose than a firefight, at least 500 officers nailed to the bar in a hail of chits, shiny irradiant faces talking war, men drinking like they were going to the front, and maybe a few of them really were. The rest were already there, Saigon duty; coming through a year of that without becoming totally blown out indicated as much heart as you'd need to take a machine-gun position with your hands, you sure couldn't take one with your mouth. We'd watched a movie (*Nevada Smith*, Steve McQueen working through a hard-revenge scenario, riding away at the end burned clean but somehow empty and old too, like he'd lost his margin for regeneration through violence); now there was a live act, Tito and His Playgirls, "Up, up, and awayeeyay in my beaudifoo balloooon," one of those Filipino combos that even the USO wouldn't touch, hollow beat, morbid rock and roll like steamed grease in the muggy air.

Roof of the Rex, ground zero, men who looked like they'd been suckled by wolves, they could die right there, and their jaws would work for another half hour. This is where they asked you, "Are you a Dove or a Hawk?" and "Would you rather fight them here or in Pasadena?" *Maybe we could beat them in Pasadena*, I'd think, but I wouldn't say it, especially not here where they knew that I knew that they really weren't fighting anybody anywhere anyway, it made them pretty touchy. That night I listened while a colonel explained the war in terms of protein. We were a nation of high-protein, meat-eating hunters, while the other guy just ate rice and a few grungy fish heads. We were going to club him to death without meat; what could you say except, "Colonel, you're insane"? It was like turning up in the middle of some black looneytune where the Duck had all the lines. I only jumped in once, spontaneous as shock, during Tet when I heard a doctor bragging that he'd refused to allow wounded Vietnamese into his ward. "But Jesus Christ," I said, "didn't you take the Hippocratic Oath?" but he was ready for me. "Yeah," he said, "I took it in America." Doomsday celebs, technomaniac projectionists; chemicals, gases, lasers, sonic-electric ballbreakers that were still on the boards; and for backup, deep in all their hearts, there were always the Nukes, they loved to remind you we had some, "right here in-country." Once I met a colonel who had a plan to shorten the war by dropping piranha into the paddies of the North. He was talking fish but his dreamy eyes were full of mega-death.

"Come on," the captain said, "we'll take you out to play Cowboys and Indians." We walked out from Song Be in a long line, maybe a hundred men; rifles, heavy automatics, mortars, portable one-shot rocket launchers, radios, medics; breaking into some kind of sweep formation, five files with small teams of specialists in each file. A gunship flew close hover-cover until we came to some low hills, then two more ships came along and peppered the hills until we'd passed safely through them. It was a beautiful operation. We played all morning until someone on the point got something—a "scout," they thought, and then they didn't know. They couldn't even tell for sure whether he was from a friendly tribe or not, no markings on his arrows because his quiver was empty, like his pockets and his hands. The captain thought about it during the walk back, but when we got to camp he put it in his report, "One VC killed," good for the unit, he said, not bad for the captain either.

Search and Destroy, more a gestalt than a tactic, brought up alive and steaming from the command psyche. Not just a walk and a firefight, in action it should have been named the other way around, pick through the pieces and see if you could work together a count, the sponsor wasn't buying any dead civilians. The VC had an ostensibly similar tactic called Find and Kill. Either way, it was us looking for him looking for us looking for him, war on a Cracker Jack box, repeated to diminishing returns.

A lot of people used to say that it got fucked up when they made it as easy for us to shoot as not to shoot. In I and II Corps it was "loose policy" for gunships to fire if the subjects froze down there, in the Delta it was to shoot if they ran or "evaded," either way a heavy dilemma, which would you do? "Air sports," one gunship pilot called it, and went on to describe it with fervor, "Nothing finer, you're up there at 2,000, you're God, just open up the flexies and watch it pee, nail those slime to the paddy wall, nothing finer, double back and get the caribou."

"Back home I used to fill my own cartridges for hunting," a platoon leader told me. "Me and my father and my brothers used to make a hundred a year between us maybe. I swear to God, I never saw anything like this.'"

Who had? Nothing like it ever when we caught a bunch of them out in the open and close together, we really ripped it then, volatile piss-off, crazed expenditure, Godzilla never drew that kind of fire. We even had a small language for our fire: "discreet burst," "probe," "prime selection." "constructive load," but I never saw it as various, just compulsive eruption, the Mad Minute for an hour. Charles really wrote the book on fire control, putting one round into the heart of things where 50 of ours might go and still not hit anything. Sometimes we put out so much fire you couldn't tell whether any of it was coming back or not. When it was, it filled your ears and your head until you thought you were hearing it with your stomach. An English correspondent I knew made a cassette of one of the heavy ones, he said he used it to seduce American girls.

Sometimes you felt too thin and didn't want to get into anything at all and it would land on you like your next-to-last breath. Sometimes your chops for action and your terror would reach a different balance and you'd go looking for it everywhere, and nothing would happen, except a fire ant would fly up your nose or you'd grow a crotch rot or you'd lie awake all night waiting for morning so you could get up and wait on your feet. Whichever way it went, you were covering

the war, your choice of story told it all and, in Vietnam an in-
fatuation like that with violence wouldn't go unrequited for
very long, it would come and put its wild mouth all over you.

"Quakin' and Shakin'," they called it, great balls of fire,
Contact. Then it was you and the ground: kiss it, eat it, fuck it,
plow it with your whole body, get as close to it as you can
without being in it yet or of it, guess who's flying around
about an inch above your head? Pucker and submit, it's the
ground. Under Fire would take you out of your head and your
body too, the space you'd seen a second ago between subject
and object wasn't there anymore, it banged shut in a fast wash
of adrenaline. Amazing, unbelievable, guys who'd played a lot
of hard sports said they'd never felt anything like it, the sudden
drop and rocket rush of the hit, the reserves of adrenaline you
could make available to yourself, pumping it up, and putting it
out until you were lost floating in it, not afraid, almost open to
clear orgasmic death-by-drowning in it, actually relaxed.
Unless of course you'd shit your pants or were screaming or
praying or giving anything at all to the hundred-channel panic
that blew word salad all around you and sometimes clean
through you. Maybe you couldn't love the war and hate it inside the same instant, but sometimes those feelings alternated
so rapidly that they spun together in a storbic wheel rolling all
the way up until you were literally High On War, like it said
on all the helmet covers. Coming off a jag like that could really make a mess out of you.

In early December I came back from my first operation
with the Marines. I'd lain scrunched up for hours in a flimsy
bunker that was falling apart even faster than I was, listening
to it going on, the moaning and whining and the dull repetitions of whump whump whump and dit dit dit, listening to a
boy who'd somehow broken his thumb sobbing and gagging
thinking, "Oh my God, this fucking thing is on a loop!" until

the heavy shooting stopped but not the thing: At the LZ waiting for choppers to Phu Bai one last shell came in, landing in
the middle of a pile of full body bags, making a mess that no
one wanted to clean up, "a real shit detail." It was after midnight when I finally got back to Saigon, riding in from Tan
Son Nhut in an open jeep with some sniper-obsessed MP's,
and there was a small package of mail waiting for me at the
hotel. I put my fatigues out in the hall room and closed the
door on them, I may have even locked it. I had the Corps
DT's, livers, spleens, brains, a blue-black swollen thumb moved
around and flashed to me, they were playing over the walls of
the shower where I spent a half hour, they were on the bed-
sheets, but I wasn't afraid of them, I was laughing at them,
what could they do to me? I filled a water glass with
Armagnac and rolled a joint, and then I started to read my
mail. In one of the letters there was news that a friend of mine
had killed himself in New York. When I turned off the lights
and got into bed, I lay there trying to remember what he had
looked like. He had done it with pills, but no matter what I
tried to imagine, all I saw was blood and bone fragment, not
my dead friend. After a while I broke through for a second
and saw him, but by that time all I could do with it was file
him in with the rest and go to sleep.

Between what contact did to you and how tired you got
between the far-out things you saw or heard and what you
personally lost out of all that got blown away, the war made a
place for you that was all yours. Finding it was like listening to
esoteric music, you didn't hear it in any essential way through
all the repetitions until your own breath had entered it and
become another instrument, and by then it wasn't just music
anymore, it was experience. Life-as-movie, was-as-(war)
movie, war-as-life; a complete process if you got to complete

it, a distinct path to travel, but dark and hard, not any easier if you knew that you'd put your own foot on it yourself, deliberately and—most roughly speaking—consciously. Some people took a few steps along it and turned back, wised up, with and without regrets. Many walked on and just got blown off it. A lot went farther than they probably should have and then lay down, falling into a bad sleep of pain and rage, waiting for release, for peace, any kind of peace that wasn't just the absence of war. And some kept going until they reached the place where an inversion of the expected order happened, a fabulous warp where you took the journey first and then you made your departure.

Once your body was safe, your problems weren't exactly over. There was the terrible possibility that a search for information there could become so exhausting that the exhaustion itself became the information. Overload was such a real danger, not as obvious as shrapnel or blunt like a 2,000-foot drop, maybe it couldn't kill you or smash you, but it could bend your aerial for you and land you on your hip. Levels of information were levels of dread, once it's out it won't go back in, you can't just blink it away or run the film backward out of consciousness. How many of those levels did you really want to hump yourself through, which plateau would you reach before you shorted out and started sending the messages back unopened?

Cover the war, what a gig to frame for yourself, going out after one kind of information and getting another, totally other, to lock your eyes open, drop your blood temperature down under the zero, dry your mouth out so a full swig of water disappeared in there before you could swallow, turn your breath fouler than corpse gas. There were times when your fear would take directions so wild that you had to stop and watch the spin. Forget the Cong, the trees would kill you, the elephant grass grew up homicidal, the ground you were walking over possessed malignant intelligence, your whole environment was a bath. Even so, considering where you were and what was happening to so many people, it was a privilege just to be able to feel afraid.

So you learned about fear, it was hard to know what you really learned about courage. How many times did somebody have to run in front of a machine gun before it became an act of cowardice? What about those acts that didn't require courage to perform, but made you a coward if you didn't? It was hard to know at the moment, easy to make a mistake when it came, like the mistake of thinking that all you needed to perform a witness act were your eyes. A lot of what people called courage was only undifferentiated energy cut loose by the intensity of the moment, mind loss that sent the actor on an incredible run; if he survived it, he had the chance later to decide whether he'd really been brave or just overcome with life, even ecstasy. A lot of people found the guts to just call it all off and refuse to ever go out anymore, they turned and submitted to the penalty end of the system or they just split. A lot of reporters, too. I had friends in the press corps who went out once or twice and then never again. Sometimes I thought that they were the sanest, most serious people of all, although to be honest I never said so until my time there was almost over.

"We had this gook and we was goona skin him" (a grunt told me), "I mean he was already dead and everything, and the lieutenant comes over and says, 'Hey asshole, there's a reporter in the TOC, you want him to come out and see that? I mean, use your fucking heads, there's a time and place for everything....'"

"Too bad you wasn't with us last week" (another grunt told me, coming off a no-contact operation), "we killed so many gooks it wasn't even funny."

Was it possible that they were there and not haunted? No, not possible, not a chance, I know I wasn't the only one. Where are they now? (Where am I now?) I stood as close to them as I could without actually being one of them, and then I stood as far back as I could without leaving the planet. Disgust doesn't begin to describe what they made me feel, they threw people out of helicopters, tied people up and put the dogs on them. Brutality was just a word in my mouth before that. But disgust was only one color in the whole mandala, gentleness and pity were other colors, there wasn't a color left out. I think that those people who used to say that they only wept for the Vietnamese never really wept for anyone at all if they couldn't squeeze out at least one for these men and boys when they died or had their lives cracked open for them.

But, of course, we were intimate, I'll tell you how intimate: they were my guns, and I let them do it. I never let them dig my holes or carry my gear, there were always grunts who offered, but I let them do that for me while I watched, maybe for them, maybe not. We covered each other, an exchange of services that worked all right until one night when I slid over to the wrong end of the story, propped up behind some sandbags at an airstrip in Can Tho with a .30-caliber automatic in my hands, firing cover for a four-man reaction team trying to get back in. One last war story.

The first night of the Tet Offensive we were in the Special Forces C Camp for the Delta, surrounded, as far as we knew, and with nothing but bad news filtering in: from Hue, from Danang, from Qui Nhon, from Khe Sanh, from Ban Me Thuot, from Saigon itself, "lost' as we understood it at the moment, they had the embassy, they had Cholon, Tan Son Nhut

was burning, we were in the Alamo, no place else, and I wasn't
a reporter, I was a shooter.

In the morning there were about a dozen dead Vietnamese
across the field there where we'd been firing. We sent a truck
over to load them on and get them away. It all happened so
fast, as they say, as everyone who has ever been through it has
always said; we were sitting around smoking grass and listening to what we thought were Tet fireworks coming from the
town, and then coming closer until we weren't stoned anymore, until the whole night had passed and I was looking at
the empty clips around my feet behind the berm, telling myself that there would never be any way to know for sure. I
couldn't remember ever feeling so tired, so changed, so happy.

Thousands of people died in Vietnam that night, the twelve
across the field, a hundred more along the road between the
camp and the Can Tho hospital compound where I worked
all the next day, not a reporter or a shooter but a medic, un-
skilled and scared. When we got back to the camp that night,
I threw away the fatigues I'd been wearing. And for the next
six years I saw them all, the ones I'd really seen and the ones
I'd imagined, theirs and ours, friends I'd loved and strangers,
motionless figures in a dance, the old dance. Years of thinking
this or that about what happens to you when you pursue a
fantasy until it becomes experience, and then afterward you
can't handle the experience. Until I felt that I was just a
dancer too.

From outside we say that crazy people think they hear
voices, but of course inside they really hear them. (Who's
crazy? What's insane?) One night, like a piece of shrapnel that
takes years to work its way out, I dreamed and saw a field that
was crowded with dead. I was crossing it with a friend, more
than a friend, a guide, and he was making me get down and
look at them. They were powdered with dust, bloodied like it

had been painted on with a wide brush, some were blown out of their pants, just like they looked that day being thrown onto the truck at Can Tho, and I said, "But I've already seen them." My friend didn't say anything, he just pointed, and I leaned down again and this time I looked into their faces. New York City, 1975, when I got up the next morning I was laughing.

Michael Herr is the author of The Big Room *and* Walter Winchell, *and co-author of the screenplays for* Apocalypse Now *and* Full Metal Jacket. *He is also the author of* Dispatches, *from which this story was excerpted, which John le Carré called "the best book I have ever read on men and war in our time."*

CRAIG VETTER

Into the Abyss

A renowned cave diver descends into
his own Heart of Darkness.

EARLY LAST MAY, MEMBERS OF THE U.S. DEEP CAVING TEAM who had quit the Huautla expedition began to arrive back in the United States from the mountains of Oaxaca, Mexico, with reports of bitter dissension among team members and news of a death. There were rumors that the team's leader, Bill Stone, was planning to salvage something of the troubled expedition by diving alone into the unknown depths of Sistema Huautla, through flooded passages nearly a mile below the entrance, into territory so remote and so dangerous that if anything went wrong there would be little chance of recovering his body, much less of rescuing him. The word suicidal was used. The name Kurtz came up, evoking the Conrad character who was finally overtaken and destroyed by madness on the ragged upper reaches of an African river.

Those who knew Stone could hardly have doubted that his eighteen-year obsession to prove Huautla the deepest cave in the world might well have pushed him into the mind-set that would choose death over outright failure. He had been born to map this cave, he told friends: to explore its shafts and great rooms; to ford its underground rivers, whitewater canyons, and waterfalls; to dive through the still, dark pools, called sumps, that had stopped all the other cavers who had tried to follow this monstrous labyrinth from the light at the entrance through the long dark to the light at the other end, where the system emptied into a gorgeous jungle canyon. Above ground, the distance from entrance to exit was eight miles. Below ground, nobody knew. For Stone—a technical wizard, a physical warhorse, proud and driven—the mystery of Huautla's unseen depths fit his ambitions perfectly: a cave as hard as Everest. Maybe harder.

It was the middle of May when I made the six-hour drive from the city of Oaxaca up into the cloud forests of the Sierra Mazateca, where the town of Huautla floats on stilts atop ridges overlooking the sinkhole valleys of these beautiful blue mountains.

Huautla (pronounced "wowt-la"), a town of 30,000 or so, is the Kathmandu of caving. It lies within striking distance of several large cave systems, and during the months between January and the onset of the rainy season in June, caving teams from all over the world gather here to provision their expeditions, to use the telephone and mail service, to spend one last night in a hotel.

Huautla is also the market center for the large population of Mazatec Indians who have lived and farmed in these steep hills for more than a thousand years. They speak an ancient language, Mazateca, which they supplement with a vocabulary of whistles as musical and complex as the birdsong that fills the forest. Their spirituality is a weave of Catholicism and old beliefs that they saw no need to abandon when the Roman faith stormed in with Cortés. They are among the few Mexican tribespeople who still practice the sacred psychedelic mushroom ceremony to cleanse their souls and keep them in harmony with the world of spirits and myth that surrounds them in the clouds, trees, rivers, and especially the caves that make lacework under their limestone highlands. According to legend, Huautla is the underworld from which the first Mazatecs walked into the light and were born. For centuries they buried their dead in the caves, where the gods they still revere make their immortal home. They do not go into the caves these days, nor do they take it lightly when others do. In 1969, a Mazatec used his machete to chop the rope from which American caver Meri Fish was suspended. (She fell, uninjured, onto a ledge.) Stone himself had a brief scuffle with locals at the cave entrance on one of his early expeditions. The Indians retreated, hurling curses that Stone was a *brujo,* a warlock.

I spent the night in one of Huautla's small hotels and the next morning drove half an hour up a steep rock-and-dirt road to the *pueblito* called San Agustin, perched on the rim of the sinkhole that holds the primary entrance to the Huautla cave. The fog that is generated each morning when the mountain air meets the atmosphere of the cave hung in the crater like milk in a blue bowl.

It had been more than two weeks since any news of the expedition, so I had no idea as I rolled slowly into the village whether the team was in the cave or out. Then I spotted team doctor Noel Sloan washing at a standpipe along the road. His face and upper body were the pale color of a salamander's belly. His greeting was affable but tired. The team had come up that morning, he said, a ten-hour trip with heavy loads after a final underground push that had lasted fourteen days. "Everybody's in the kitchen shack," he said, pointing 50 yards down the hillside to a small wooden hut with a tin roof. "We haven't slept yet. It's been an extremely intense expedition."

Inside the hut I found the tatters of the team seated around a large makeshift table taking their first aboveground meal. There were seven of them, and they were a picture of dirt-eating exhaustion. Stone's face was gaunt and filthy. His fingers were wrapped in duct tape. He stopped a forkful of salad halfway to his mouth as I came in and greeted me with words that reflected the sullen, almost surly mood that seemed to be on him in the wake of his great adventure. "My God," he said. "There's only one person I'd be more surprised to see down here, and I'd have to kill that person."

It was a reference to one of the people who Stone thought had let him down, one ancillary player in the many disputes, disappointments, and disasters that had befallen him on the long way to this bittersweet—and perhaps last—Huautla expedition.

Huautla put its spell on Stone in 1976, the first time he climbed into it. He was a 23-year-old engineering student at the University of Texas, a member of an expedition that pushed the cave to a Western Hemisphere depth record of 2,624 feet. Another team that same year got only 200 feet deeper before it was stopped by a flooded room, a dead end that the cavers called the San Agustin sump. The only way past it was to dive, and in 1981 Stone took measure of the barrier by swimming a thousand underwater feet before the limits of his open-circuit scuba gear turned him back.

Three years later he led an expedition that attempted to connect the cave from the opposite direction: from the jungle plateau up to the high entrance. The probe took three months and turned out to be a logistical nightmare: 600 dives through six sumps using 72 scuba tanks. The team mapped six cave miles, which covered only a quarter of the aboveground distance to the San Agustin sump.

Stone returned from that trip to the drawing board with

another idea: to design and build a "rebreather," a sophisticated piece of machinery that would give him greater range than ordinary scuba gear and allow him, perhaps, to dive through the unknown distance of the San Agustin sump into the air bells that he expected to find farther down the cave.

He began work on his high-tech backpack in 1984 in the basement of his Maryland home. He and several friends built the machine by hand on weekends, in the early hours before Stone went to his job as a structural engineer at the National Institute of Standards and Technology, and in the late hours after he got home. By 1987, they had a prototype: a 195-pound, computerized gas-processing plant that would scrub and remix exhaled air, making it possible for a diver to stay underwater for up to 48 hours. Stone called his backpack the MK1R, and it was a testament to his great problem-solving aptitude, his tenacity, and his two-headed passion for science and adventure. It was a rare and powerful combination: a kind of tough brilliance that took the mapping of a circuit board to be the same as the mapping of a cave. In the summer of 1987, Stone began testing the rebreather and looking for teammates to train for an all-out assault on Huautla's last secrets.

I met Stone and four members of his prospective team five years later, during a training mission at northern Florida's Jackson Blue Spring. For three weeks they had spent their days tinkering with the rebreathers and diving with them into a long, deep, clear-water cave at the head of the spring. Tagging along on one of their practice dives, I tried to imagine the double whammy of climbing nearly 3,000 feet into the earth and then diving through a flooded snakehole. I decided I'd sooner light my hair and try to roast hot dogs over the flame.

As it turned out, the combined job of caving and diving was going to be one of the most serious challenges Stone would face in building his team. The underground athletes of the world tend to fall into two distinct groups: dry cavers, who have mastered the climbing, rappelling, and hauling techniques necessary to live and travel underground, and cave divers, mostly from Florida, who park their trucks at the edge of cave-ridden springs like Jackson Blue, wade in, and spend the limits of their air in purely submarine explorations. The Huautla team needed members who could do both, and bridging the gap between the mole people and the eel people was going to be difficult.

On his 1984 expedition, Stone had discovered that because most cave divers didn't take well to the spartan and spooky experience of life underground, it was easier to turn skilled dry cavers into divers than the other way around.

"Easier, but not safer," according to team member Tom Morris. A 35-year veteran of cave-diving expeditions, Morris talked about the dangers of underwater caving from close, bitter experience. "I personally know fifteen people who have drowned in Florida," he said. "And dry cavers are at particularly high risk when they dive, because they're at home in caves, at ease, which is no way to be underwater."

Rolf Adams, a strong and experienced caver, put the proportions of the Huautla challenge into perspective one morning at Jackson Blue as he lugged the cumbersome rebreather out of the water and over a small seawall. "In Huautla," he said, "this single step is going to be a rock climb."

Adams was one of the five international members of Stone's team: a 26-year-old Australian with a wry spirit and a willing attitude, he was in Florida trying to make the conversion from dry caver to cave diver. Along with his rebreather training, he was spending several days a week completing a basic cave-diving certification course. He was learning fast. Stone expected that when the expedition got to Huautla in February 1993, Adams would probably be one of the lead team. Then, on their last day at Jackson Blue, Adams was lost in the kind of accident that is every cave diver's nightmare.

It was Easter Sunday, and the team was packed to leave. Adams was anxious to make a last dive, purely for the practice, in a cave called Hole in the Wall, about half a mile up the spring from camp. He and veteran cave diver Jim Smith donned traditional open-circuit dive gear and then, using the fixed line on the cave's bottom as a guide, swam about 2,000 feet into the tunnel before making their turn for the trip out. Halfway back, Smith looked to see Adams on the ceiling of the cave, struggling to switch from his primary regulator to his backup. That done, he gestured that he was OK, and Smith led on, only to be overtaken moments later by a panicked Adams, who was signaling that he was out of air. Smith immediately put his regulator into Adams's mouth and deployed his own backup as the two sank to the cave floor, where they were enveloped by a blinding storm of silt. They rose again to the cave ceiling; then the regulator fell from Adams's mouth, and he pulled loose from Smith's hold, fell away into the murk, and was gone.

Smith made it out with virtually no air in his tanks. Sheck Exley, the world's most respected cave diver and a friend of the team, was called in to recover the body. The postmortem found ample air in Adams's tanks and blamed the accident on "pilot error" rather than equipment failure. Stone, who counted Adams as one of his best friends, flew to Australia to deliver a eulogy at the funeral and then postponed the expedition several months.

It would not be the last delay. In fact, two years would pass between Adams's death and the team's arrival in Mexico. Over that time, Stone would beg money and gear from sponsors, redesign his machine, recruit and train team members, go into debt, and watch a contract for a documentary film fall into contention and then ultimately collapse under an injunction that would prevent him from making any film at all. It was the sort of run-up that tests the perseverance of an explorer before he ever reaches the unknown territory, a gauntlet of personal and logistic struggles that required Stone to fold salesman, accountant, clerk, teacher, politician, and adventurer into a single fierce and unstoppable personality.

"We call him the bulldozer," said Sergio Zambrano that first day in San Agustin. Zambrano was one of two Mexican members of the team. A seasoned mountaineer, diver, and caver, he had been responsible for obtaining the expedition's permits and for acting as liaison with federal, state, and village officials. And though he is a soft-spoken, gentlemanly spirit, Zambrano made it plain that being Stone's diplomat was not easy work.

"He went from a D-9 to a D-10 on this trip," he said, emphasizing Stone's big-tractor, get-out-of-the-way leadership style.

I'd seen what Zambrano was talking about on my visit with the team at Jackson Blue Spring. Stone rarely walked anywhere. Instead, he moved from task to task at a lope that made everybody else look slow and lent a general feeling of impatience to his manner. He talked fast and rarely yielded a point, no matter what the subject. And when he got rolling on one of his pet harangues—the bureaucracy at NASA, for instance, through which he had made it to the final cut as a candidate for astronaut training in 1989—he sprayed a sorehead kind of judgment that cast any approach but his own as the work of fools and incompetents. He could have gone to the moon on one-tenth of what the space agency spent, maybe less, he told me, and someday he was going to prove it by organizing a group of disgruntled former NASA employees into an independent team that would make it into space. Given Stone's technical abilities and the obsessive lens through which he focuses on the job at hand, I couldn't help thinking that he might just do it. The only thing that might stop him would be the kind of personality problems that bedeviled him throughout the Huautla expedition. Over the week I was in San Agustin, nearly all of the team members took me aside to grumble about the personal tensions that had plagued the expedition almost from the day they crossed the border at Reynosa. "We were a crew, not a team," was how one of them summed it up.

The affinities and differences within the team showed themselves early. The pairs that formed on the drive to Mexico remained partners throughout the expedition. Kenny Broad, 27 years old, an anthropologist at Columbia University and a veteran of ten cave-diving expeditions, rode with 29-year-old Ian Rolland, a jet mechanic for the Royal Air Force and one of Britain's most experienced sump divers. Noel Sloan, a 40-year-old anesthesiologist in Indianapolis and one of the team's founding members, rode with Steve Porter, a 40-year-old property analyst from Minnesota, and Don Broussard, a 46-year-old Texas mathematician. Stone made the drive with 34-year-old Barbara am Ende, the only woman on the expedition, a Ph.D. candidate in marine geochemistry at the University of North Carolina, and a dry caver with twenty years' experience. The two of them had met on a cave rescue two years before, and their romantic involvement had evolved naturally into her training as a cave diver and her inclusion on the team. Jim Brown, an accomplished cave diver from Pennsylvania, along with Mexican cavers Angel Soto and Sergio Zambrano and British cave diver Rob Parker, completed the eleven-member core team.

From the moment they arrived in San Agustin, Stone set the team to work at a feverish pace: unloading gear, digging latrines, building tables and benches for their aboveground camp. On March 3, they went to work rigging the cave with fixed rope that began at the entrance and descended 2,824 feet to camp five at the San Agustin sump. Visiting cavers who dropped by on their way to or from other expeditions volunteered to hump 35- and 40-pound loads on the twelve-hour round-trip to camp three, the huge room that stood 750 vertical feet above the sump and served as the main bivouac. Altogether, visitors and team members made more than a hundred antlike trips into the cave, carrying nearly two tons of gear and food. Through it all, Stone pushed as if he were late for something, as if he were Hannibal crossing under the Alps.

"I've never seen him so possessed," said Sloan. "If there was a minute when gear wasn't being hauled, he went crazy."

By the middle of March, with camp three in place, Stone and Ian Rolland began to rig camp five, a twelve-by-four-foot platform they had designed to hang above the water in the narrow rock chamber of the sump room. This cramped space, a difficult hour-and-a-half rappel from camp three, was where the dive teams would work, eat, and sleep. The roaring noise of an upstream waterfall provided a nerve-racking bass note, exacerbating the restless energy already on them as they anticipated slipping into the cold, murky water that led they didn't know where, or how deep, or how far.

Stone chose Sloan, Porter, and Rolland as the point team, and on March 23 they began a series of dives that lasted three days. Each man went alone into the water, laying guide line on the cave floor as he went. The decision to make solo dives was based on the worry that if they dove in pairs and one man got in trouble, there would be a double drowning as the second man tried to save his partner.

Stone visited them during their first probes and returned to camp three saying that the short, tentative dives they were making were an indication that they were scared. In three days they had laid only 750 feet of line. He expected a breakthrough, and was getting impatient.

Kenny Broad, who was waiting in camp three for his turn in the water, wasn't surprised at the timid first efforts. "They were not bold dives," he said, "except for Ian, who was pushing ahead well. Noel was freaked-out, but I'm not knocking that. The water was cold, and the visibility was poor. And we had just beaten the shit out of the rebreathers, dragging them to the center of the earth."

By the time the lead team returned to camp three, the expedition had been underground for thirteen days, and the tension was beginning to unstitch things. Jim Brown, who had the most experience on the rebreather after Stone, had decided he wasn't going to dive. "I just didn't like the feel of the place," he said. "It was just one thing after another. And Bill was pushing the whole way. He'd yell at you not to do something, then turn around and do the same thing himself." Meanwhile, Sloan and Porter, rattled and exhausted by the initial dives, told Stone that they needed R-and-R time out of the cave before diving into the sump again. Stone took their request badly. "He just couldn't believe that we wanted to take a break," said Sloan. "He wanted us to stay down there forever, and when I told him we were going up, he became despondent. He sat there for ten minutes totally speechless. I have never seen him so depressed."

The two of us were standing on the road above the kitchen shack watching the Mazatec farmers scattered here and there in the steep cornfields, carefully hoeing each plant.

"I just had a really bad feeling that something was going to happen," said Sloan, remembering his unease after those first dives. "It was the same feeling I had before Rolf died on Easter

Sunday in 1992. I mean, I knew when he asked to borrow my regulator that he was going to die."

With Sloan and Porter back in Huautla and Brown serving only as support, the work of cracking the sump fell to Broad and Rolland.

"I was itching to dive," said Broad of the moment Stone gave him the nod. "I hadn't gone to Mexico to sleep on the rocks. I went to dive, and I was particularly happy to be diving with Ian. He and I had become very close friends by then. He was a great dry caver, which I'm not, and he took great pains to teach me the ropes. And he was a fine cave diver, too, the only one on the team, really, whom I felt comfortable having as my support down there. And he told me the same thing."

Broad's reading of Stone's leadership was by turns understanding and critical. "As the leader of an expedition, you have certain things you want to get done and you're going to piss people off regardless," he said. "But Bill can be hyperinsensitive in the way he says or does things. He doesn't back down on things. He's not a people person."

Broad and Rolland made the trip back down to camp five the same day that Sloan and Porter climbed out. Broad made the first dive, laying 280 feet of line beyond the 750 feet already in place, and came up with news that the flooded passage was growing larger. This was a sign, he thought, that they were nearing an air bell. Rolland made the next dive and came back with further signs that they were about to break through: the ceiling of the sump was beginning to slope upward more drastically, and the sediment on the bottom was getting deeper.

"We were pretty excited," said Broad. "This was what the expedition was all about for me: good friends alone down there, things going like clockwork. Ian and I really knew each other by that time. He talked a lot about his wife and his kids, and we ran a spectrum of philosophical issues. When you're with the right person, you open up pretty fast in an intense situation like the one we were in down there."

Broad went back into the sump on the second day of their push. In just under 50 minutes he covered a distance of 1,411 feet and poked his head up into a long, narrow room full of air.

He was the first person ever to see the lonely rock chamber that lay beyond the San Agustin sump. A sandbar ran down the middle of the room—3 feet wide, 100 feet long—but he didn't climb onto it. He knew that Rolland was better equipped to survey the room, and he was excited to get back to tell his friend that they had cracked the seal on Huautla's dark heart.

Meanwhile, at camp three, Stone, Brown, am Ende, and Parker waited for news. Broussard was off on one of his many Sherpa-like trips to camp five and arrived on the afternoon of the breakthrough. He found Broad and Rolland rigging the rebreather for a second dive, chatted with them for a few minutes, and made the climb to camp three to report that the sump had been cracked.

According to Broussard, there was no particular celebration at the news. "It wasn't joyous," he said. "The crew expected it. Everyone breathed a sigh of relief that we were finally on the other side, but the attitude was more like, 'Yes, the sump has been pushed. Now we can start the next phase of the work.'"

Sloan and Porter were in Huautla on their break as Rolland began his dive to the other side at about four o'clock on March 27. Sloan, still spooked by his experience in the sump, hired a *curandero,* a shaman, to read the tarot for him. "It was kind of weird," he said. "He dropped the cards in four piles. The first three were for yourself, your family, and any question you had. When he dropped the fourth, which is for friends and those around you, it was the death card. That was four o'clock in the afternoon. Which is when Ian died."

By seven o'clock that night, Broad had begun to worry. He had boiled tea water in expectation that Rolland's dive would take two, maybe three hours. Their agreement was that if Rolland wasn't back in six hours, Broad would go for help. As the fourth hour passed, Broad began to fix the platform pulley system so that Rolland could get himself out of the water should he return while Broad was gone. Then he turned off the teapot, left a carbide lamp within easy reach, and on the stroke of the sixth hour quickly began the climb to camp three to organize what he still expected to be a rescue.

On the way up, he considered the possibilities. Rolland was an insulin-dependent diabetic, and although he was extremely vigilant in monitoring his blood sugar, Broad thought it possible that he had become hypoglycemic in the air bell, decided not to risk the swim back, and was waiting for help to arrive.

Broad reached camp three at about 11:30 that night. Anxious to return to the sump, he woke the sleeping crew and told them that they needed to begin rescue preparations immediately. Stone argued that the exhausted team, including Broad, needed sleep before they began the technically demanding work of putting a second rebreather together. He reasoned that if Rolland was trapped in the air bell, he would be on the sandbar and in no danger of hypothermia. He consulted Broussard, also an insulin-dependent diabetic, and decided that if Rolland had suffered a low blood-sugar reaction, the candy bars he was carrying would sustain him overnight. Broad left the discussion angry and frustrated, but he was eventually calmed by Broussard, who agreed with Stone that the team needed rest. "No one slept too well," said Broussard. "But it was better than nothing."

At five the next morning, the team was up and at work:

Some of them went to the surface to summon further help, including Sloan and Porter and a group of British cavers who
were camped at a cave nearby. Stone and Broad assembled the
second rebreather at camp five, and Broad began his dive. He
made it through the sump in 30 minutes and surfaced in the air
bell calling Rolland's name. When there was no answer, he
began to swim around the sandbar and noticed footprints going
over the top and then back into the water. Moments later he
spotted Rolland: motionless on the bottom in ten feet of water,
the regulator hanging from his mouth, the lights on the rebreather flashing. Broad dove fast in the hope that perhaps he
had arrived just in time. Only when he touched his friend's arm
did he know for sure that the worst was true.

He made a visual inspection of Rolland's body and equipment, but disturbed nothing. "That's standard," he said. "You
don't move anything unless you're taking detailed notes on a
slate. Essentially, you treat it like a crime scene." From what
Broad could see, the rebreather seemed to be functioning
perfectly, a verdict that was later confirmed by three hyper-
baric physiologists who analyzed the machine's black-box
computer readouts.

As Broad surfaced below the platform in camp five, he
could see on Stone's face the realization of what had happened. "I don't remember what I said or what his reaction
was," said Broad. "It was just numbing. We stayed on the platform that night, and Stone and I talked for a long time. He
was sad for Ian's wife and kids. And the death had the added
dimension for him that he had lost an important cog in the
expedition machine. As for me, I could have given a rat's ass
about a hole in the ground compared to my friend's life."

Stone himself recovered the body from the air bell. It took
five days to make the hard, sad trip to the surface. Twenty-five
people, including cavers from nearby expeditions, converged

to help, and on the morning when they finally lifted the body over the lip of the sinkhole, they were greeted by a scene that was, for Broad, touchingly surreal. "It was amazing," he said. "The Mazatecs were waiting for us with flowers in their arms, incense burning on a little altar. They'd cut hundreds of steps in the steep hillside, and they helped carry Ian to their church, where they had a memorial service with singing and prayers. I'm an anthropologist, so I'm used to analyzing rituals. I don't really take part in them. But this was different."

"I was very proud of my people," said Sergio Zambrano, who along with Rob Parker accompanied the body to the Oaxaca airport, from which it was flown to London. "Bill didn't want the Mazatecs to hold the service. I had to talk him into it. I told him, 'These caves have belonged to them for thousands of years. They have deep and sacred beliefs about them. And in a way, those who die here belong to them as much as they belong to their friends and family.'"

A few days later, as Stone spoke to a gathering of officials in Huautla, he heard again how deeply the Mazatecs are connected to the mythology of their caves. One of the town's mayors listened to Stone's report of the accident, then rose to chide what he felt was the caver's gringo arrogance. You come down here with all your technology, he said, and you still don't understand why you have suffered this tragedy. Perhaps it is because you did not ask the permission of the god of the caves to enter the sacred domain. This death might have been avoided had you made peace with the gods of the mountain, had you asked a *curandero* to make the proper sacrifice.

Veteran cave photographer Wes Skiles, who was on assignment to photograph the expedition for *National Geographic,* arrived with a crew the day before Rolland's body reached the surface. Skiles photographed the Mazatec memorial service and then went into Huautla and made a phone call during which he learned of another cave-diving death: Sheck Exley, the best-liked and boldest cave diver in the world, mentor to Skiles, Stone, and many others, had drowned just days before while trying to set a deep-diving record in a cave called Zacatún in northern Mexico.

By the time Stone's shattered team met in the kitchen shack under the weight of the double tragedies, morale had reached its nadir. Everyone except Stone and am Ende was of a mind to end the expedition. Stone, in fact, had already pushed a second sump—which began at the end of the air bell—by himself. On April 8, while the rest of the team had been struggling to pull themselves together emotionally, he had left am Ende at camp five and dived past the room where Rolland drowned. He'd made it 557 feet through the second sump and surfaced on the other side into a dry passage large enough to pitch a camp from which to explore the low end of the system.

There were those who took his quick return to the sump as a sign of callousness, a lack of grief. For Stone, the opposite was true. He believed that to abandon the project in the wake of Rolland's death would have rendered the death a waste. It was a question of debt: huge financial debt, to begin with, and then a deeper sense that as leader you owed it to a lost team member to accomplish something with what had been spent. For a man like Stone, to quit with no payoff was impossible.

"I figured I had to set an example," he said. "We had to keep this thing going." He returned from his successful reconnaissance dive suggesting to the team that they were on the verge of accomplishing what they'd come for; all they really needed was some time off before a final do-or-die push. He proposed a trip over the mountain to the jungle resurgence of the Huautla system, where everyone could relax, think things through, give the depression and the personal hostilities that were haunting the group a chance to dissipate.

Just before leaving for the jungle canyon, Broad told Stone that he couldn't go on with the expedition, that he would be a danger to himself and the rest of the team if he did. He would stay, he said, long enough to help his friend Skiles get photographs, and then he would leave. Stone said that he understood. He respected Broad—the work he'd done, the trauma he'd suffered—and though his absence was going to leave the team desperately short of people willing and able to make the dives beyond the sump, Stone acquiesced gracefully to Broad's feeling that he had reached his limits. Porter, who had come to feel that the expedition was operating under a dark cloud, said that he would stay on as part of the support team but was not going to dive again. That left Stone facing what he felt could well be the utter failure of the expedition. Time was running out; further dives through the sump would be on hold while the team helped Skiles haul his gear and take photographs. The crew members who remained were tired and depressed, and some of them were angry. And the rainy season was only six weeks away.

It was almost the middle of April by the time Skiles and his team reached camp three. The morning after their arrival, they rose to what Broad thought was a louder roar than usual from a waterfall that was within earshot of the camp. In fact, it had rained hard that night, and the runoff surge had raised the level of the river gorges by six feet, making the way out of the cave impassable. On their first foray upstream, Skiles and the team got only 150 feet before the current they were battling turned them back. That night there was talk of rationing food and carbide for their lamps if the water continued to block the way to the top.

Stone, who had been delayed in a gear hunt on the surface, was stopped in his attempt to climb down to the group by five-foot standing waves in the passage called Upper Gorge. He left

food and gear and a note that said he would begin rigging another route to camp three if the water continued to rise.

The next day, Skiles and his crew were turned back again,
although the flood had begun to abate somewhat. By the third
day, the water was low enough that the group decided to
move out. It was hard, wet going, and especially dangerous for
the diving specialists whose climbing skills were weak. At the
top of one waterfall, Porter slipped and was trapped on the
rope under the heavy flow. Sloan heard him yell, scrambled
down, grabbed his chest harness, and managed to pull him
from the powerful cataract. The team then decided to abort its
try and head back to camp three. As they began their rappel,
Porter fell again, this time to the plunge pool at the bottom of
the falls. No one on the rope was close enough to reach him.
Long, tense moments passed before Porter was able to surface.

The team made it out the next day, but for Broad, Porter's
close call was the last ominous straw. As he made his good-
byes, Porter decided to go with him. Stone turned on Porter
in a rage, telling him that he had signed on for the whole trip,
that leaving would let the team down, that by damn he was
staying, no matter what. Porter relented.

Skiles, who had other commitments, made a final photo
trip into the cave before leaving with his team. It was the end
of April. The known extent of the cave was barely past the
point to which Broad and Rolland had pushed it a month before. And the expedition had dwindled to eight people.

As Skiles and the others arrived back in the States with reports of the death and delay and the animosities that were
loose among those who remained, it became clear that if
Stone did make a final push beyond the sump, he would be
working on a desperately thin margin of error. The team was
down to three divers: Stone, Sloan, and am Ende, whose exploratory cave-diving experience was virtually nil.

Then Sloan demurred. He was still under the sway of his premonitions and had come back into the cave with a talisman called Ojos de San Pedro, a small paper bundle tied with straw and full of green dust and a garlic clove, that had been given to him by a *curandero* in Huautla. Since his first dives, he had been wrestling with the question of whether to go back into the sump. Finally he decided that the risks were too high and the support too thin for him to be comfortable on this kind of exploratory reach. He did agree, however, to remain in the cave as emergency backup for Stone's dive to the other side, which was to include am Ende.

As Stone's partner and the only woman on the core team, am Ende had worked long and hard to organize the logistics of the expedition. In the cave she had rigged and hauled with the straightforward energy and mental toughness that had seen her through twenty years of caving alongside men. "In a way, caving with these guys was frustrating," she said. "I ran, lifted weights, climbed stairs to get in shape, and some of the men on the team who didn't do anything to get ready for the trip were still faster and stronger than me. But I pulled my weight. I worked my butt off."

To many of those involved in the expedition, Stone's final push seemed a desperate and dangerous stroke. They were concerned with am Ende's lack of experience, about the fact that she and Stone were going to dive together instead of solo, about the slim chance that a rescue could be mounted if their equipment failed or if one of them so much as sprained an ankle in whatever lonely terrain waited for them beyond the sump.

"I was very concerned for their safety on that dive," said Broussard, who was to wait in camp three with Sloan. "Bill was pushing the equipment and personnel real hard at that point. And we didn't have nearly the backup that cavers like to have in risky situations. Barbara had only been diving for a couple of years, so no matter what, it took a lot of guts for her to do what she did."

Stone and am Ende got into their dive gear on April 30 at camp five, which was by then being called "camp fear." Am Ende was using Rolland's rebreather, which Stone had refitted after a careful examination convinced him that the machine had not been at fault. For her part, am Ende shared Stone's faith in the equipment and in her own abilities.

"I know there were people who worried about my lack of cave-diving experience," she said. "And with Ian's death there were a lot of people with less than positive thoughts about the whole thing, and some of that rubbed off on me. But mostly, what I felt when I slipped into the water was great excitement."

Am Ende went ahead on the dive through the first sump. Stone followed, dragging the 150-pound duffel bag packed with their camping gear, food, lights, and ropes. It took them half an hour to swim the 1,411 feet to the air bell, and Stone said he spent every minute of the dive rehearsing in his mind exactly what he would do if am Ende had a problem.

"Underwater, you think about the technology every moment," he said. "My eyeball was glued to the lights on her machine, the buddy display that goes from green to flashing red and then to solid red if there's a gas-mixture screwup. I knew that in the worst case we could have aborted to one of the open-circuit bailout bottles we were carrying or to one of the gas bottles that Ian and Kenny had stashed at 400 and 750 feet into the sump, but when you dive as a team the worry is always increased."

They spent about twenty minutes in the air bell where Rolland had died and then dove 557 feet through the second sump, surfacing into a dry passage that opened onto a large tunnel that became their base camp. They stashed their rebreathers on a high ledge so that the rigs they were going to need for the trip out would not be carried off by high water if the rains arrived ahead of schedule.

"The water level in the cave was way down when we got on the other side, which was very fortunate," said Stone. "If it had come up while we were beyond the sump, we would have had serious problems."

Just how serious a flood would have been became clear the next day as the two began their explorations: fifteen feet above the cave floor they found the wrapper from a Snickers bar lodged against the rock wall of a tunnel. "That was the only thing that really spooked me while we were over there," said am Ende. "I knew that it could only have come from our group, and that it had been washed down there in the flood that trapped Wes. Seeing it that high on the wall was disconcerting."

Stone and am Ende spent six days exploring the lower reaches of Sistema Huautla. Altogether, they surveyed two miles of subterranean territory that no human had ever seen before. They traveled through large tunnels and huge rooms, past seven lakes and two waterfalls to a final sump that stopped them at a depth of 4,839 feet. "I never felt so remote," said Stone, "especially on that last day. We were 22 hours from camp five, and I kept thinking, Don't fall, don't make a mistake, because there ain't gonna be any rescue."

Sloan and Broussard waited at camp three for the duration of Stone's and am Ende's dangerous push. Porter had changed his mind again in the middle of the anxious vigil and had left Huautla.

"I was almost as nervous as Noel even though he was the primary backup," said Broussard. "We spent the time organizing camp and beginning to haul gear out to keep busy, but we were nervous the whole time. And when they finally walked back into camp with news of their success, we were tickled no end. It was a day to remember."

On my last day in San Agustín, Stone and I stood overlooking the valley as he prepared to make a final trip into the cave, to haul out the last of the gear. By then we'd already talked about the success of his last dive, which had established Huautla as the fourth-deepest cave in the world; about Rolland's death, which doctors would finally attribute to complications of diabetes; and about the bitterness that was even then evident among the bone-tired crew that remained There were only seven of them now, and the feelings they confided to me about the expedition in general and about Stone's leadership in particular were not gracious. Stone himself was bitter about what he called the laziness of certain members of the group. "I wish it had been a military operation," he said. "There would have been a few people I would have keelhauled."

When we talked about another attempt to make Huautla's final connection, Stone said maybe: from the bottom, a dive into the resurgence and then upstream toward the sumps. Others on the expedition wondered where he would find a team. "The puzzle of Huautla won't be solved, I'd say, for a decade," said Sloan. "We looked long and hard to find people to put this expedition together, and none of them will want to come back and do it again. The thing is, you never know the cost of a world-class caving expedition until it's too late to ask for a refund."

"Good luck," I said as Stone turned down the steep trail for his final trip into the cave that had defined his life for twenty years.

"Luck," he said, "is not a factor."

It was a pompous remark in light of all that had happened. It had taken a million dollars, two lives, and the efforts of something like 50 people to see Stone's grand mission through. But perhaps it shouldn't come as a surprise that luck, or fate, or the blessings of the gods of the cave, held no place in Stone's own version of what he had experienced. His rough charisma and galloping hubris lay at the center of everything right and everything wrong about the whole Herculean endeavor. And in the end, it may be that prizes like Huautla go only to those who rarely ask anyone's permission for anything, and who rarely stop to count the price.

Craig Vetter has been a freelance writer for more than 30 years. He is a contributing editor for Outside *magazine, a frequent contributor to* Playboy, *and the author of the novel* Striking it Rich.

* * *

Kharkov and the Lubyanka

He did not abandon hope as he entered hell.

IT WAS ABOUT NINE O'CLOCK ONE BLEAK NOVEMBER DAY
that the key rattled in the heavy lock of my cell in the
Lubyanka Prison and the two broad-shouldered guards
marched purposefully in. I had been walking slowly round left
hand in the now characteristic prisoner's attitude of supporting the top of the issue trousers, which Russian ingenuity sup-
plied without buttons or even string on the quite reasonable
assumption that a man preoccupied with keeping up his pants
would be severely handicapped in attempting to escape. I had
stopped pacing at the sound of the door opening and was
standing against the far wall as they came in. One stood near
the door, the other took two or three strides in. "Come," he
said. "Get moving."

For me this day—twelve months after my arrest in Pinsk
on 10 November 1939—was to be important. I was being
marched off to my trial before the Soviet Supreme Court.
Here in Moscow, shambling through the echoing narrow
corridors of the Lubyanka between my two guards, I was a

man almost shorn of identity, ill-fed, abysmally lonely, trying to keep alive some spark of resistance in the dank prison atmosphere of studied officers' loathing and suspicion of me. Just a year before, when the Russian security men walked into the welcome-home party my mother had arranged for me in the family house at Pinsk, I was Lieutenant Rawicz of the Polish Cavalry, aged 24, slim and smart in my well-tailored uniform and whipcord breeches and shining riding boots. My condition now was a tribute to the unflagging brutalities and the expert subtleties of N.K.V.D. (Soviet Secret Police) interrogators at Minsk and Kharkov. No prisoner can forget Kharkov. In pain and filth and degradation, they try to turn a man into a whimpering beast.

The air struck chill as we turned a last bend in the corridor, walked down some steps and emerged into a cobbled courtyard. I gave my trousers a hitch and stepped out to keep up with my guards, neither of whom had spoken since we left the cell. On the other side of the yard, we pulled up in front of a heavy door. One of them pulled me back a pace by tugging at the loose unfastened blouse which, with the trousers, formed my prison outfit. They stepped up as the door opened, jogging me forward into the arms of two other uniformed men who quickly ran their hands over me in a search for hidden weapons. No word was spoken. I was escorted to another door inside the building. It opened as though by some secret signal, and I was pushed through. The recess of the door on the inside was curtained, and I was shoved through again. The door closed behind me. Two guards, new ones this time, fell in behind me at attention.

The room was large and pleasantly warm. The walls were cleanly white-painted or whitewashed. Bisecting the room was a massive bench-type table. On this side, bare of the smallest stick of furniture, I and the guards had the whole space to

ourselves. Ranged along the other side of the table were about
fifteen people, about ten of them in the blue uniforms of the
N.K.V.D., the rest in civilian clothes. They were very much at
ease, talking, laughing, gesticulating, and smoking cigarettes.
Not one of them spared me even a casual glance.

After ten minutes or so, I shuffled my feet in their canvas
shoes (they had lace-holes but no laces) on the polished
wooden parquet floor and wondered if a mistake had been
made. Somebody has blundered, I thought. I shouldn't really
be here at all. Then an N.K.V.D. captain looked our way and
told the guards to stand at ease. I heard their boots thump behind me.

I stood there trying not to fidget, and looked round. I surprised myself with the discovery that for the first time in
weary months I was faintly enjoying a new experience.
Everything was so clean. There was a comforting air of in-
formality all round. I was almost in touch with the world
outside prison walls. In and out of the room passed a steady
stream of people, laughing and chatting with the crowd behind the table, elbows sprawling over the magnificent red
plush covering. Someone asked when an N.K.V.D. major expected to get his holidays. There were happy inquiries about
someone else's large family. One man, impeccably dressed in
a Western-style dark grey suit, looked like a successful diplomat. Everyone seemed to have a word for him. They called
him Mischa. I was to remember Mischa very well. I shall
never forget him.

On the wall facing me on the other side of the table was
the Soviet emblem, cast in some kind of plaster and lavishly
coloured. On each side of it were the portraits of Russian
leaders, dominated by a stern-faced Stalin. I was able to look
round now with frank interest. No one bothered me. I
switched my trousers grip from my left hand to my right

hand. I noted there were three curtained doorways into the room. There was a single telephone, I observed, on the long table. In front of the central position on the great table was an old-fashioned, solid brass pen-stand in the form of an anchor and two crossed oars, with a glass inkwell, both standing on a massive marble or alabaster base.

And all the time, the everyday conversation flowed across to me from the other side of the table, and I, to whom no single kind word had been spoken for a year, who had drifted deeper and deeper into isolated depression under the rigidly-enforced prison rule of absolute silence, felt this was a most memorable day.

Standing there in my dirty, shapeless, two-piece prison rags, I was not conscious of any sense of incongruity before the cheerful and well-dressed Russians. The fastidious pride of the Polish cavalry officer had been the first thing they attacked back in Minsk ten months before. It was a callous public stripping, the preliminary to my first interrogation. The Russian officers lolled around smiling as I was forced to strip off my uniform, my fine shirt, my boots, socks, and underwear. I stood before them robbed of dignity, desperately ashamed, knowing fearfully that this was the real start of whatever foul things were to befall me. And when they had looked me over and laughed and finally turned their backs on me, then, a long time afterwards, I was thrown my prisoner's trousers and *rubashka*, the Russian shirt-blouse. Gripping those damned, hateful trousers, closely watching my tormentors, I heard for the first time the questionnaire that was to become the theme of my prison life.

Name? Age? Date of birth? Where born? Parents' names? Their nationality? Father's occupation? Mother's maiden name? Her nationality? The pattern was always the same. The questions at the start came in the order they were set out in the documents flourished in the hands of the investigators. They were quite pleasant at that first interrogation. They gave me coffee and appeared not to notice my awkwardness in handling the cup with my one free hand. One of them handed me a cigarette, turned back in nicely simulated dismay at the apparent realisation that I could not one-handedly light it for myself and then lit it for me.

Then the other questions. The dangerous questions.

Where were you on 2 August 1939? In the Polish Army mobilised against the Germans in the West, I would say.

But, they would say, you know Eastern Poland very well. Your family lived at Pinsk. Quite near the Polish border with Russia, is it not? Quite easy for a well-educated young man like you to take a trip across, wasn't it?

Careful denials, blacking out of my mind the memories of teen-age trips to the villages across the Russian border. Then the speeding up of the tempo. Two of them firing alternate questions. A string of Russian border village names. Do you know this place or that place. This man you must have met. We know you met him. Our Communist underground movement had you followed. We always knew the people you met. We know what passed between you. Were you working for the *Dwojka* (Army Intelligence)?

You speak Russian fluently?—Yes, my mother is Russian.

She taught you Russian?—Yes, since I was a boy.

And the *Dwojka* were very happy to have a Polish officer who could speak Russian and spy for them?—No. I was a cavalry officer. I fought in the West, not the East.

Then would come the payoff line. In this first interrogation it was delivered in an affable, we-are-all-good-fellows-together manner. A document was placed before me, a pen put in my hand. "This," said the smiling N.K.V.D. major, "is the questionnaire to which you have given us your answers.

Just sign here and we shan't have to bother you any more." I didn't sign. I said I could not sign a document the contents of which were withheld from me. The major smiled, shrugged his shoulders. "You will sign, you know—some day you *will* sign. I feel sorry for you that you do not sign today. Very, very sorry."

He must have been thinking of Kharkov.

So opened the battle of wills between Slavomir Rawicz and the men of the N.K.V.D. Quite early I realised they had no specific information against me. They knew only what my Army dossier revealed and what they could pick up in Pinsk about my family background. Their charges were based entirely on the conviction that all Poles of middle or upper class education living on the Russian border were inevitably spies, men who had worked stealthily and powerfully against the Russian Day of Liberation. I knew none of the places they mentioned, none of the men they sought to get me to acknowledge as confederates. There were times when I was tempted to relieve the anguish of soul and body by admitting acquaintance with the strangers they mentioned. I never did. In my mind, even in my deepest extremity of spirit, I knew that any such admission would be surely fatal.

The great stone fortress prison of Kharkov opened its grim gates to me in April 1940. Mildly conditioned by the rigours of Minsk, I was still unprepared for the horrors of Kharkov. Here the phenomenal genius of an N.K.V.D. major nicknamed The Bull flourished. He weighed about fifteen stone. He was ginger-haired, with luxurious growths on head, on chest, and on the backs of his huge red hands. He had a long, powerful body, short, sturdy legs and long, heavy arms. A shining red face topped a bulging great neck. He took his job as chief interrogator with deadly seriousness. He hated with frightening thoroughness the prisoner who failed to capitulate. He certainly hated me. And I, even now, would kill him, without compunction and with abounding happiness.

The Bull must have been something special even in the N.K.V.D. He ran his interrogation sessions like an eminent surgeon, always showing off his skill before a changing crowd of junior officers, assembled like students at an interesting operation. His methods were despicably ingenious. The breakdown process for difficult prisoners started in the *kishka*, a chimneylike cell into which one stepped down about a foot below the level of the corridor outside. Inside a man could stand and no more. The walls pressed round like a stone coffin. Twenty feet above there was the diffused light from some small, out-of-sight window. The door was opened only to allow a prisoner to be marched for an appointment with The Bull. We excreted standing up and stood in our own filth. The *kishka* was never cleaned—and I spent six months in the one provided for me at Kharkov. Before going to see The Bull, I would be taken to the "wash-house"—a small room with a pump. There were no refinements. No soap was provided. I would strip and pump the cold water over my clothes, rub them, stamp on them, wring them, and then put them back on to dry on my body.

The questions were the same. They came from the same sheaf of documents which travelled with me from prison to prison. But The Bull was far more pressing in his absorbing desire to get my signature. He swore with great and filthy fluency. He lost his temper explosively and frequently. One day, after hours of unremitting bawling and threatening, he suddenly pulled out his service pistol. Eyes blazing, the veins on his neck standing out, he put the barrel to my temple. He stood quivering for almost 30 seconds as I closed my eyes and waited. Then he stood back and slammed the pistol butt into my right jaw. I spat out all the teeth on that side. The next day, my face puffed out, the inside of my mouth still lacerated and bleeding, I met him again. He was smiling. His little knot of admirers looked interestedly at his handiwork. "You look lopsided," he said. And he hit me with the pistol butt on the other side. I spat out more teeth. "That will square your face up," he said.

There was the day when a patch of hair about the size of a half-crown was shaved from the crown of my head. I sat through a 48-hour interrogation with my buttocks barely touching the edge of a chair seat while Russian soldiers took over the duty in relays of tapping the bare spot on my head at the precise interval of once every two seconds. While The Bull roared his questions and leered and, with elephantine show of occasional pleasantry, cajoled me to sign that cursed document.

Then back to the *kishka*, to the clinging, sickening stench, to hours of awful half-sleep. The *kishka* was well named: it means "the intestine" or "the gut." When I came to—usually when my tired knees buckled and I had to straighten up again—I had only The Bull to think about. He filled my life completely. There were one or two occasions when the guard on duty pushed through to me a lighted cigarette. These were the only human gestures made to me at Kharkov. I could have cried with gratitude.

There were times when I thought I was there for life. The Bull seemed prepared to continue working on me forever. My eyes ran copious tears from the long sessions under powerful arc lamps. Strapped on my back on a narrow bench, I would be staring directly into the light as he walked round and round in semigloom outside its focus, interminably questioning, in-sulting, consigning me to the deepest hell reserved for stub-born, cunning, bastard Polish spies and enemies of the Soviet. There was something obscene about his untiring energy and brute strength. When my blurred eyes began to close, he would prop them open with little sticks. The dripping water trick was one of his specialities. From a container precisely placed over the bench, an icy drop of water hit exactly the same spot on my head steadily at well-regulated intervals for hours on end.

Day and night had no meaning. The bull sent for me when he felt like it, and that could as well be at midnight as at dawn or any other hour. There was always a dull curiosity to guess what he had thought up for me. The guards would take me down the corridors, open the door, and push me in. There was the time when The Bull was waiting for me with half a dozen of his N.K.V.D. pupils. They formed a little lane, three each side, and the mastermind stood back from them a couple of paces. I had to pass between them to reach him. No word was spoken. A terrific clout above the ear hurled me from one silent rank to the other. Grimly and efficiently they beat me up from one side to the other. They kicked me to my feet when I slumped down, and when it was over and I could not get up again, the Bull walked over and gave me one final paralysing kick in the ribs. Then they lifted me on to the edge of the same old chair and the questioning went on, the document was waved in my face, a pen was thrust at me.

Sometimes I would say to him, "Let me read the document. You can't expect me to sign something I have not read." But he would never let me read. His thick finger would point to the space where I was to sign. "All you have to do is to put your name here and I will leave you alone."

"Have a cigarette?" he said to me on one occasion. He lit one for himself, one for me. Then he walked quietly over and stubbed mine out on the back of my hand, very hard. On that occasion I had been sitting on the edge of the chair until—as always happened—the muscles of the back and legs seized up in excruciating cramp. He walked round behind me as I rubbed the burn and kicked the chair from beneath me. I crashed on to the stone floor.

As a new and lively diversion towards the end of my stay at Kharkov, The Bull showed off with a Cossack knife, of which he seemed very proud. He demonstrated its excellent steel and keen edge on my chest, and I still have those scars to remind me of his undoubted dexterity and ingenuity.

There was a day near the end when he was waiting alone for me. He was quiet. There were none of the usual obscene greetings. And when he spoke the normally harsh, strident voice was low and controlled. As he talked I realised he was *appealing* to me to sign that paper. He was almost abject. I thought he might blubber. In my mind I kept saying to myself, "No, not now, you fat pig. Not now. Not after all this...." I did not trust myself to speak. I shook my head. And he cursed me and cursed me, with violent and passionate intensity, foully and exhaustively.

How much can a man, weakened with ill-feeding and physical violence, stand? The limit of endurance, I found, was long after a tortured body had cried in agony for relief. I never consciously reached the final depth of capitulation. One small, steadfast part of my mind held to the unshakable idea that it was death to give in. So long as I wanted to live—and I was only a young man—I had that last, uttermost strength of will to resist them, to push away that document which a scrawl of pen on paper might convert into my death warrant.

But there was a long night when they fed me with some dried fish before I was taken to the interrogation room. I retain some fairly clear memory of all the many sessions except this one. My head swam, I drooled, I could not get my eyes to align on anything. Often I almost fell off my chair. The cuffings and shakings seemed not to worry me and when I tried to talk my tongue was thick in my mouth. Vaguely I remember the paper and the pen being thrust at me, but, like a celebrating drunk might feel after a heavy night, there is no memory of the end of that interview.

In the morning when I came back to life, I pulled my face away from the wall of my cell and smelt a new and peculiar smell. In the dim light the wall where my mouth had rested showed a wide, greenish stain. I was really frightened as I stood there, weighed down by a truly colossal feeling of oppression, like the father of all hangovers. They drugged you, I kept telling myself. They drugged you with the fish. What have you told them? I didn't think I could possibly have signed their damned paper, but I couldn't remember. I felt ill and low and very worried.

Quite soon afterwards I was moved to Moscow and the Lubyanka. The guards were chatty and smiling as I left. This was a feature of Pinsk and Minsk, now Kharkov and later Moscow. The guards acted on my departure as if they were glad I was leaving. They talked freely, joked a little. Maybe it was their way of showing a sympathy in which earlier they could not indulge.

Conditions at the Lubyanka were a little easier. My reputation as a recalcitrant had obviously preceded me because I was very soon consigned to the *kishka*. But this *kishka* was clean and the periods I was forced to spend in it were shorter.

The interrogation team at the Lubyanka nevertheless tried out their special powers of persuasion on me. It was possibly a matter of metropolitan pride to try to succeed where the provincial boys had failed. There were the usual questions, the repeated demands for my signature, some manhandling, references to the filthy, spying Poles. But there was only one torture trick of which The Bull might have been envious.

They strapped me with my feet pulled stiffly out under the now familiar "operation table." My arms were stretched out along the table surface, each hand tied and held separately. My body was arched in a straining bow around the table end, and the pain grew into searing agony as they hauled taut on the straps. This, however, was preparatory stuff like climbing into the dentist's chair with a raging toothache. The operation was yet to come. Over the table was suspended an old-fashioned small cauldron fitted with a spout. It contained hot tar. There followed the usual pressing invitation to sign, with a promise that if I agreed I should be released immediately and returned to my cell. I think they would have been most disappointed if at that stage I had agreed to sign. The first drop of tar was hell. It burned savagely into the back of my hand and held its heat a long time on the puckered and livid skin. That first drop was the worst. It was the peak of pain. The rest were faintly anti-climax. I held on to consciousness and to my will to resist. When they said I should be glad to sign with my left hand at the end of the session, I proved them wrong. I had learned my fortitude in a very hard school.

That was the last major assault. I had been in the Lubyanka only about two weeks when I was led forth to my first and only experience of a Soviet court of justice.

Slavomir Rawicz escaped with a small group of fellow prisoners from a Soviet labor camp in 1941, marching out of Siberia, through China, the Gobi Desert, Tibet, and over the Himalayas to British India. His story is told in The Long Walk: A True Story of the Trek to Freedom, *from which this piece was excerpted. He now lives in England.*

EARL PERRY

✦ ✦ ✦

The Thrill

*The author reveals a hunter's secret
when someone gets under his skin.*

WE ARE STANDING AROUND THE CAMPFIRE, AFTER A PORK chop dinner. I am talking to some of the other passengers about hunting. Ursula interrupts, leaning in over the shoulders, banderilleras high, planting one: "I bet you get a real Thrill out of killing something, eh, Earl?" Her tone leaves no doubt of the nature of the "Thrill." I have encountered this before: mental chyme, comprising some partly digested and uncomprehended chunks of Freud that someone else had read for her, and a lot of acid.

I can never tell when it will happen. There is not usually much point in conversing with people who have their opinions adsorb onto them, so generally I don't. But sometimes it happens. Yes, it does happen. Rather to my own surprise, something about Ursula bores through the shell of my denial. On the sudden I determine to out myself and my fellow hunters. I decide to confess.

"Well, yes, Ursula, though it isn't something we hunters usually talk about. I don't know how you figured it out. But you're right. I do get a Thrill out of it. But it's maybe not what you think, not quite. You probably think it has to do with the way we mark the young hunters, and you're right, that's a Thrill, but that's not the *real* Thrill."

"Mark the young hunters?" She is momentarily interested, but she sees through the diversion and comes back to the matter at hand. "Oh, I think I've got a pretty good idea just what kind of a Thrill you get from murdering some helpless creature," she says. She leans in over the horns to plant another banderillera. "Excites you, eh? Stiffens you right up, I bet. About all that does, eh? Maybe that's what the young hunters are for, Earl?" I concede: she is quick, to have integrated the young hunters like that.

I narrow my eyes and fix them on Ursula's. I widen my shoulders a little and lean very slightly toward her. There is a sudden tautness near her eyes, and she sways back almost imperceptibly. Good. I am not looking at Snake, but I am very conscious of him. He is registering. This will go into the annals. I want to do it right.

"You know, Ursula," I say mildly, "There's real excitement when you settle behind the scope of Old Flintheart and peer across the canyon and you see that buck over there, Ursula, pawing through the snow, eating. And Ursula, he has no idea that you've become Death. He has no idea he's become food. And you look into his eyes, his huge, brown, unsuspecting eyes, Ursula, and you take just a moment to caress it through your mind before you start the trigger squeeze. And he's the symbol of the forest quiet, and he's the symbol of the forest loveliness, and you're about to shatter it, Ursula. You're about to shatter *him*, Ursula. And that's good, Ursula, that's very good. But that's not the *real* Thrill."

"God," says Ursula. "You make me sick. You know that?" She is listening intently.

I move a little toward Ursula. I use a yogic technique to make myself long in front. "And then those crosshairs get very still. And then you do it, Ursula, you send that slow-spinning bullet across the canyon in a lazy parabola. And while it's lifting into the rising limb of that curve, and while it's arching down through the falling limb of that curve, you have just time to register the intertwining of destinies, Ursula, and then that bullet hits. And you walk across the canyon, Ursula, and you stand over that blasted loveliness, the symbol of the forest, and his eyes are powdering, Ursula, and that's a Thrill, yes, Ursula, that's a Thrill, but that's not the *real* Thrill."

One of the passengers moves up on the other side of Ursula. By now my eyes have turned from blue to gray, but in the red of the firelight it is doubtful she can perceive that. "And you put the knife in below the sternum, Ursula. And you run that knife down toward the thighs, Ursula. And behind the knife the guts are bulging in ropy pearlescence, welling from the incision behind the knife, and that's good, Ursula, that's *very* good, but that's not the Thrill."

I am near to chanting now. "And you smell the scent of the summer in him, the scent of the grass eaters, the scent of the prey. And you run the slit past the coarse hairs around his penis, and past the quiescent heft of his scrotum, and they lie there. And now they're soft forever. And all their dreams of battle and all their dreams of does have entered eternity."

"And you get between his thighs, Ursula, and you want them open, Ursula, and you cut down through the thighs to the pelvis, Ursula, and crack it open and lay him wide in the snow." I have lowered my voice, and it is growing more intense. "And that's a Thrill, Ursula, but that's not the *real* Thrill." Ursula's mouth is open, and she has raised one hand to it.

"And it's cold, Ursula, and the snow is creaking under your feet. And your feet have gone past pain into bluntness. And your hands ache and sting, Ursula. And you run your fingers down in among the steaming, still-contracting snakes of the intestines, Ursula. And that gives you feeling again, Ursula, and that's *good*. But that's not the Thrill."

"And you cut past the great dome of the diaphragm, up where all the destruction is, Ursula, and a hot flood of clotting blood spills down at you, and it's beginning to string, Ursula. You reach on up and grab the slippery corrugation of the windpipe and slash it, and you pull it all out, and that buck is shrunken now, Ursula. And that's *good*. But that's not the Thrill, Ursula. No, that's not the Thrill." Ursula is motionless and aghast.

"You look down on the reddened smear of your arms, Ursula, and against the red are dark carmine crescents formed of the hairs of your hands, your forearms, your elbows, your biceps, your shoulders, Ursula. The red life of the buck is crusting on your arms, Ursula. And that's *good*. But that's not the Thrill, Ursula."

"Oh my God. Oh my God. I didn't want to hear this," says Ursula. Her eyes are wide and horrified. She has made herself smaller.

"And when you've raked all the guts out, Ursula, you stand over it for just a moment. And there's a wind blowing down 5,000 miles from the far north country, across all that barrenness, a freezing wind, and those guts, Ursula, they smoke and they steam, and the blood is denting the snow. And it's cold, Ursula, and you *want* it cold."

"And you stand there looking down at it, Ursula, and you take off all your clothes, Ursula, and just for a minute you stand there, and you let that icy death-wind from the north country lick you all over, Ursula, and it tightens your skin,

Ursula, until your whole body is as hard as root and stone, and you're with the *ice*, Ursula, and *then*, Ursula, THEN." I move in closer to her, and lock my eyes on hers. The others have grayed out.

"Ursula." I run my tongue hard on the first syllable of her name, let it glide off the others. "*Ursula. Then. Then* is when it happens. Then you slide yourself into that hot reeking body cavity. And you work yourself *up*, and *in*, until you can't get any deeper. And I'm telling you, Ursula, that's good, Ursula, that's the *Thrill*, Ursula, that's the *real* Thrill. And Ursula, we all do it. Grandfather and child, uncle and nephew, father and son, we *all* do it."

"Please," she says quietly. "I didn't. I don't want to know this. Oh my God. I'm going to be sick." She is wrapping herself around her solar plexus.

Then a passenger cracks the moment. He points across the fire at her and begins to whoop with laughter. "Oh my God," he says, "Ropy pearlescence! Oh magnificent. Old Flintheart! Oh my God. Carmine crescents! Crawling inside!" He points at her and gasps with delight. The others break out laughing, some very uncertainly. Riva looks angry. Her husband is loud in his laughter.

Ursula shakes slightly and straightens. "Well," she says furiously, "You don't suppose I believed all that crap? No. *No way.*" She looks around the campfire. "I was just playing along to see what he'd say."

"Of course you were. Of course. Just playing along. We all do it. Crawling inside!" The man crows happily and points at her again. Fresh laughter. Ursula essays some haughty and vespine remarks. These fail. She withdraws into the darkness.

Riva looks at me for a long moment. "You son of a bitch," she says flatly.

I look back at her. "Riva," I say. "Yes." I smile. She leaves the circle of the fire.

Snake catches my eye. He inclines his head slightly, acknowledging. I incline my head, accepting.

Earl Perry was a professional boatman, and is both a hunter and a student of yoga. His patience is not infinite.

PART FOUR

INTO THE LIGHT

✦ ✦ ✦

No Like A-feesh?

Is he only a man, or something more?

I'D MADE UP MY MIND TO SPEND JUST THE DAY AT SATHYA SAI Baba's ashram, returning to Bangalore after evening prayers. I hadn't seen him in fourteen years, and he hadn't spoken to me privately since that interview more than seventeen years before. But hardly a week had passed throughout the preceding years when I hadn't thought of him. And occasionally I had dreams that bore the unmistakable stamp of his presence—love—and held relatively important messages, ones I had no trouble deciphering. When I least expected it, I'd feel that embracing glow of being loved, the sheer sweetness of Baba's enigma.

"Don't try to understand me, because you never will," he'd said.

This was true. I'd often decided it was all over, that he and I were through—I'd descend back into unalloyed matter, and he'd go…wherever it was he needed to go. But the bond never broke. As he'd promised, he was always there, hidden at times, but there, in the heart.

And as the years passed, I came to see the pendulum swing of my soul, from matter to spirit, darkness to light, the unreal to the real, back and forth—endlessly. I also came to understand that the momentum needed for leaps of faith was generated this way. I accepted more now, too, was kinder to myself, more forgiving, more *objective*. Slightly.

I never went to meetings of local Sathya Sai groups; but I did on occasion pray, in mosques, churches, synagogues, temples—whatever was handy. I realized that the image of God I'd chosen, besides his formless, nondualistic eternal oneness, was that of Sathya Sai Baba. He'd stood the test of time.

But the idea of seeing the reality, rather than the idea and the image, filled me with trepidation, even with dread. I knew I was drinking heavily—too heavily—and finding reasons not to go. But now I was on my way.

We drove from the West End Hotel at 3:30 a.m. I estimated that would get me there around 11:00—generally in time for morning darshan—*if* things were still the same. The driver I'd chosen was someone I knew to be untalkative.

Memories of driving out with Abdul and Joy came back, but I just couldn't relate *this* me to *that* me. We were different people. I'd been a mere child then.

I wondered who I was kidding while I tried to snooze. This might be the most important day I would have for years, maybe *ever*. Because part of me wanted to exorcise Baba forever, or satisfy itself concerning his reality enough to make a serious commitment. Make or break: that was the attitude I took.

Hovering up above the parched plains of Andhra Pradesh, the bloody sun sat like a mothership bearing galactic emperors to an appointment at the end of the world. The sudden, awesome beauty of this spectacle felt like a punch to the heart. As we hurtled through the primeval landscape, I felt like the first man, or the last one. Slipping on headphones, I started listening to Ravi Shankar's *Shanti–Dhwani* where I'd left off after buying it the day before. Dedicated to Indira Gandhi—its sole shortcoming—it is a shimmering masterpiece, transcending musical definition. That dawn, however, I felt the hairs on my neck stand up as, instead of Ravi's orchestral sitar assembly, I heard the chanting of Sanskrit mantras, one of them the sole piece of Vedic wisdom I can still quote with the proper intonation: the *Gayathri*. It is the supreme and most profound plea to the Lord of this universe that humanity has ever uttered: Baba had once said that it was the only request worth making of God:

> *Om Asatomah sat gamayah*
> *Tamaso mah jyotir gamayah*
> *Mnityoman amrtam gamayah*
> *Om Shantih Shantih Shantih*
>
> Eternal One
> Lead me from the Unreal to the Real
> From Darkness to Light
> From Death to Immortality
> To be with Eternity in everlasting peace

With around five hours to go, by my estimate, I was very surprised to see a sign reading PUTTAPARTHI 30 KM, assuming it was an error for 300 km. I mentioned it to the driver, who'd shot past the turnoff indicated by this sign, anyway, and he brought us to a slithering halt, backed up to the sign, nodded, and then turned off down the side road.

"Thirty kilometers?" I inquired, laughing sagely.

"Half hour more arriving," he replied.

"Arriving *where*?"

"Sai Baba place."

"It's only six o'clock!" I yodeled. "We've only been driving

for two and a half hours. How can we bloody well arrive there in *half an hour?"*

"Journey is three hours only."

"No it's not," I snapped. "It's at least *seven* hours."

"Three hours only."

First the *Gayathri*, and now—What? A warp in the space-time continuum?

"It took *seven* hours in 1974," I added, trying to sound less hysterical. "Why does it take three hours now? Hmm? Why?"

Because they'd built a new road was the answer. Instead of weaving north, then east, you could now go straight, on the new road. Humbled, I sank back, not wanting to be so near to Puttaparthi so soon.

Before long, we swerved around a corner I remembered well.

"Sai Ram, Sai Ram," rasped a familiar voice.

The old blind beggar Joy had condemned as a phony devotee and millionaire stood with his usherette's tray of framed Baba pictures, and his eye sockets like a dead dog's nose. I told the driver to stop and gave the millionaire some more rupees to fatten his bank account, for auld lang syne.

In no time, I gasped slightly at the start of that breathtakingly elegant landscape that I'd never forgotten, with its giant outcrops of sculptured rock, its blackened mountaintops, its verdant paddies, its sense of timeless peace. I wasn't sure whether I'd change into Baba-devotee regulation white, but I'd brought the clothes along in case I felt like conforming. And I did.

Hopping around by the roadside, trying to find the hole in my pants for a foot, I looked up as a small bus hurtled into view. It was painted with Baba slogans and his emblem, and full of kids from one of his colleges. Most schoolkids, encountering a foreigner in the middle of nowhere with his big pale butt exposed to the elements, would have hooted lewd and humiliating remarks through the windows. These students merely looked away politely, and I could hear the singing of *bhajans* as they passed. The kids who attended Baba's educational establishments had been unnaturally well behaved every time I encountered them.

Vaguely recalling the lay of the land, I was surprised to find an ornate concrete arch spanning an otherwise empty stretch of road, WELCOME TO PRASANTHI NILAYAM, it read, ABODE OF BHAGAVAN SRI SATHYA SAI BABA.

It wasn't premature, however. Around the next bend appeared a small, towerlike structure with a radar scanner on top of it—much like what you'd find in a minor airport. As we got closer, there was a sign proclaiming SRI SATHYA SAI AIRPORT. Beyond the tower was also, as one might expect, a runway large enough to land a medium-size jet on. *Jesus!* I thought. But beyond it I saw another unfamiliar structure. This one was massive: several wings, surrounded by many three-story officelike blocks, all in a compound recently planted with trees. Another sign: SRI SATHYA SAI INSTITUTE OF HIGHER MEDICAL SCIENCES.

"Holy shit!" I said out loud. "What's *that?*"

"Baba hospital."

"Oh."

There had always been a hospital in the ashram, but that one had been the size of a small family bungalow. This one was bigger than any in Toronto. Before I could be more amazed, we turned onto a shady, tree-lined boulevard that had been a stretch of country dirt road the last time I saw it. On either side were more colossal, immaculately maintained buildings. The Sri Sathya Sai University, the SSS Sports Arena, the SSS College of Arts and Sciences, and many others that seemed to be hostels and administrative buildings.

It gradually dawned on me that this *was* Puttaparthi. High on a hill to the left stood a 70-foot-high painted concrete statue of Hanuman, the monkey god whose burning tail had scorched these mountains as he flew to Lanka and a showdown with the demon Ravana. Beyond this, just up from where "Nagamma's Hotel" had been, I saw what looked like a repro Hindu palace. *Oh dear,* I thought, *Baba's built himself a palace. That's it—he's sold out.* I was almost pleased. I asked the driver about it.

"Not palace," he corrected. "That place museum of spirituality."

What would you exhibit there? I wondered, suddenly noticing dozens and dozens of buses parked everywhere in sight. Baba was certainly more popular than he'd been twenty years before, when the Puttaparthi bus terminal had handled one bus per day and had trouble coping with that.

"Today big festival," the driver explained.

"Which one?"

"Guru Poornima."

Guru Poornima: the festival held on the full-moon night nearest to mid-July, according to the lunar calendar, and dedicated to your guru. It was the one festival I'd never attended at Prasanthi Nilayam. What a coincidence! Of all the days on which to come—a festival. There had never been much chance of contact with Baba during festivals—even twenty years before—because of the crowds. Indians love festivals, attending every one they can justify attending. A holy day, a holiday. I hated the crowds, mostly, and the chaos that disrupted my tranquil pastoral idyll. Baba seemed to place great importance on them, though, taking pains to ensure that the arrangements for the influx of people were adequate, and putting on a lavish display of Hindu pomp—Brahmans chanting the Vedas, elephants dressed up for parades, bands, free food, and always making a speech himself, then leading *bhajans*. Festivals were also where he performed some of the more extraordinary public materializations—but that was then. Now he apparently never materialized anything more than *vibhuti* in public.

I remembered watching him wave his hand inside a small jar, showering a three-foot-tall silver image of Shirdi Sai Baba with enough *vibhuti* to completely cover it—about 300 times as much as the jar could have contained had it contained any at all before he put his hand inside.

Coming back to the present, I saw something I *did* recognize: the ashram wall. Over that wall, somewhere, was the person who had dominated half my life.

Then I recalled the time in 1974 when he'd said to us that Puttaparthi would be a city one day, and that the crowds around him would be so vast we would be lucky to catch a distant glimpse of him. I'd forgotten about it.

Now the memory made me tremble. Everything he'd said had come true. At the time it had seemed absurd, impossible. Yet here it was. I told the driver to pull over, jumped out, and went in the back gate to the ashram, as I'd always done, where the little shrine to Ganesh stood.

Prasanthi Nilayam was packed. Possibly 100,000 people milled around—Indians, Westerners, Chinese—all dressed neatly, all fairly orderly, too. The ashram had also grown, rows of dormitories stretching off farther than I even wanted to see. But the Mandir, the temple where Baba still lived, had not changed at all. The sand around it had been replaced by concrete; but the three domes and the wedding-cake sculptures, and the atrocious pastel pink-blue-green color scheme, were exactly as I remembered.

Someone had once asked Baba what these colors signified.

Bad taste, I'd said to myself, but Baba had answered: "Blue is for the sky; green is for the earth; and pink...pink is for babies." I'd never been sure if this was a joke or some mighty profundity.

I was being jostled by a thousand bodies—all men; women were still on the "Ladies Side." It took some minutes before I realized that Baba was actually giving *darshan* as I stood there. Attempting to squeeze around the side, I found myself borne along by a human tide, eventually thrust toward a spot just outside the central compound. Craning my neck, I got some idea where Baba was by following the eyelines of other devotees. He was under the Mandir porch, where amplified lead singers snag *bhajans.* Even without seeing him, I knew he was there.

Pressed by the mob behind me, claustrophobic and suddenly very hot and sweaty, I angrily jabbed back with my elbows. Somehow I found myself shunted around until I ended up in the front row, right by the passage formed by seated devotees that Baba used to walk down.

Unaccountably irritable by now, I told myself, *If he's really who he says he is, he'll come down that line and stand just there. Then he'll smile at me. That's all.*

I saw the familiar orange robe. He walked with that strange, majestic, gliding step, as he'd always done during *darshans,* his hand poised in the lotus mudra, the index finger occasionally writing in the air—*altering the Akashic records of human destiny.* He'd scarcely aged at all. Nearly 67, he looked no more than 45, which was how he'd looked when he *was* 45.

He drew nearer, pausing to take notes or speak to someone here and there, nimbly stepping back if someone breached protocol and tried to touch his feet. I expected to feel something; instead, I felt nothing at all. This pleased me, too. Emotion wouldn't cloud my perception. He reached the end of the human aisle leading to where I stood, pausing motionless, as he'd always done, staring into worlds within worlds.

The denizens of all three Hindu *lokas* were said to seek the Avatar's *darshan*. I'd often thought how much more crowded the ashram must be than it already was. Half the population of the universe was out there—or in there. Then he walked closer, and I felt myself thinking, *No, I don't believe. Don't make me believe, either. But if you come and stand there and smile—I'll believe.* The reality confused me after years of living with the idea and the image. He drew closer. As I realized I knew what he was going to do, someone reached out to touch his feet. He skipped away with a reprimand. Then he stood, not twenty feet away, and looked straight into my eyes. Not a muscle on his face moved. Abruptly he turned and walked back down the aisle, heading across the compound.

That's that, I thought. *There's the answer: You feel nothing at all, and he doesn't even know who you are....*

This seemed a perfect conclusion to the whole thing. I could probably get back to the West End in time for lunch, too, at this rate. Instead, I decided to walk where I'd once found unsurpassed serenity in the natural world.

First I offered a flower to Ganesh—good old Ganesh. Then I left the ashram, heading down the track that led to the Chitravati River. Or at least used to lead there. A hundred yards off the main drag, houses and minihotels for devotees ended and country began.

"Sai Ram, *appa*," a crafty-looking, well-coiffed sadhu announced, holding out his *kamandalam* bowl.

"Fuck off," I told him with satisfaction. I'd never have said that back in 1974.

Turning the bend where I should have seen the river's edge, I found only a 200-yard expanse of sand. The monsoon had failed here, too. All that was left was a twisting sand runway, with herds of goats being driven down it, and deep holes being dug to reach the shallow Chitravati underground. Baba

had always warned people not to dig so many wells. It lowers
the water table, he had explained. At the time, I had wondered
what that had to do with us devotees, concluding it might be
some sort of parable. Maybe it hadn't been.

I followed the dry bed. This aridity depressed me in a landscape that had once been so lush. After half a mile, I turned
back, heading to the old part of Puttaparthi village—where
Baba had been born. It looked exactly the same, charming and
chaotic, full of fat water buffalo and happy children. Baba's
house had been torn down, I was surprised to learn. He didn't
want it to become a shrine. You can't stop Indians building
shrines, though.

With a bicycle and a ledger, Baba's brother appeared. *He*
looked older, but was as pleasant as he'd always been.

I remarked how the place had changed.

"It is amazing what he has done" was the reply.

Did he get to see his brother the god much these days?

"It is not possible now," he answered. "Swami is too busy
with important matters. *Very* few see him now."

I asked if it was strange having such a…successful sibling.

"Swami is not my brother," he said patiently. "Long ago he
ceased to be tied to these worldly bonds. He has come for
everyone. I am no more important than…you."

Bad analogy, I thought. So he believed in Baba the way any
other devotee did. The brother he'd grown up with was like
someone who'd died—not someone who'd become too famous
to speak to relatives who were no longer on his social level.

What an odd fate. I said good-bye to God's brother and
walked back toward the main ashram gate. There, the little
strip of lean-tos and stalls and mud-brick eateries had transformed itself into a thriving commercial street of concrete
triplexes, covered bazaars, and air-conditioned coffee shops,
bookstores, and even travel agents. There were banks, Kashmiri

carpet vendors, and even a photographic-supply store that specialized in blowing up your favorite Baba snap to life-size posters or prints of any dimension.

I hated this ugly face of spiritualism. In the coffee shops and bookstores I heard Westerners engaged in the same conversations that had begun to sicken me by the time I finally left Puttaparthi, twenty years before:

"Did you see the expression on his face as he touched that old man?"

"Wow!"

"Remember how he took the jasmine *mala* and gave it to Raja Reddy?"

"He's so beautiful!"

"Sai Ram!"

"Sai Ram, Sai Ram!"

"What time is the discourse?"

"Eight. But we should get there by three to get a good seat."

"Or two?"

"Sai Ram!"

You can never go home. And I should never have come back to a place where I'd even willed my ashes to be scattered before July 14, 1992. It was just as well: You can't scatter ashes on a dried-up river. Unless you're a little too interested in symbolism.

The driver was disappointed to find we were leaving at 9 a.m., not 9 p.m. He was enjoying the holy day, had even found some friends to play with.

"Business meeting," I explained.

"Accha."

I took a last look at the city of Prasanthi Nilayam, feeling no regrets at all knowing I'd never see it again.

Before I even realized it, we were approaching the outskirts of Bangalore. I noticed a huge sign reading WINE SHOP and asked the driver to stop. A cocktail before lunch would be just the thing, no?

Knowing wine was probably the one alcoholic beverage the place *didn't* sell, I walked over, attracting much local attention on the way. Inside was a dingy room with a fenced-in counter, behind which were arranged many rows of bottles. Two yards away was a stone quarry: this dive evidently existed to part the quarry workers from their paychecks before they could get home. I realized why so many people supported Prohibition so keenly.

The rogues who ran this demons' den exhibited great joy at having foreign custom. It would hardly have amazed me to learn I was the first Westerner ever to step through their portals. I asked for a bottle of rum. This proved troublesome. They were not accustomed to such big spenders, and had only mickeys in stock. No problem—I asked for two half bottles, unfazed by having to pay three cents more for the same quantity of rum.

This freewheeling spirit moved them. One man set about laboriously wrapping the two mickeys in separate sheets of newspaper and enmeshing them in string. His colleagues disappeared through a door to the rear.

Wondering whether they had ever cleaned the place, I heard the man who'd disappeared out back going Psst! Psst! behind me.

"Afisth…afifeeth?" he asked me in covert tones.

"What?"

"Afeetsch…afhish?" He beckoned me to join him, to see for myself what it was he had.

He wants to sell me hashish, I realized, thinking these boys certainly covered their market well. I followed him into an even dingier back room that smelled like the Bangalore

cabaret-brothel. I wondered how they smuggled their drugs—
or in *what* they smuggled them.

"Ah!" the man said eagerly, indicating a mound wrapped in
newspaper sitting on a wooden table so sodden with grease it
was almost liquid itself.

He began to unwrap the mound. I was curious to see what
sort of hashish one could find this far south of Swat. Instead
of hashish, however, as a final sheet of virtually transparent
newsprint was peeled away, I saw a small pile of very dead fish.

"Afhish," the man announced in triumph.

"A *fish*! Yes, yes—they're fish, all right. For eating?" I
pointed at my mouth.

"Ah! *Accha!*" he said enthusiastically.

Very far from the sea, with no fishable rivers within 500
miles—indeed, with no monsoon, no rivers at all to speak
of—fish would have to travel some distance to arrive on the
outskirts of Bangalore. Without the benefit of refrigeration,
and *with* the benefit of humid 130-degree heat, these speci-
mens smelled as if they were some weeks into their own pu-
trefaction. I now remembered reading warnings in the press
about illegal sales of poisonous fish, too.

"Very nice," I said, "but no thanks. I'm a vegetarian."

"Vesh darian, ha?" the man inquired, crestfallen.

I returned to collect my bottles.

"Very darian," the man explained to his partner.

"No like a-feesh?" he replied, astounded.

"Nor meat."

"But a-feesh goot, yes?"

"A-feesha ne," the other man reminded the partner.

This man tried again. "Goot a-feesh."

I walked back to the car, wondering who'd be having a fish
dinner tonight near the quarry. Their last supper, probably.

In my hotel room, I went to unswaddle one of the rum bottles from its paper and string and accidentally dropped it. The container shattered on the thick wool pile of my carpet, its dark contents seeping out like blood.

The moment it happened, I remembered that the fish symbolized Christ and the soul. Wondering why this irrelevancy had occurred to me, I was suddenly overwhelmed by the sense of Baba's presence, of divine love. The fragrance of the incense that burned in Baba's temple distinctly permeated the room. It was a fragrance I hadn't smelled in decades. Staring at the rum stain, I knew. Beyond all doubt, Baba *was* omnipresent. Beyond *all* doubt. He who is one with the Father is no different from the Father. And the Father was very, very close right then—or really just more *accessible*.

The power of this incident engulfed me. Never before had I experienced such a feeling of God's proximity. It was and *is* undeniable.

Going for a swim later, I ran into Dick Workman, an IBM executive here to hook up his company to the Tata empire, forming Tata Business Machines—TBM. I liked Dick, and I didn't envy him his task. His job would be to train Indians in IBM work habits. A personable American from Georgia, he'd spent much of his life stationed in the East for his company, and he was married to a beautiful young Korean girl, Soo-Hyon—"Sue."

When he heard I'd once lived here, Dick was eager to pump me for useful information. Our conversations had been more on the secular side of profundity. I'd never mentioned Sai Baba before, and I told him only that I was going out of town for the day. But now I had the urge to mention Baba, wondering whether to give him the copy of Howard Murphet's *Sai Baba: Man of Miracles,* which I'd picked up again, for old times' sake, in Puttaparthi. The book provided a

readable introduction, one that had attracted many people to
Baba's ashram. As I decided Dick wasn't Baba material, and
that I wanted to keep the hard-to-find book myself, anyway,
an orange butterfly fluttered at my face. I whacked it away,
reaching for my rum and fresh lime. Within seconds, the butterfly was back, swooping to batter itself against my lips. I
brushed it off again. Seconds later, the thing flapped around
my lips again, until I was spitting out wing dust. This happened several times more before Dick exclaimed. "That's the
darnedest thing I *ever* seen!"

As he said it, the tidal sensation of Baba's love, the glow of
being loved, washed over me. I could even smell that incense
in the air again. It all clicked: orange butterfly; battering at my
lips. And the whole time I'd been trying to decide whether
to mention Baba. I excused myself, saying I had to fetch
something I wanted Dick to read.

Back in the room, divinity was so tangible I started to weep
from sheer joy. *I believe, I believe,* I told Baba, told myself. The
room felt hallowed; I felt humbled and absurdly happy. I *hadn't*
wasted my time. But, on the other hand, that bastard just
wouldn't go away, would he?—and I'd have to take this into
serious account before long. Time was running out, after all.
It always is. Eighteen years had just trickled away without my
noticing them.

I rejoined Dick and, now, Soo-Hyon, handing them *Sai
Baba: Man of Miracles*, saying just that I thought they might like
a glimpse of the local fauna.

"Soo-Hyon'll read it," Dick announced, pushing the book
at her. "She likes that sort of thing, don't you, sweetheart?"

As he said that, and Soo-Hyon reached for the book, I
knew it was intended for her, not him.

I was grateful. I promised I'd never let myself forget who
Baba really was again. There was only one kingdom left in the

empire of the soul that I needed to revisit now. Suddenly, I could see the end of the road.

Although God is omnipresent, there are places, as well as people, through which it is *easier* to look upon the Eternal.

Paul William Roberts has written for many magazines and newspapers, including The Toronto Star, Saturday Night, *and* Harper's, *and is an award-winning writer-producer for Canadian television. Born in Britain and educated at Oxford, he currently lives in Toronto. He is the author of* In Searach of the Birth of Jesus: The Real Journey of the Magi, The Demonic Comedy: Some Detours in the Baghdad of Saddam Hussein, *and* Empire of the Soul: Some Journeys in India, *from which this story was excerpted.*

WILLIAM ASHTON

⋆ ⋆ ⋆

A Room of Men

The author rediscovers the community of his own sex.

My first memory of an art gallery is my father lifting me above the crowd in the National Gallery of Art in Washington, D.C. He raised me above his head to catch a glimpse of the painting we patiently waited to study. I recall being eight or nine years old and wondering why people were slowly filing past the painting with such silence and respect. The woman in the painting sat with her hands folded, her head slightly turned and framed by straight long black hair. Her lips formed a peculiar smile, an expression I had not seen before—or since. Only years later did I realize this woman was the *Mona Lisa,* one of Leonardo da Vinci's masterpieces. My father's patient desire to show his son the work of a master planted a seed.

Twenty-two years later, during a sabbatical from my professional life in Alaska, I wandered through Southeast Asia and Eastern Europe. My travels included the national galleries of art in Tokyo, Jakarta, Singapore, Kuala Lumpur, Bangkok, Athens, and Sofia. During my stay in Sofia, in the rapidly changing atmosphere of post-Communist Bulgaria in April 1992, I found the right mixture of earth, air, fire and water to sprout the seed planted by my father.

As soon as I walk through the door of the Bulgarian National Gallery of Art I feel slightly off-balance, slightly different. I chalk it up to the greasy food Sofia's less expensive restaurants offer a budget traveler. I wander through room after room of 18th- and 19th-century art. None of the stories told through color capture me until I reach a particular room. The walls are full of paintings of men planting fields, clearing a battlefield, saying prayers on a hilltop, and displaying their wealth.

Walking into the room my eyes immediately focus on one painting: men gathering in a tavern on a late winter day. The patrons gather around many small tables, some standing, others sitting. They are deeply immersed in the atmosphere of the moment. Most of the crowd faces the center of activity. Their hands are raised clapping a rhythm; they shout encouragement to the men in the center of the room. Red cheeks highlight expressions of good feeling.

In the foreground of the painting, two men are in the middle of the local gathering place stripped of their winter clothes, naked to the waist. They are lost in a trance, driven by impulses flowing through every muscle. Around the room, eyes focus on these two with awe, with respect, for their dancing ability and passion for life.

The faces radiate a kinship between men, a connection of strong male friendships. The way they are focused on a common shared experience makes me realize how seldom I feel such a focus with my men friends back home in Anchorage. The last time I felt this in tune with my gender was with my Boy Scout troop during summer camp. During those summer retreats, boys came together through shared scouting adventures to learn the companionship of our gender. The men in this painting share this companionship with their neighbors. I suspect they could not conceive of a community where the brotherhood of men no longer carries on this tradition.

Drawn in by the colors, lighting, and facial expression, the story brings a rise within me. A surge begins at the base of my spine, an awakening; of what I know not. In a moment of discomfort, I look around to see if anybody else is in the room. I am lucky. No one is watching, no other human is in the room. No one except the men on the walls.

I return to the painting. Now I notice some men are bored and unexcited. They look away from the center, they look down at the floor, and they distance themselves from the other men. These men are worn down by life. Their bodies sag, like summer ripe corn enduring a three-week dry spell. The zest for life does not flow through their arteries. They can not, or do not, tap into the flow of life force that binds men between heaven and earth.

Their eyes and body tell the story; the signs are subtle, but distinct. The eyes are downcast, weak, and withdrawn. The windows to the soul are cloudy. The light inside indicates the inner fire is about to die out for lack of fuel. The bodies are slouched, flaccid, and pasty. The vessel of the soul suffers from poor maintenance. The reservoir within that holds a man's nourishment suffers from leaks and cracks in the container.

I study the scene some more. Now I notice the contrast between men who feed the internal flame, the hearth of creation, and the men who neglect the fire. Another shiver flutters up my spine. Studying the faces of the lifeless men, I recognize the expression I saw so often in my father's face in the years leading to his death the year before my sabbatical. This is the expression that I started to see in my face while shaving. This lifeless expression convinced me to leave a secure job and set out on my journey.

My attention returns to the moment, to the men in the middle of the room.

What are these men so passionately engaged in?

They are carrying on the unspoken traditions of their father, and their father before them, and their father before them—a tradition that cleanses men's souls. They are dancing.

One is crouched in a deep knee bend characteristic of Cossacks or Greek dancers. He is kicking out the deep bass notes. The other stands tall dancing the fine steps of a tenor. Each is engulfed in emotion, entwined in the energy of the other. Each is embraced in a tradition of manhood.

The mixture of pigments on the canvas captures me; I sense the room is moving, or is it just me that is shifting. I feel dizzy. The density of my body disperses like a drop of food coloring dissipating in a pool of water. While standing before these men a subtle current swirls through me, a current that binds me with these men. The men in the tavern open their brotherhood to welcome me. They welcome me for what feels like an eternity, though I have no idea how long in clock time. I stand joined in a way that nurtures my body and soul. The seed planted by my father finds a new source of nourishment. I savor the feelings these men spark within me.

Boundaries of time and space return, the timeless moment retreats, the density of my body returns. My body armor reforms, bringing the return of restrictions on my feelings. Timeless clarity quickly becomes a fleeting memory. The traditional circle of men dissipates; linear words and time return. I return to the world of flat, two-dimensional paintings of men in this land between Europe and Asia. It takes me a few moments for me to readjust to being in the art gallery.

As I readjust, I remember how seldom my father bonded

with men the way the men in the tavern are connected with one another. I realize how seldom I connect with other men. Like father, like son.

My visit with Bulgarian men of the early 19th century draws to a close. I walk over to a bland Stalin-era museum bench and sit down. I need a moment to regain my equilibrium, a moment to survey the painting once more. I doubt fifteen minutes have passed since entering the room. Somehow this painting, or this place, binds me with men in a way that knows no time clock, work shift, or assembly line. For a brief moment I return to one of the traditional practices of men, the power of nurturing transformation.

In that moment of transformation, standing with the gathering of men, I entered a cauldron created by opposites. The opposites of fire and water, of radiant passion and flowing emotions, combined with the opposites of air and earth, of ephemeral thoughts and the power of place. They demonstrated the alchemical tradition of joining opposites together to form the crucible of transformation. The medieval tradition of turning lead into gold. I feel the leaden life I walked in the door with is transformed. Though I sense the transformation is not complete.

Six years after that day in Sofia I now understand one of the few times I felt my father come alive was the day he held me high above the crowd to see the *Mona Lisa*. His instinctual response of raising his son in offering to a master passed on a timeless male tradition. In that moment he intuitively combined the four alchemical elements to create the crucible, the vessel, that men draw upon to sustain them in their daily life. He instinctively passed on a lesson from father to son of how to recharge one's vessel.

My father passed on his passion of learning about the

treasures of the world. That moment in front of Leonardo's masterpiece set deep within me the seed of tradition. The tavern of men in Sofia awakened a conscious appreciation for the alchemical traditions of men necessary to sustain life. I sense my journey, my transformation, is incomplete until I pass on the traditions of my father, and forefathers, to my son.

William Ashton is a reformed environmental engineer with twenty years experience in Alaska. His travels to power places and sacred sites has "reformed" his view of the environment and our relationship with the planet. His transformation from an engineer out-of touch with nature to being in-tune with nature came to completion when he started working with the "spirits of the land" on restoration projects. He recently moved to Portland, Oregon.

✦ ✦ ✦

Heading for Home

Dreams can come true.

WHAT WOULD IT FEEL LIKE TO PLAY BASEBALL AGAIN? THE question lingered for weeks after the phone call that invited me to a reunion of my Minnesota high school's back-to-back state champion baseball teams. It was a rhetorical question, really, because I knew how it would feel. It would feel terrific.

I hadn't swung at a baseball in so many years I could hardly count back that far. Softball, yes, but not baseball. I was in my 40th year, and had stopped playing in my 21st, when childhood dreams found their final resting place in an inability to hit curveballs to the opposite field and I moved on to adult ambitions.

But to play ball again, if only once, would recapture those long-lost days of hope and promise, those days of dirt and grass and clean white lines, of leather and wood and the unparalleled crack of bat on ball. Good wood, we used to say. Do ballplayers still say that, *Good wood,* when they make solid contact?

Would I be young again? Of course not. But of course! One last round with old friends to celebrate the champions we once were. It may sound childish, but it kept me awake at night, rekindled dreams, brought back with stunning clarity specific plays in the field, heroic at-bats, game winning hits that were so vivid they could have happened that afternoon. It invaded me with a nostalgic eagerness.

At that time I was working nights in a bar, fueling the itinerant writer's life, covering the mortgage, building for a future while mining the present for all I could get. The Friday night before I flew from San Francisco to Minneapolis for the Saturday afternoon game, I had to work till closing time, impatiently herding the stragglers out at 2 a.m. and turning to the task of cleaning up the joint. It had been an especially busy night and I was way behind schedule. By the time I got home it was nearly 4 a.m. and my flight left at 7. I fell into bed and slept maybe two hours, rising with little time to spare.

After a quick shower, I nicked myself with an unsteady hand while shaving. The blood wouldn't stop flowing and my window of time shrank. By the time I headed for the car with Paula, who would drop me off, I was running very late.

Traffic was light so early in the morning, but my heart sank when I saw the gridlocked cars trying to drop passengers at the terminal. Why was the airport so busy so early on a Saturday? It made no sense. But Paula diverted onto the adjacent road to avoid the jam and got close to my airline's check-in. I gave her a quick kiss good-bye, vaulted a low wall, and wedged through the stalled cars.

I had fifteen minutes to departure now, but was confident I could make it. When I entered the terminal, though, it was utter chaos. Crowds pushed and pulled, and to get to a monitor to locate the gate for my flight I had to wrestle with desperate people dragging overstuffed luggage. With bags slung over my shoulders, I began to sweat, and the nick on my upper lip began to bleed again. The only tissue I had was already stained, but I pressed it against my lip hoping to stanch the flow.

A large woman with enormous suitcases blocked my way. Impatient children squeezed past my legs and almost tripped me. A sweaty man cursed as my bag bumped his shoulder. He looked vile, but he couldn't have looked worse than I did, with sweat dripping from my nose, blood seeping through the tattered tissue, a frantic look in my eyes. I was having trouble breathing now, but finally I found a monitor, located my flight number, and cursed aloud when I saw the gate listed. It was at the satellite farthest from the check-in counter, a long haul on the best of days.

Luckily I had a first-class upgrade provided by a brother who flew more than 100,000 miles annually on this airline. But I still had to get through the interminable line at security and out to the gate. Blood now covered my fingers and probably half my face as I waited for the line to creep through the metal detectors.

When I finally cleared security, I ran, dripping blood, the half mile, it seemed, to the gate, where a long line of people shuffled their feet trying to check in. I ran to the counter waving my first class upgrade.

"First class!" I said. "I'm in first class!"

The agent looked at me as if I'd just stormed across the Tiber in animal skins. "All seats are assigned. Please go to the end of the line."

"But I have a confirmed seat, in first class!"

"All seats are released ten minutes before departure, and all seats have now been assigned. Please go to the end of the line."

"But I'm in first class."

The agent scowled at me as if dealing with a stupid child. "It's too late. You have lost your seat. Go to the end of the line."

I was stunned. My watch read 6:55. I'd lost my seat. Blood dripped to the floor. My hand was sticky; the tissue was shredded, sopping. I shambled to the end of the line, numb.

Five minutes later the agent announced that the flight had been closed, and anyone holding tickets for this flight could catch the next one in two hours. Two hours meant I would arrive in Minneapolis after the game was over. There'd be baseball, but there wouldn't be any for me.

I don't remember ever being so depressed. I wandered away from the line, closer to the gate, as if by doing so I might somehow find a way aboard the plane. I stood there, one hand on my bleeding face, the other holding my ticket and upgrade limply at my side, feeling a gnawing emptiness as the reality sank in: I would miss the game.

I was standing to the left of the check-in desk. The ramp to the plane was to my left. I was staring at it like a man in an emergency room watching a silent TV while waiting to be sewn back together, when a gate agent strode off the ramp toward me and announced, "I have one more seat. Who wants it?"

"I do!" I shouted and almost tackled her. By sheer luck I was closer to her than any other would-be passenger and no one was going to get that seat ahead of me. She grabbed my ticket and hurried up the ramp with me in tow, handing me a boarding pass on the fly and returning my upgrade.

"The seat's near the back," she said as I followed her on board, and I shuffled down the aisle feeling the other passengers looking at me in barely suppressed alarm because of my bloody face. Each one seemed to breathe a sigh of relief as I passed, knowing I wouldn't be sitting anywhere near them. I went all the way to the rear without finding the seat, and I just stood there, waiting to be rescued. No way would they get me off this plane.

"What are you doing?" an attendant asked.

"I have a seat, but I don't know where."

The attendant who'd brought me aboard returned and beckoned me forward. A few rows up there was a middle seat and she held my bags while I crammed in, then helped stow them.

I leaned back in my seat trying to catch my breath. I'd never felt so wrung out. The tissue in my hand was reduced to powder and the blood still seeped from my lip. It took an hour in the air for me to gather the strength to go clean myself up, and when I witnessed the spectacle of my face in the mirror I cringed. I looked as though I could have climbed aboard the plane after three weeks of sleeping on the street.

But I made it to Minneapolis. My good friend Louie was waiting for me at the gate and hustled me to his car. I threw my bags in the trunk after dragging out my sweats and changed clothes as we drove. Game time was in 30 minutes and we had about a 20-minute drive to the field.

Louie hadn't played on the baseball team. He'd tried out every year, but never moved higher than junior varsity. But I couldn't imagine him not being part of this day, and he hoped he'd get a chance to swing a bat if there weren't enough players.

I was in a fog when we arrived at the field. Everything was so familiar, the green grass, the old dugouts, the pond and park beyond right field. Oh! How could nothing have changed through all these years? Everything seemed the same except the outfield fence which hadn't existed when I played here more than twenty years ago.

The field was full of ballplayers in uniform. Who were they? I wondered. Then I began to recognize people. There was lanky Jim who batted fourth, played right field, and sometimes pitched; and Max, who'd always been big, was even bigger now, who'd hit a dramatic home run to cap a five-run rally that won a game early in that final season. And Dave, left fielder, good power hitter, with the volatile personality. It wasn't till I got down on the field and got a closer look at the guys that I realized I knew them all from those long ago years.

There wasn't time for me to go into the school and change into a uniform. The game was about to begin.

I took my old position at shortstop wearing a sweat shirt and shorts and began warming up. The fertile smells of damp grass and dirt after a summer rain unlocked years of memories, when summer meant slinging my glove onto my bike's handlebars, wedging my bat over the bars between my thumbs, and riding off to one of the two neighborhood ballfields to play with friends. Every day of summer was filled with baseball, and the names and faces of those neighborhood kids came back to me like characters in a play. I remembered the first time I suffered a bad hop in the balls, at age seven, and the unrelenting pain that made me think I was going to die on the spot. I remembered the joys of sunny days, the disappointments of rain, the thrill of my father saying, "Let's go shag some balls," and he'd pitch in the golden evening light to every kid who showed up, and there was always a crowd.

Somehow these reveries took me through the first inning and in the bottom of the second I would get a chance to bat. What would this be like? Could I still hit the ball? I stood in the on-deck circle loosening up, watching Tom, who'd spent most of his career warming the bench, foul off a couple of pitches. He'd had a mysterious neurological disorder just a year ago that doctors thought would leave him bedridden for life, but here he was, playing ball again as if in the glow of youth.

On the next pitch he lined the ball into center field for a single, but he could hardly run to first. Louie was down there coaching first base, and he stepped in to run for Tom.

It was fitting to have Louie on base when I stepped up to the plate. We'd been through so much together in the years after high school. Even though I left Minnesota to go to college and never returned to live there, Louie and I would get together every year and keep in touch by mail and phone, sharing in each other's joys and frustrations, supporting each other as only true friends do. He grinned broadly, a sign that he was as thrilled as I was to be out on the field, in the game.

The first pitch came at me like a missile out of fog. My eyes seemed to be playing tricks. The whole experience seemed to be playing out in another world. After my ordeal to get here I was hardly "here" in a conscious sense. Everything seemed to be dripping with fantasy and dream, with an unreality that left me floating around the field as if watching from afar.

The next pitch came in and I swung, fouling it back into the screen. That first contact brought me home a little. Now I felt as if I were there in the batter's box. I looked at Louie on first base and he clapped and yelled. I waited for the next pitch.

When it came I swung, not really seeing the ball, seeing rather a flash of movement, something white against the backdrop of trees. My body initiated the action, not my mind. From deep in the recesses of my muscles, I swung and felt the contact, the "good wood" of the past and watched in astonishment as the ball arced high and deep toward left field. I stumbled down the first base line trying to keep my eye on the ball, watching it soar farther, and farther, and finally over the fence.

There was a whoop from somewhere. The voice of an old coach carried across the diamond, "Hey, you still know how to turn on a fastball!" Louie pranced around second base, doing a little jig and shouting. I rounded the bases in a dream. How had this happened? How had I hit that ball out of the park?

I rounded third base and headed for home, seeing Louie standing behind the plate grinning, feeling a lightness and fullness one only feels when touched by the hand of the divine. It was just one swing of the bat, but in baseball parlance, sometimes that's all it takes.

Larry Habegger is executive editor of Travelers' Tales, coauthor of the syndicated newspaper column "World Travel Watch," and a lifelong sports fan.

Acknowledgements

We would like to thank our families and friends for their usual forbearance while we are putting a book together. Thanks also to Lisa Bach, Susan Brady, Deborah Greco, Raj Khadka, Cynthia Lamb, Jennifer Leo, Natanya Pearlman, Tara Weaver, and the staff at O'Reilly & Associates, especially Susan Bailey and Kathryn Heflin, and to Sleeping Lady Retreat and Conference Center in Leavenworth, Washington, for a wonderful and supportive creative environment.

Frontispiece excerpted from *The Meaning of Culture* by John Cowper Powys. Published by W. W. Norton. Copyright © 1929. Reprinted by permission of Laurence Pollinger Ltd and the Estate of John Cowper Powys.

"The Perfect Punch in the Face" by Richard Sterling published with permission from the author. Copyright © 1999 by Richard Sterling.

"Devils Thumb" by Jon Krakauer excerpted from *Into the Wild* by Jon Krakauer. Copyright © 1996 by Jon Krakauer. Reprinted by permission of Villard Books, a division of Random House, Inc. and Macmillan Publishers Ltd.

"The World's Most Dangerous Girlfriend" by Christopher Cook Gilmore reprinted from the December 1998/January 1999 issue of *Men's Journal*. Copyright © 1999 by Men's Journal Company, L.P. Reprinted by permission. All rights reserved.

"The Lure of Danger" by Sebastian Junger originally appeared in the April 1998 issue of *Men's Journal*. Copyright © 1998 by Sebastian Junger. Reprinted by permission of Stuart Krichevsky Literary Agency, Inc.

"Wild Turkey" by Ray Isle reprinted from the Volume 2, Number 4 issue of *Terra Nova: Nature & Culture*. Copyright © 1997 by Ray Isle. Reprinted by permission of the author.

"A Fine Boyo" by Frank McCourt excerpted from *Angela's Ashes: A Memoir* by Frank McCourt. Copyright © 1996 by Frank McCourt. Reprinted by permission of Scribner, a division of Simon & Schuster, Inc., and the Aaron Priest Agency.

"Fire Beneath the Skin" by Tim Ward excerpted from *Arousing the Goddess* by Tim Ward. Copyright © 1996 by Tim Ward. Reprinted by permission of the author.

"In Chief Yali's Shoes" by Tim Cahill excerpted from *Pass the Butterworms: Remote Journeys Oddly Rendered* by Tim Cahill. Copyright © 1997 by Tim Cahill.

Reprinted by permission of Villard Books, a division of Random House, Inc., and Fourth Estate.

"Applause in Calcutta" by George Vincent Wright published with permission from the author. Copyright © 1999 by George Vincent Wright.

"Trail Mix" by Bill Bryson excerpted from *A Walk in the Woods: Rediscovering America on the Appalachian Trail* by Bill Bryson. Copyright © 1997 by Bill Bryson. Used by permission of Broadway Books, a division of Random House, Inc., and Transworld Publishers Ltd.

"Turn the Tables" by Richard Sterling published with permission from the author. Copyright © 1999 by Richard Sterling.

"Original Sin" by Michael Quinn Patton excerpted from *Grand Canyon Celebration: A Father-Son Journey of Discovery* by Michael Quinn Patton (Amherst, NY: Prometheus Books). Copyright © 1999 by Michael Quinn Patton. Reprinted by permission of the publisher.

"An American Hero" by Michael Paterniti first appeared in the November 1998 issue of *Esquire* magazine. Copyright © 1998 by Michael Paterniti. Reprinted by permission of International Creative Management.

"The Pilot and the Elements" (*"Le Pilote et les puissances naturelles"*) by Antoine de Saint-Exupéry excerpted from *A Sense of Life* (*Un sens a la vie*) by Antoine de Saint-Exupéry. Copyright © 1956 by Editions Gallimard. Translation copyright © 1965 by Funk and Wagnalls Company. Reprinted by permission of HarperCollins Publishers, Inc. and Editions Gallimard.

"The Longing" by Phil Cousineau excerpted from *The Art of Pilgrimage: The Seeker's Guide to Making Travel Sacred* by Phil Cousineau. Copyright © 1998 by Phil Cousineau. Reprinted by permission of Conari Press.

"On the Road" by Eddy L. Harris excerpted from *South of Haunted Dreams: A Ride Through Slavery's Old Back Yard* by Eddy L. Harris. Copyright © 1993 by Eddy Harris. Reprinted by permission of Sterling Lord Literistic, Inc.

"The Blue Man" by Emily Jenkins excerpted from *Tongue First: Adventures in Physical Culture* by Emily Jenkins. Copyright © 1998 by Emily Jenkins. Reprinted by permission of Henry Holt & Co., Inc.

"Crevasse" by James Wickwire and Dorothy Bullitt excerpted from *Addicted to Danger: A Memoir* by James Wickwire and Dorothy Bullitt. Reprinted with the permission of Pocket Books, a division of Simon & Schuster, Inc. Copyright © 1998 by James Wickwire and Dorothy Bullitt.

"Breathing In" by Michael Herr excerpted from *Dispatches* by Michael Herr. Copyright © 1968, 1977 by Michael Herr. Reprinted by permission of Alfred A. Knopf, Inc. and Donadio & Ashworth, Inc.

"Into the Abyss" by Craig Vetter reprinted from the November 1994 issue of *Outside*. Copyright © 1994 by Craig Vetter. Reprinted by permission of the author.

"Kharkov and the Lubyanka" by Slavomir Rawicz excerpted from *The Long Walk: The True Story of a Trek to Freedom* by Slavomir Rawicz. Copyright © 1956, 1984, 1997 by Slavomir Rawicz. Reprinted by permission of The Lyons Press and Aitken Stone Literary Agency.

"The Thrill" by Earl Perry reprinted from the Winter 97-98 issue of *Boatman's Quarterly Review*. Copyright © 1998 by Earl Perry. Reprinted by permission of the author.

"No Like A-feesh?" by Paul William Roberts excerpted from *Empire of the Soul: Some Journeys in India* by Paul William Roberts. Copyright © 1994 by Paul William Roberts. Used by permission of Putnam Berkley, a division of Penguin Putnam Inc., and Stoddart Publishing Co., Limited, Don Mills, Ont.

"A Room of Men" by William Ashton published with permission from the author. Copyright © 1999 by William Ashton.

"Heading for Home" by Larry Habegger published with permission from the author. Copyright © 1999 by Larry Habegger.

About the Editors

Sean O'Reilly is a former seminarian, stockbroker, and prison instructor who lives in Arizona with his wife Brenda and their four small boys. He's had a life-long interest in philosophy and theology, and is at work on a book called *How to Manage Your Dick: A Guide for the Soul*, which makes the proposition that classic Greek, Roman, and Christian moral philosophies, allied with post-quantum physics, form the building blocks of a new ethics and psychology. Widely traveled, Sean most recently completed an 18,000-mile van journey around the United States, sharing the treasures of the open road with his family. He is editor-at-large and director of international sales for Travelers' Tales.

Larry Habegger, executive editor of Travelers' Tales, has been writing about travel since 1980. He has visited almost fifty countries and five of the six continents, traveling from the frozen arctic to equatorial rain forest, the high Himalayas to the Dead Sea. In the early 1980s he co-authored mystery serials for the *San Francisco Examiner* with James O'Reilly, and in 1985 the two of them began a syndicated newspaper column, "World Travel Watch," which still appears in major newspapers throughout the USA. He was born and raised in Minnesota and lives with his family on Telegraph Hill in San Francisco.

James O'Reilly, president and co-publisher of Travelers' Tales, wrote mystery serials before becoming a travel writer in the early 1980s. He's visited more than forty countries, along the way meditating with monks in Tibet, participating in West African voodoo rituals, and hanging out the laundry with nuns in Florence. He travels extensively with his wife Wenda and their three daughters. They live in Palo Alto, California when they're not in Leavenworth, Washington.

TRAVELERS' TALES GUIDES

LOOK FOR THESE TITLES IN THE SERIES

FOOTSTEPS: THE SOUL OF TRAVEL

A NEW IMPRINT FROM TRAVELERS' TALES GUIDES

An imprint of Travelers' Tales Guides, the Footsteps series unveils new works by first-time authors, established writers, and reprints of works whose time has come...again. Each book will fire your imagination, disturb your sleep, and feed your soul.

KITE STRINGS OF THE SOUTHERN CROSS
A Woman's Travel Odyssey
By Laurie Gough
ISBN 1-885211-30-9
400 pages, $24.00, Hardcover

THE SWORD OF HEAVEN
A Five Continent Odyssey to Save the World
By Mikkel Aaland
ISBN 1-885211-44-9
350 pages, $24.00, Hardcover

ℐPECIAL INTEREST

THE FEARLESS SHOPPER
How to Get the Best Deals on the Planet
By Kathy Borrus
ISBN 1-885211-39-2, 200 pages, $12.95

Check with your local bookstore for these titles
or visit our web site at www.travelerstales.com.

$\mathscr{S}$PECIAL INTEREST

THE GIFT OF BIRDS:
True Encounters with Avian Spirits
Edited by Larry Habegger & Amy Greimann Carlson
ISBN 1-885211-41-4, 275 pages, $17.95

TESTOSTERONE PLANET:
True Stories from a Man's World
Edited by Sean O'Reilly, Larry Habegger & James O'Reilly
ISBN 1-885211-43-0, 300 pages, $17.95

THE PENNY PINCHER'S PASSPORT TO LUXURY TRAVEL
The Art of Cultivating Preferred Customer Status
By Joel L. Widzer
ISBN 1-885211-31-7, 253 pages, $12.95

DANGER!
Ttue Stories of Trouble and Survival
Edited by James O'Reilly, Larry Habegger & Sean O'Reilly
ISBN 1-885211-32-5, 336 pages, $17.95

FAMILY TRAVEL:
The Farther You Go, the Closer You Get
Edited by Laura Manske
ISBN 1-885211-33-3, 368 pages, $17.95

SPECIAL INTEREST

THE GIFT OF TRAVEL:
The Best of Travelers' Tales
Edited by Larry Habegger, James O'Reilly & Sean O'Reilly
ISBN 1-885211-25-2, 240 pages, $14.95

THERE'S NO TOILET PAPER...ON THE
ROAD LESS TRAVELED:
The Best of Travel Humor and Misadventure
Edited by Doug Lansky
ISBN 1-885211-27-9, 207 pages, $12.95

A DOG'S WORLD:
True Stories of Man's Best Friend on the Road
Edited by Christine Hunsicker
ISBN 1-885211-23-6, 257 pages, $12.95

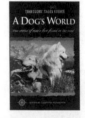

WOMEN'S TRAVEL

A WOMAN'S PASSION FOR TRAVEL
More True Stories from A Woman's World
Edited by Marybeth Bond & Pamela Michael
ISBN 1-885211-36-8, 375 pages, $17.95

SAFETY AND SECURITY FOR
WOMEN WHO TRAVEL
By Sheila Swan & Peter Laufer
ISBN 1-885211-29-5, 159 pages, $12.95

$\mathcal{W}$OMEN'S TRAVEL

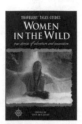

WOMEN IN THE WILD:
True Stories of Adventure and Connection
Edited by Lucy McCauley
ISBN 1-885211-21-X, 307 pages, $17.95

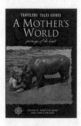

A MOTHER'S WORLD:
Journeys of the Heart
Edited by Marybeth Bond & Pamela Michael
ISBN 1-885211-26-0, 233 pages, $14.95

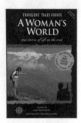

A WOMAN'S WORLD:
True Stories of Life on the Road
Edited by Marybeth Bond
Introduction by Dervla Murphy
ISBN 1-885211-06-6
475 pages, $17.95

———— ⋆ * ⋆ ————

Winner of the Lowell
Thomas Award for Best
Travel Book – Society of
American Travel Writers

GUTSY WOMEN:
Travel Tips and Wisdom for the Road
By Marybeth Bond
ISBN 1-885211-15-5, 123 pages, $7.95

GUTSY MAMAS:
Travel Tips and Wisdom for
Mothers on the Road
By Marybeth Bond
ISBN 1-885211-20-1, 139 pages, $7.95

ℬODY & SOUL

THE ADVENTURE OF FOOD:
True Stories of Eating Everything
Edited by Richard Sterling
ISBN 1-885211-37-6, 375 pages, $17.95

*Small Press Book
Award Winner and
Benjamin Franklin
Award Finalist*

THE ROAD WITHIN:
True Stories of Transformation
and the Soul
*Edited by Sean O'Reilly, James O'Reilly
& Tim O'Reilly*
ISBN 1-885211-19-8, 459 pages, $17.95

LOVE & ROMANCE:
True Stories of Passion on the Road
Edited by Judith Babcock Wylie
ISBN 1-885211-18-X, 319 pages, $17.95

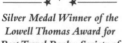

*Silver Medal Winner of the
Lowell Thomas Award for
Best Travel Book – Society of
American Travel Writers*

FOOD:
A Taste of the Road
*Edited by Richard Sterling
Introduction by Margo True
ISBN 1-885211-09-0
467 pages, $17.95*

THE FEARLESS DINER:
Travel Tips and Wisdom for Eating
around the World
By Richard Sterling
ISBN 1-885211-22-8, 139 pages, $7.95

𝒞OUNTRY GUIDES

AUSTRALIA
True Stories of Life Down Under
Edited by Larry Habegger & Amy Greimann Carlson
ISBN 1-885211-40-6, 375 pages, $17.95

AMERICA
Edited by Fred Setterberg
ISBN 1-885211-28-7, 550 pages, $19.95

JAPAN
Edited by Donald W. George
& Amy Greimann Carlson
ISBN 1-885211-04-X, 437 pages, $17.95

ITALY
Edited by Anne Calcagno
Introduction by Jan Morris
ISBN 1-885211-16-3, 463 pages, $17.95

INDIA
Edited by James O'Reilly & Larry Habegger
ISBN 1-885211-01-5, 538 pages, $17.95

$\mathscr{C}$OUNTRY GUIDES

FRANCE
Edited by James O'Reilly, Larry Habegger
& Sean O'Reilly
ISBN 1-885211-02-3, 517 pages, $17.95

MEXICO
Edited by James O'Reilly & Larry Habegger
ISBN 1-885211-00-7, 463 pages, $17.95

————— ⋆ ⋆ ⋆ —————
Winner of the Lowell
Thomas Award for Best
Travel Book – Society of
American Travel Writers

THAILAND
Edited by James O'Reilly
& Larry Habegger
ISBN 1-885211-05-8
483 pages, $17.95

SPAIN
Edited by Lucy McCauley
ISBN 1-885211-07-4, 495 pages, $17.95

NEPAL
Edited by Rajendra S. Khadka
ISBN 1-885211-14-7, 423 pages, $17.95

COUNTRY GUIDES

BRAZIL
Edited by Annette Haddad & Scott Doggett
Introduction by Alex Shoumatoff
ISBN 1-885211-11-2
452 pages, $17.95

— ★ ✱ ★ —
Benjamin Franklin
Award Winner

CITY GUIDES

HONG KONG
Edited by James O'Reilly, Larry Habegger & Sean O'Reilly
ISBN 1-885211-03-1, 439 pages, $17.95

PARIS
Edited by James O'Reilly, Larry Habegger & Sean O'Reilly
ISBN 1-885211-10-4, 417 pages, $17.95

SAN FRANCISCO
Edited by James O'Reilly, Larry Habegger & Sean O'Reilly
ISBN 1-885211-08-2, 491 pages, $17.95

ℛEGIONAL GUIDES

HAWAI'I
True Stories of the Island Spirit
Edited by Rick & Marcie Carroll
ISBN 1-885211-35-X, 416 pages, $17.95

GRAND CANYON
True Stories of Life Below the Rim
Edited by Sean O'Reilly,
James O'Reilly & Larry Habegger
ISBN 1-885211-34-1, 296 pages, $17.95

Submit Your Own Travel Tale

Do you have a tale of your own that you would like to submit to Travelers' Tales? We highly recommend that you first read one or more of our books to get a feel for the kind of story we're looking for. For submission guidelines and a list of titles in the works, send a SASE to:

Travelers' Tales Submission Guidelines
330 Townsend Street, Suite 208, San Francisco, CA 94107

or send email to ***guidelines@travelerstales.com***
or visit our Web site at **www.travelerstales.com**

You can send your story to the address above or via email to ***submit@travelerstales.com***. On the outside of the envelope, ***please indicate what country/topic your story is about***. If your story is selected for one of our titles, we will contact you about rights and payment.

We hope to hear from you. In the meantime, enjoy the stories!